## *Praise for* **The Age of Austerity**

"The economic collapse that began in 2008 and its aftermath . . . has mired us in what Thomas Edsall rightly calls 'the age of austerity.' What this means, the former *Washington Post* reporter argues in his eye-opening and hugely important account, is a transformation of U.S. politics into 'a dog-eat-dog political competition over diminishing resources.' Edsall's point is powerfully argued."     —*The Boston Globe*

"In this erudite primer on the conditions that have brought us to this moment of economic crisis, journalist and Columbia University professor Edsall argues that the U.S. faces a future of diminished resources, and, as a result of partisan intractability, the possibility that we won't overcome current challenges to long-term prosperity. . . . Providing ample sociological and economic evidence via descriptive graphs and in-depth analysis, Edsall . . . illuminates hard but necessary truths."     —*Publishers Weekly*

"*The Age of Austerity* greatly clarifies the current frightening crisis in our politics. Thomas Edsall, one of our major political commentators, sees Republicans and Democrats as competing coalitions of haves and have-nots, locked in brutal battles over the fundamentals of modern American government at a time of severe economic duress. The stakes for America's future are economic and moral as well as political, and they are as large as they have been since the Great Depression. Edsall's analysis—at once calm and insistent, upsetting and enlightening—is a singularly valuable account of these ugly times."

—Sean Wilentz, Sidney and Ruth Lapidus
Professor of the American Revolutionary Era at Princeton University,
author of *The Rise of American Democracy* and *The Age of Reagan*

"Back in 1984 Thomas Edsall followed his bloodhound's instincts into the labyrinth of Washington and produced a breakthrough account of *The New Politics of Inequality*, showing us how a quiet transfer of power had taken place in the nation's capital. . . . Here, during the 'morning in America' of the Reagan Revolution, was the beginning of the long crusade by the richest and most powerful interests to control America's taxing and spending policies. They succeeded beyond even their own expectations, finally producing a government of the 1 percent, by the 1 percent, and for the 1 percent. Now Edsall has produced another compelling and disturbing book grounded in the diligent and dogged reporting for which he is known and honored. Our present age of austerity is no accident. But there is a ray of light in this book: if our politics brought it on, our politics can change it—once we've changed the politicians." —Bill Moyers

"Most books about contemporary politics are designed for quick obsolescence. A notable exception to the rule is the work of Thomas Byrne Edsall, whose five careful books . . . are still found on the shelves and in the footnotes of everyone who writes about politics—left and right, academics and journalists alike. Edsall's distinctive method combines his own reporting with rigorous use of data from across the social sciences, including psychology and anthropology. . . . The great topic of Edsall's life's work is the breakdown of the New Deal–era liberal coalition at the intersection of race, resentment and inequality."
—*The New York Times Book Review*

"Edsall's book really comes alive . . . when it turns to the political effects of austerity." —*Financial Times*

"As economists handicap the odds of a new recession and speculate about a lost decade for the U.S. economy, Tom Edsall offers a troubling vision of American political and social conflict in circumstances of low growth and intense polarization. To avoid what he dubs a 'brutish future,' our divided leaders will have to come together around a plan for renewed growth that is bound to offend the core constituencies of both political parties. If Edsall is right, the outlook for such an agreement is dim at best, and the alternative is the decline of the United States."
—William Galston, Senior Fellow at the Brookings Institution and former policy advisor to President Clinton

*Thomas Byrne Edsall*

## The Age of Austerity

Thomas Edsall is an American journalist and academic, best known for his twenty-five years covering politics for *The Washington Post*. He holds the Joseph Pulitzer II and Edith Pulitzer Moore Professorship in Public Affairs Journalism at Columbia University, and is a correspondent for *The New Republic* and an online columnist for *The New York Times*. In addition, he was the former political editor of *The Huffington Post*. He is the author of *Chain Reaction*, a Pulitzer Prize finalist (1992), *The New Politics of Inequality* (1984), and *Building Red America* (2006), among other works. Edsall is also the winner of the Carey McWilliams Award of the American Political Science Association. Mr. Edsall lives in New York and Washington, D.C., with his wife, Mary.

# The Age of Austerity

# THE AGE OF AUSTERITY

*How Scarcity Will Remake American Politics*

## Thomas Byrne Edsall

Anchor Books
A Division of Random House, Inc.
New York

FIRST ANCHOR BOOKS EDITION, SEPTEMBER 2012

*Copyright © 2012 by Thomas Byrne Edsall*

All rights reserved. Published in the United States by Anchor Books, a division of Random House, Inc., New York, and in Canada by Random House of Canada Limited, Toronto. Originally published in hardcover in the United States by Doubleday, a division of Random House, Inc., New York, in 2011.

Anchor Books and colophon are registered trademarks of Random House, Inc.

Pages 239, 241–43 constitute an extension of this copyright page.

The Library of Congress has cataloged the Doubleday edition as follows:
Edsall, Thomas Byrne.
The age of austerity : how scarcity will remake American politics /
Thomas Byrne Edsall. — 1st ed.
p. cm.
Includes bibliographical references and index.
1. Divided government—United States.
2. Political parties—United States.
3. Social conflict—United States.
4. United States—Politics and government.
I. Title.
JK2261.E37 2012
320.973—dc23
2011029939

*Charts and graphs by Mapping Specialists, Ltd.*
*Book design by Pei Loi Koay*
*Author photograph © Michael Lionstar*

**Anchor ISBN: 978-0-307-94645-4**

www.anchorbooks.com

Printed in the United States of America
10   9   8   7   6   5   4   3   2   1

*To those who, in an age of austerity, have provided me with an abundance of joy—my wife Mary, my daughter Alexandra Tileston Victor Edsall, her husband Robert Salomon Victor, my grandson Thomas Edsall Victor, and my granddaughter Lydia Edsall Victor.*

# Contents

# The Age of Austerity

# The Noose

This book will argue that the broad, tacit compromise of long standing between one political party promoting a social safety net and the other party asserting that hard-earned tax dollars unjustly finance those benefits is no longer sustainable. That compromise between right and left required a growing economy to fund an array of social programs while keeping taxes relatively low in order to moderate hostilities in a politically charged resource war.

Now we have entered a period of austerity markedly different from anything we have seen before. The two major political parties are enmeshed in a death struggle to protect the benefits and goods that flow to their respective bases, each attempting to expropriate the resources of the other. A brutish future stands before us.

A taste of that brutish future arrived in August of 2011. On August 2, a Republican Congress successfully forced House and Senate adoption of $2.2 to $2.5 trillion in spending cuts over ten years. The Budget Control Act of 2011 specified just under $1 trillion in spending reductions by setting binding caps on annual appropriation bills for "discretionary"—nonentitlement—programs such as defense, education, national parks, the FBI, the EPA, low-income housing assistance, medical research, and other nonmandatory programs. In addition, the act ordered the creation of a Joint Select Committee ("Super Committee") to draft legislation reducing the deficit by an additional $1.5 trillion by November 23, 2011. Failure to enact deficit reduction by December 23, 2011, was set to trigger automatic cuts ("sequestration") at the start of 2013, half of which targeted military programs and half of which targeted nondefense entitlement and discretionary programs, including Medicare, farm price supports, and other domestic spending.[1] Under the August 2 legislation, Social Security, Medicaid, food stamps, veterans' benefits, Pell grants, and child nutrition were to be exempt from cuts.[2]

There are clear consequences to these actions.

First, the cuts, painful as they are to various constituencies, are inadequate to resolve the danger of long-term debt. Henry Aaron of the Brookings Institution estimates that "We would have to sequester $1.2 trillion every two years for at least a decade to prevent the debt/GDP ratio from getting 'too high.' . . . Any deficit reduction which cuts a flat amount each year (as the August 2011 cuts and sequestration do) simply pushes the day of reckoning off a couple of years."[3]

Second, the very ineffectiveness of the 2011 Budget Act in addressing long-term debt ensures that austerity will continue to dominate public discourse. "My guess is that we are entering into a decade of fiscal retrenchment, so that this won't be the only Congress that makes austerity a political imperative," said John Feehery, former aide to GOP House Majority Leader Tom DeLay and House Speaker J. Dennis Hastert.[4] That does not mean, however, that Congress will solve the deficit and debt issues: "They always seem to find a way—either through obscure accounting tricks or simply undoing what was put in place—in order to avoid confronting the harsh realities of the country's deficit problem," noted Columbia political scientist Gregory Wawro. "The smart money is on them doing the same this year."[5]

Third, in the short term such cuts threaten to undermine already anemic economic growth.

Fourth, insofar as austerity towers above all other issues, the prospects for the political system to deliver significant long-term stimulus to break increasingly structural unemployment are diminished.

The politics of retrenchment have, in effect, placed politicians in a vise, exacerbating the struggle for smaller pieces of a shrinking pie. Each party has veto power over policy, and the two parties share little or no common ground. Each party is guided by an ideology, and a profoundly ingrained value system, diametrically opposed to that of the other.

Republicans believe government and taxes kill jobs, bleed the economy, and deplete the private sector. Democrats see government as a driving force producing growth, wealth, and innovation. Republicans see government spending as a cause of economic stagnation; Democrats see government outlays as a crucial tool in kick-starting a "virtuous cycle of invention and manufacturing."[6]

Paradoxically, many, if not most, voters hold internally contradictory views on the role of government—strongly supportive of major deficit reduction while opposed to paring back the most costly and fast-growing programs from which they themselves benefit. When pressed on specifics, the public has no stomach for the kind of fiscal consolidation that would rein in the growth of long-term debt.

Gallup, for example, found in an April 2011 survey that 73 percent of respondents blamed the deficit on government "spending too much money on federal programs that are either not needed or wasteful."[7] At the same time, voters are adamantly opposed to cuts in the two programs that are doing most to push up the deficit, Medicare and Social Security. A CNN poll conducted August 5–7, 2011, asked respondents if Congress should reduce federal spending through "major changes to the Social Security and Medicare system." The answer was a decisive "No" by a margin of 64–35, with Democrats adamantly opposed, 71–28, and independents only slightly less so, 62–37. A majority of Republicans were also against the idea, 57–42. While many leaders of the Tea Party movement back sharp reductions in Medicare for future generations, Tea Party supporters themselves—the roughly 20 percent of the electorate who are the propelling force behind the drive to reduce the size and cost of government—were divided on the issue of whether there should be major changes in Social Security and Medicare, opposing such action by a 52–47 margin.[8]

Such apparently contradictory views grow out of a set of underlying beliefs, widely espoused but most firmly held by those on the right: that government disproportionately benefits the "undeserving" poor, and that government benefits can undermine work incentives and the drive to improve one's economic position.

These beliefs, which are explored in later chapters, are evident in survey data revealing the issues on which Tea Party supporters hold much stronger views than the general public. An April 5–12, 2010, *New York Times* poll found, for example, that 27 percent of all voters are convinced that the Obama administration's policies favor the poor, compared to twice that,

56 percent, among Tea Party backers. Similarly, 11 percent of all respondents said administration policies favor blacks over whites, less than half the 25 percent of Tea Party supporters who hold that view. A plurality of all those queried, 47 percent, said providing government benefits to poor people "helps until they're on their own," and 38 percent said such benefits encourage "them to remain poor." Among Tea Party backers, an overwhelming 73 percent said government benefits encourage poor people to remain in poverty, and only 16 percent said the benefits help poor people get back on their own. Finally, when asked "do you think too much has been made of the problems facing black people, too little, or is it just about right," 28 percent of all those surveyed said "too much," 16 percent "too little," and 42 percent said "about right." Among the Tea Party backers, fully 52 percent said "too much," 6 percent said "too little," and 36 percent said "about right."[9]

As Congress struggles to balance the competing interests of the poor, on the one hand, and of middle-class beneficiaries, on the other—of Republican budget hawks on the right, and of Democratic redistributionists on the left—it is fast running out of accounting manipulations, budgetary maneuvers, and other mechanisms to mask red ink. Legislators have adopted year-by-year "temporary" laws to extend the Bush tax cuts, to avoid reducing the level of Medicare payments to doctors, and to prevent the Alternative Minimum Tax (AMT) from hitting the middle class. These provisional policies have been adopted to evade public acknowledgment of real long-term costs in five- and ten-year budget projections required by the Budget Control Act of 1974.[10]

In the midst of the current "great contraction"—with sustained high levels of unemployment, economic volatility, and pessimistic anticipation of lowered living standards—the political system is tied in knots, resulting in incoherent and often destructive responses to an ongoing crisis.[11]

Immediately after the August 2011 enactment of the debt ceiling legislation, the White House struggled to put the best face on what was clearly a defeat at the hands of the GOP. On August 4, the White House Office of Public Engagement declared that the "budget compromise removes the cloud of uncertainty over the economy, and takes important steps toward reducing our deficit. In that sense, it's a win for all Americans."[12]

The August 2011 debt ceiling deal was not treated as a win by Wall Street and the market. On August 5, Standard & Poor's lowered its rating of

U.S. debt from AAA to AA+. S&P's rationale for the downgrade accurately described the state of American politics, and, by specifically citing the use of threats of default as "bargaining chips in the debate over fiscal policy," placed much of the onus for the downgrade on the GOP. The S&P released a communiqué on the day of the downgrade, noting that:

> The political brinksmanship of recent months highlights what we see as America's governance and policymaking becoming less stable, less effective, and less predictable than what we previously believed. The statutory debt ceiling and the threat of default have become political bargaining chips in the debate over fiscal policy. Despite this year's wide-ranging debate, in our view, the differences between political parties have proven to be extraordinarily difficult to bridge, and, as we see it, the resulting agreement fell well short of the comprehensive fiscal consolidation program that some proponents had envisaged until quite recently.[13]

The political conflict that led to the debt ceiling debacle first gained strength well before the emergence of the Tea Party in the summer and fall of 2009. On January 15, 2009, five days before he was inaugurated, Obama announced that he would sponsor a White House Fiscal Responsibility Summit on February 23, 2009, an event that became a key turning point in the fiscal policy debate. Obama set in motion a focus on the deficit and national debt that would come to dominate his presidency. In his opening statement at the summit, the new chief executive declared: "We cannot and will not sustain deficits like these without end . . . we cannot simply spend as we please and defer the consequences to the next budget, the next administration, or the next generation." The president promised "to cut the deficit we inherited by half by the end of my first term in office."[14]

With those words, Obama turned over control of the political agenda to the Republican Party. Government budget deficits are a winning issue for the right; instead of preempting the opposition, Obama was thrown on the defensive, compelled repeatedly to backtrack.

For Obama's core Democratic constituencies, the Fiscal Responsibility Summit—a bid to proactively engage the deficit—was a strategic error, undermining the power of the administration to manage the forces of austerity and allowing a sustained assault on the liberal welfare state.

More than a year and a half later, in November 2010, after enactment of the administration's $780 billion stimulus program,[15] the $938 billion health care reform initiative,[16] the $80 billion bailout of General Motors and Chrysler,[17] and the recession-driven $142 billion surge in means-tested welfare spending,[18] the Republican Party scored a landslide victory in the midterm elections, taking decisive control of the House of Representatives.

Obama acknowledged that his attempt to steer the debate on government budget shortfalls had failed: "Republicans were able to paint my governing philosophy as a classic, traditional, big government liberal . . . the Republicans were successful in creating a picture of the Obama administration as one that was contrary to those commonsense, Main Street values about the size of government."[19]

In early 2011, Obama tried once again to portray himself as in control of the deficit freight train. On February 14, fully two years after he had opened Pandora's box, Obama announced a budget for 2012 calling for one trillion dollars in spending cuts: "It will mean cutting things that I care deeply about; for example, community action programs in low-income neighborhoods and towns, and community development block grants that so many of our cities and states rely on. But if we're going to walk the walk when it comes to fiscal discipline, these kinds of cuts will be necessary."[20]

For many Democratic voters, the proposed cutbacks were brutal. Office of Management and Budget (OMB) Director Jacob "Jack" Lew struggled in congressional testimony and in television appearances that day to portray the administration's slashed spending plan as painful but carefully considered. "We're beyond the easy, low-hanging fruit," Lew told Candy Crowley on CNN. "We're reducing programs that are important programs that we care about, and we're doing what every family does when it sits around its kitchen table. We're making the choice about what do we need for the future."[21]

For Republicans, the Obama proposals were blood in the water. Obama, Lew, and others in the administration were playing on Republican turf, under rules determined by conservatives who held the trump cards. Alabama senator Jeff Sessions, the senior Republican on the Senate Budget Committee, dismissed Obama's cuts as inadequate: "A one-trillion dollar reduction is insignificant and does not get us off on the right course. We are facing a fiscal crisis."[22]

The next day, February 15, Lew ran into a buzz saw when he appeared before the House Budget Committee. Paul Ryan of Wisconsin, the new Republican committee chairman, told Lew:

Because we face a crippling burden of debt, this year's budget in particular presented the president with a unique opportunity to lead our country. The president has disappointed us all by declining that opportunity. He punted. Instead of confronting our debt head-on, the president has presented us with a budget that spends too much, borrows too much, and taxes too much. And that costs jobs and opportunities. His budget would double the amount of debt held by the public by the end of his term, and triple it on the 10th anniversary of his inauguration.[23]

On March 18 the nonpartisan Congressional Budget Office (CBO) dealt the Republicans a royal straight flush. In a report to the Senate, the CBO described its projection of the effect of the administration's 2012 proposal: "In all, deficits would total $9.5 trillion between 2012 and 2021 under the President's budget (or 4.8 percent of total GDP projected for that period). . . . Federal debt held by the public would double under the President's budget, growing from $10.4 trillion (69 percent of GDP) at the end of 2011 to $20.8 trillion (87 percent of GDP) at the end of 2021."[24]

Levels of debt approaching 90 percent of gross domestic product (GDP) by 2021 and trending higher afterward could, according to the CBO and leading economists, trigger a "financial crisis." The CBO described the ensuing process:

> [I]nvestors would require the government to pay higher interest on its securities . . . other countries' experiences suggest that a loss of investors' confidence can occur abruptly and might well come during an economic downturn . . . policymakers would need to make fiscal policy choices that would be much more drastic and painful than if policies had been adjusted sooner. The exact point at which such a crisis might occur is unknown . . . because the ratio of U.S. debt to GDP is heading into territory outside the modern experience of most developed countries.[25]

The pressure for additional retrenchment forced Obama to abandon his own February 14 plan, acknowledging, in effect, that the "tough choices" he had called for were not tough enough. In an April 13, 2011, speech, Obama raised his original target for one trillion dollars in savings to a "grand bargain" of four trillion dollars in savings over the next twelve years. Obama's grand bargain included tax hikes in addition to spending cuts. After months of negotiation, Obama could not win Republican support for such a plan. Instead, with his back to the wall, forced by the GOP's refusal to raise the debt ceiling to prevent the United States from defaulting on its obligations, Obama acceded to the August 2 "compromise" that required cuts of $2.2 to $2.4 trillion over ten years.

The August legislation provided no stimulus to boost employment, and none of Obama's "investment" agenda. Contrary to Obama's promise to preserve Medicare, the legislation called for automatic cuts—triggered sequestration—in the event that Congress failed to reduce spending in other areas. "I got 98 percent of what I wanted," boasted House Speaker John Boehner about the outcome of the legislative negotiations.[26]

Austerity had become the watchword for the Democratic administration. There was no evidence, however, that austerity was the path to recovery. Instead of rebounding, the stock market swung wildly, with the Dow Jones Industrial Average dropping 512 points from the close of trading on Wednesday, August 3, to Thursday, August 4, rising a modest 61 points on Friday, August 5, only to fall 635 points on Monday, August 8, rising 430 points on Tuesday, falling 520 on Wednesday, rising 423 on Thursday, and closing the week with a 126-point hike. Overall, from August 1, 2011, the day before the debt ceiling and budget cuts became law, to the end of the month, the Dow dropped 609.32 points, from 12,186.30 to 11,576.98, or 5 percent.

From July to August, the Conference Board's consumer confidence index plummeted from 59.2 to 44.5. "The index is now at its lowest level in more than two years (April 2009, 40.8)," said Lynn Franco, director of the Conference Board Consumer Research Center. "A contributing factor may have been the debt ceiling discussions since the decline in confidence was well underway before the S&P downgrade."[27] Instead of winning plaudits from the private sector, the debt ceiling/budget cuts legislation contributed to market anxiety—in fact causing a degree of panic.

The brinksmanship on display in the August political battle over raising the debt ceiling appeared likely to have damaging long-term consequences, both domestically and on the international front.

Republican pollster Bill McInturff described the debt ceiling negotiations as a "signal event"—on a par with the Iranian hostage crisis, Iraq's invasion of Kuwait, 9/11, Hurricane Katrina, the Lehman Brothers collapse, and the recessions that defined the 1980, 1992, and 2008 presidential campaigns. The debt ceiling negotiations "led to a scary erosion in confidence in both [the economy and the federal government], at a time when this steep drop in confidence can be least afforded," McInturff warned. "Americans' attitudes about the debt ceiling are not only based on the actual outcome, but are primarily derived from the manner in which this issue was debated and resolved. Their views about this process are clear, and are overwhelmingly negative."

McInturff backed up his argument with poll data: In October 2010, voters were split on the question of whether they had confidence in "the government in Washington to deal with economic problems": 47 percent yes, 52 percent no. In August 2011, after the debt ceiling debate, only 26 percent of respondents said they had confidence in government and 73 percent said they did not. Similarly, the level of voter dissatisfaction had been almost the same in 2007 and 2009—34 satisfied, 64 dissatisfied in 2007, 38–61 in 2009—but in August 2011 the ratio of satisfied to dissatisfied shot up to 21–78.[28]

On the international front, the damage done by the debt ceiling debate was incalculable. John N. Gray of the London School of Economics wrote in the *Financial Times*: "If America's loss of economic primacy is simply the logic of globalisation in action, the speed of America's decline is a result of political failure—not least the failure to deal with debt. The last-minute cosmetic agreement on the deficit ceiling may well go down as the moment when the world began to suspect that America's political class is incapable of addressing the country's problems."[29]

The 2008–2009 economic collapse and its aftermath—growing inequality; mounting debt; partisan polarization; long-term unemployment at levels not seen since the 1930s; the empowerment of a progovernment coalition on the left, and of an ultraconservative populist movement on the right, each armed with a moral vision; wars in Iraq and Afghanistan; and the decline of America's global stature—have converged to generate a dog-eat-dog political competition over diminishing resources.

The politics of scarcity favor the right, which is better equipped ideologically than the left to inflict the hardship measures a sustained economic crisis invites. Nonetheless, Republicans in power have frequently overestimated their mandate, forfeiting public support.

For four decades conservatives have won elections by mobilizing white voters, especially white married Christians. This bedrock GOP foundation is steadily eroding, while Democratic voting blocs—Hispanics, African Americans, other minorities, and single women—are expanding as a share of the electorate.

Republican leaders see the window closing on the opportunity to dismantle the liberal state. The prospect looms that the GOP will be forced to accommodate changing demographics as proponents of big government gain traction and as an ever-growing cohort of Americans becomes dependent on social welfare initiatives. These stresses create an incentive within the conservative movement to pull hard right and to pursue increasingly high-risk strategies.

The 2012 election is positioned to be the most ideologically consequential contest since 1932, setting the stage for a new complex of differences and tensions—no longer confined to this continent. As rising expectations meet diminishing resources on a global scale, political conflict resolution mechanisms with which we are familiar are likely to be swept away.

The optimism underpinning our politics and our social policy depends on the conviction that success in this country is not zero-sum. This belief is fast eroding. In its place, a creeping distrust is sapping the optimism from our system, perhaps the most crucial quality in what has made us an "exceptional" nation.

The stakes could not be higher. The politics of scarcity reach beyond our borders. Past crises serve as warning. The economic deprivation of the Great Depression was among the fundamental causes of the rise of totalitarian regimes, the bloodshed of the 1930s, and World War II, with the eruption of mass violence stemming, in large part, from the rapidly spreading economic collapse.[30] "Germany, Italy, and Japan considered themselves unjustly handicapped in trying to compete with other nations for markets, raw materials, and colonies. They believed that such countries as Belgium, France, Great Britain, the Netherlands, and the United States unfairly controlled most of the world's wealth and people. . . . Germany, Italy, and Japan began to look for lands to conquer in order to obtain what they considered to be their share of the world's resources and markets."[31]

Mass unemployment and the impoverishment of once-viable sectors led to populations in desperate need of food, clothing, and shelter. Desperate need inexorably led to war. Between 1939 and 1945, it is estimated, between fifty and sixty-six million people perished.[32] Only someone unacquainted with, or oblivious to, the dark turns that history can take would say that such events are unrepeatable.

From its founding, Americans have been convinced that their nation is exempt from those constraints of class and history that have bound the rest of the world. This autonomy provided the chance to build an economy and a democratic system of governance based on unconstrained opportunity in a liberal marketplace, putting the United States on a never-ending path of growth. This vision was reinforced by the postwar economic boom from 1945 to 1973, with circumstances favoring the victorious United States over its depleted allies and defeated adversaries.

In past crises the American people have proved relatively adept at translating the forces of lethal competition into political combat rather than violence. As the country once again stands on the brink, whether we can continue down that path is an open question.

# Chapter One

## Austerity

In a matter of just three years a bitter struggle over limited resources has enveloped political discourse at every level in the United States.

Pitched battles between haves and have-nots over health care, taxes, union rights, and unemployment benefits—as well as, at a local level, cuts in police protection, garbage collection, and the numbers of teachers—have dominated public debate. A stagnant economy, ballooning deficits, and the mushrooming strength of antigovernment forces are producing a set of wedge issues centered on fiscal conflict and budget shortages to create a new politics of scarcity.

The ranks of the disadvantaged have exploded. A total of 28.9 million American men and women in July 2011 were either out of work or under-employed, including 13.9 million unemployed actively looking for work, 8.4 million classified as "involuntary part-time workers," and 6.6 million who wanted a job but had given up looking, according to the Bureau of Labor Statistics.[1]

The severity of joblessness and the prospects for finding work have only minimally abated: in June 2011 there were 4.01 million men and women who had been out of work for at least a year,[2] and nine unemployed job seekers for every two job openings, according to the Bureau of Labor Statistics.[3]

Resource competition between Democrats and Republicans now leaves each side determined to protect what it has at the expense of the other.

Worklessness and an underfunded safety net are forcing elected officials to make zero-sum choices—or worse, to enter negative-sum negotiations in which gains and losses add up to less than zero.

There are additional measures of distress. Financial pressures on the working and middle classes have escalated, forcing survival strategies that leave no room for sharing with the less well off. Millions of homeowners who were banking on real estate appreciation to carry their education, medical, and/or retirement costs have seen the average value of their properties drop by 21 percent, from $329,400 in March 2007 to $260,300 in early 2011.[4] In July 2011, 11 million homeowners, or 23 percent, were underwater (owed more than their homes were worth) by an average of $65,000, and another 2.4 million, or 5 percent, had equity of $5,000 or less.[5] From the start of the recession in December 2007 to the end of 2010, banks repossessed just over 2.5 million homes, according to RealtyTrac.com.

With the disappearance of defined-benefit pensions from the private sector, a substantial proportion of those approaching the end of their working lives are depending on inadequate or nonexistent savings that will leave them radically short of what they need to get by, according to Boston College's Center for Retirement Research.[6]

Half of those already retired receive 90 percent or more of their total income from Social Security, which has an average annual benefit of fourteen thousand dollars.[7] "Even before the financial crisis that began in the fall of 2008, Americans were woefully unprepared for retirement. . . . Today, one-third of American households do not have any form of retirement savings plan beyond Social Security. . . . While lower- and middle-income households are least prepared, most Americans—even in middle- to higher-income households—will fall well short of their retirement expectations," reports the management consultant firm McKinsey & Company.[8] An AARP poll released on February 3, 2011, found that among those between the ages of forty-six and sixty-five, 25 percent had no retirement savings.[9]

Pressures on the Social Security trust fund are mounting. The leading edge of the baby boom generation turned sixty-five in 2011. The average age of retirement has dropped sharply over the past hundred years. With prolonged schooling and increased longevity, the proportion of the life span in which people actually work and contribute to Social Security and Medicare is declining.[10] At the start of the twentieth century, more than two-thirds of men who survived past the age of sixty-five worked. By 1950 that proportion had shrunk below 50 percent, and by 1985 only 16 percent were employed. The result is a transformation of the *dependency ratio*: "the number of people 65 and older to every 100 people of traditional working ages [20 to 64] is projected to climb rapidly from 22 in 2010 to 35 in 2030," according to the U.S. Census Bureau.[11]

Compounding these developments, the population of the very poor is also swelling and increasingly turning to the government for help. In 2010, according to the U.S. Census, 15.1 percent of the population was living in poverty, the highest level since 1993 and up from 11.3 percent in 2000. The poverty rate for whites was 13 percent; for blacks, 27.4 percent; and for Hispanics, 26.8 percent. The number of households receiving Temporary Assistance to Needy Families (TANF), the post-1996 welfare-reform program, increased from 2.27 million in 2000 to 4.49 million by May 2011.[12]

Reflecting the increased need for emergency food, the number of food stamp recipients grew from 17.2 million in 2000, at an annual cost of $17.1 billion, to 44.1 million at the end of 2010, at a cost of $69.6 billion, the highest number in the history of the program.[13] The number of food stamp recipients has grown over just the past three years by 61 percent, with the average monthly per person SNAP (Supplemental Nutrition Assistance Program) benefit in 2010 being $133.70.[14] This amount is available only to persons beneath the government's designated poverty level, who do not have more than $2,000 in liquid assets or own a home, a population currently estimated at one-fifth of all Americans. At the same time, only two-thirds of those eligible under Department of Health and Human Services criteria enroll in SNAP. In 2006, the last year for which there is data, 44 percent of SNAP household heads reported their race/ethnicity as Hispanic or African American.[15]

Medicaid, the program providing health care to the indigent, has grown by 5 million recipients in a decade, from 41.4 million in 2000 to 46.5 million in 2010. Over the course of the next decade, if the Obama administration's health care reform survives court and congressional challenges, Medicaid will be required to provide essential coverage for everyone at or below 133 percent of the poverty line; this will add an estimated 15.9 million more recipients between 2014 and 2019, at a five-year cost of $443.5 billion to the federal government and $21.1 billion to be paid by the states.[16]

### "Getting Something for Nothing"

As the numbers of recipients of government benefits—ranging from welfare, Medicaid, and unemployment compensation to veteran's benefits, Social Security, and Medicare—have exploded, the potential for political manipulation has become apparent. In June 2009, for example, the publication of a study by the Urban Institute and Brookings Institution Tax Policy Center showing that 46.9 percent of all households paid no federal income tax in the previous year, as illustrated in Figure 1.1,[17] spurred a flurry of conservative political reaction. The outpouring from the right only intensified with the April 29, 2011, release of a Joint Committee on Taxation analysis showing that 51 percent of tax filers in 2009 paid no income tax.[18] Curtis Dubay, senior tax policy analyst at the Heritage Foundation, argued: "We have 50 percent of people who are getting something for nothing."[19]

Sean Hannity of FOX News raised the stakes, declaring: "You know, we saw stories this week where people were saying, all right, health care, where do I sign up for my free Obama health care? We saw stories this week, 50 percent of American households no longer pay taxes. What does that mean for America if you have a voting electorate that's not paying any taxes?"[20]

In May 2010, the Tax Policy Center story was followed by a second that provided further ammunition for the GOP and for the nascent Tea Party movement. Figure 1.2 demonstrates a long-term trend that had accelerated sharply with the onset of the Great Recession: the steady decline of private sector earnings as a share of total personal income, accompanied by a steady rise in government transfer payments financed by tax dollars.[21]

By midsummer 2011, Republican presidential candidates were calling for legislation to make payment of federal income taxes mandatory for all workers, targeting the bottom third of the income distribution whose income was too low to meet federal income tax thresholds at that time.

As the economy continued to falter, massive growth in demand for government services threatened to add substantially to the debit side of the government ledger. The 2010 federal deficit stood at $1.3 trillion[22] and was predicted by the Congressional Budget Office to hit $1.5 trillion in 2011.[23] But those figures tell only a small part of the story. The CBO reported that total federal debt held by the public exceeded $9 trillion at the end of FY 2010, or 62 percent of the GDP, up from 36 percent of GDP in 2007, just as the recession began.[24] The ratio of debt to GDP has never exceeded 50 percent except

**Percentage of Tax Units with Zero or Negative Individual Income Tax Liability by Filing Status and Cash Income Level, Current Law, 2009[1]**

| Cash Income (2009 dollars)[2] | Tax Filing Status | | | | | | All Tax Units |
|---|---|---|---|---|---|---|---|
| | Single | Married Filing Jointly | Head of Household | Married Filing Separately | Elderly Tax Units | Tax Units with Children | |
| Under $10,000 | 99.9 | 100.0 | 99.7 | 97.3 | 100.0 | 99.9 | 99.8 |
| $10,000–$20,000 | 74.3 | 99.9 | 99.3 | 57.9 | 89.5 | 99.8 | 83.6 |
| $20,000–$30,000 | 36.7 | 90.2 | 92.3 | 26.2 | 76.5 | 98.9 | 61.8 |
| $30,000–$40,000 | 16.0 | 79.8 | 77.9 | 13.7 | 61.4 | 89.3 | 47.5 |
| $40,000–$50,000 | 7.4 | 71.7 | 45.1 | 17.1 | 48.2 | 68.3 | 35.7 |
| $50,000–$75,000 | 5.0 | 34.2 | 21.2 | 4.9 | 22.5 | 40.9 | 21.5 |
| $75,000–$100,000 | 3.6 | 11.3 | 8.2 | 8.8 | 8.1 | 15.1 | 9.2 |
| $100,000–$200,000 | 4.0 | 3.4 | 2.1 | 9.3 | 4.9 | 4.0 | 3.5 |
| $200,000–$500,000 | 3.0 | 1.8 | 2.5 | 4.8 | 3.9 | 1.6 | 2.0 |
| $500,000–$1,000,000 | 2.6 | 1.8 | 5.3 | 0.0 | 1.6 | 2.1 | 2.0 |
| Over $1,000,000 | 2.0 | 1.5 | 0.0 | 0.0 | 1.1 | 1.3 | 1.5 |
| All | 46.7 | 38.1 | 71.9 | 25.8 | 55.3 | 54.1 | 46.9 |

*Source: Urban-Brookings Tax Policy Center Microsimulation Model (version 0509-2)*
[1]Calendar year. Includes both filing and nonfiling units but excludes those that are dependents of other tax units.
[2]Tax units with negative cash income are excluded from the lowest income class but are included in the totals. For a description of cash income, see http://www.taxpolicycenter.org/TaxModel/income.cfm.

*Figure 1.1 shows the percentage of households that pay no federal income tax in 11 income categories, ranging from those making less than $10,000 a year, 99.8 percent of whom pay no income tax, to those making over $1 million annually, 1.5 percent of whom pay no federal income tax.*

during World War II and the decade afterward. The CBO projects that debt held by the public will reach 101 percent of GDP by 2021, the highest level since 1946, and 187 percent by 2035.[25]

The consequences, according to the CBO, will be disastrous: higher interest rates for all borrowers; more borrowing from China, Germany, and other countries; declining domestic investment; an inability to respond to future recessions; a growing likelihood of new financial crises; higher interest charges on new government debt; and a severely diminished safety net.[26] And if the past is any guide, the potential for global chaos.

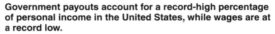

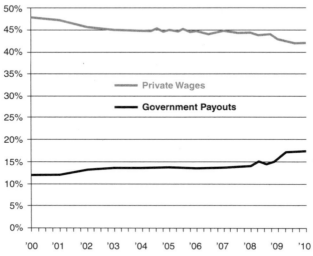

Source: Bureau of Economic Analysis

*Figure 1.2*

### Your Loss Is My Gain

The major issues of the next few years—long-term deficit reduction; a graying population (in 2050 the number of Americans sixty-five and older is projected to be 88.5 million, more than double the aged population of 40 million in 2010); entitlement reform, notably of Social Security and Medicare; and defense spending—suggest that "your loss is my gain" politics will inevitably intensify.

Competition between the Pentagon, entitlement spending, and what remains of discretionary spending on behalf of the poor ensures that among the most incendiary issues will be the attempt of each major party to blame the other for the conclusive demise of the American Century.

The threats to individual well-being inherent in such negative-sum conflicts cut against the American grain. A brutal squeeze on resources is evident in venues from Colorado Springs—where more than a third of the city's 24,512 streetlights were extinguished, police helicopters sold, the police vice team laid off, and money for water and fertilizer in city parks eliminated—to

Prichard, Alabama, where monthly pension checks to the town's 150 retired workers were halted.[27]

At the height of the 2011 battles between Republican governors and public sector unions, New Jersey governor Chris Christie defined the polarized struggle in terms of the deserving taxpayers and the elderly of New Jersey joined together, on one side, against a protected class of public employees seeking to line its pockets, on the other. Christie told the state legislature on February 22, 2011:

> Enacting reform of our public employee health insurance program now will enable us to take another vital step—providing critical property tax relief to those who need it most: hard working, middle-class New Jerseyans and seniors. But let me be clear: the chance for middle class taxpayers and seniors to receive double the property tax relief without raising taxes on anyone else is solely up to you, the Legislature. The ability to provide doubled property tax rebates involves a tradeoff and requires real reform to pay for it.[28]

Along parallel lines, shortly after he won election in 2010, Wisconsin governor Scott Walker declared, "[W]e can no longer live in a society where the public employees are the haves and taxpayers who foot the bills are the have-nots"—a clear bid to establish polarizing divisions to the advantage of the GOP.[29]

There are, however, obvious dangers for the Republicans who, galvanized by Tea Party success, emerged in 2010 and 2011 as self-proclaimed advocates of the new austerity. First and foremost, substantial numbers of Republican voters have no appetite for cuts in the two programs that virtually every economist and budget analyst says must be chopped down to size: Medicare and Social Security.

### Chased by a Tiger

When voters were asked in a March 3, 2011, Wall Street Journal/NBC poll if Medicare cuts were necessary to "significantly reduce" the deficit, 18 percent agreed and 54 percent said no. In the case of Social Security, 22 percent said cuts were needed, while 49 percent said they were not. Bill McInturff, a Republican strategist who co-ran the poll, said the results are "a huge flashing yellow sign for Republicans on how much preparation will be needed if they propose to change Social Security and Medicare." Asked why the House Republican leadership is preparing to go ahead with entitlement cuts, McInturff said, "It may be hard to understand why someone would try to jump off a cliff . . . unless you understand that they are being chased by a tiger, and that tiger is the Tea Party."[30]

In addition to the difficulty in persuading sufficient numbers of Republicans to slash the most popular—and expensive—entitlements, the GOP is in danger of splintering over the question of whether to cut defense spending. While the House leadership and many of the more senior Republicans in both branches of Congress consider the Pentagon budget untouchable, that is not the case for newly elected GOP members, many of whom have ties to the Tea Party.

On February 16, 2011, for example, the House voted 233–198 to eliminate funding for additional engines for the F-35 aircraft. The action was taken over the objections of the Republican leadership and a majority of the Republican caucus, 130 of whom voted to preserve the F-35 appropriation. Funding for the additional aircraft engines was eliminated, however, by an alliance of 110 Republicans, many of whom were freshmen elected with Tea Party backing, and 123 Democrats.[31]

## Girding for Battle

On one side, Republicans and Tea Party activists are convinced that their rights, freedoms, and economic stability are under assault by the Democratic-led expansion of the state. "Now that the Democrats have added trillions to our national debt, unemployment has more than doubled, and millions of Americans have lost their jobs," declared Senator Jim DeMint (R-SC) on September 3, 2010. "The Democrats' experiment with socialism must end: government spending, debt, and takeovers will not put Americans back to work."[32]

On the other side, liberals and many Democrats are determined to protect the flow of government benefits to key constituencies.

When President Obama's National Commission on Fiscal Responsibility and Reform, aka the Deficit Commission, proposed a collection of hard-nosed savings measures—among them, reducing Social Security benefits and raising the retirement age to sixty-eight, freezing federal salaries for three years, eliminating earmarks, and capping the tax deductibility of health insurance coverage and of mortgage interest payments—Democratic House Minority Leader Nancy Pelosi declared:

> This proposal is simply unacceptable. Any final proposal from the Commission should do what is right for our children and grandchildren's economic security as well as for our nation's fiscal security, and it must do what is right for our seniors, who are counting on the bedrock promises of Social Security and Medicare. And it must strengthen America's middle class families—under siege for the last decade, and unable to withstand further encroachment on their economic security.[33]

Both left and right are girding for battle. Liberals, for example, are preparing to call for shoring up Social Security by raising the cap on payroll taxes for higher-income earners, while conservatives are looking toward finding ways to trim benefits—by shrinking, for example, the cost-of-living adjustment (COLA) to 1 percent below inflation (and/or adopting a new yardstick—the Chained Consumer Price Index—for setting COLAs that would lower benefits), as well as raising the age at which such benefits can be collected.[34]

Underlying these ideological battles is the corrosive power of political money in Washington, which also drives partisan polarization and an embattled mind-set. The relentless fund-raising pressures on elected officials have eroded the capacity for independent judgment in two ways. First, the power of the Speaker, the majority leader, and others in the congressional hierarchy to direct campaign contributions from PACs and lobbyists, along with the crucial role of the Republican and Democratic congressional and senatorial committees, forces members to accede to leadership demands. Second, and more subtly, the pervasiveness of fund-raising demands in each representative's and senator's daily life requires perpetual accommodation to special interests.

The influence community—lobbies, trade associations, public relations and media advisory firms—has become the single biggest source of second careers for retired and defeated members of Congress, their staffs, and ranking officials throughout the executive branch. As of this writing, 370 former members of the House and Senate are lobbyists. Members of the House and Senate have substantially higher returns on their stock investments than the general public—6 percent higher annually for representatives, 10 percent for senators, according to a study published in 2004 in the *Journal of Financial and Quantitative Analysis*, "Abnormal Returns from the Common Stock Investments of Members of the U.S. House of Representatives." The study concluded, "We find strong evidence that Members of the House have some type of nonpublic information which they use for personal gain. . . . Our results indicate that Representatives, like Senators, also trade with a substantial information advantage."

The conservative drive to dismantle the welfare state occurs in the context of a multibillion-dollar annual flow of private sector cash to shape political decisions in Washington. In 2010, a non–presidential election year, a total of $3.48 billion was spent by House and Senate candidates, the political parties, and independent expenditure groups, according to the Center for Responsive Politics at OpenSecrets.org. In addition, lobbyists reported receipts of $3.5 billion, according to the center. The $6.98 billion combined total does not include undisclosed money spent by tax-exempt independent expenditure groups or the fees collected by strategic and media consulting firms. In 2012, a presidential election year, total spending by all groups will be substantially higher than in 2010. Thus, even as the government is drowning in debt, and as the two parties fight incessantly over money, the political system itself is awash in cash, setting the stage for the most significant partisan confrontation since 1932.

## A Flood Tide of Red Ink

After the Democratic electoral rout on November 2, 2010, which President Obama called a shellacking, power at the federal level was split, with Republicans in control of the House of Representatives after winning 63 new seats, and Democrats in command of the Senate and the White House. In the states, however, Democrats suffered devastating defeats. Republicans won 675 new state legislative seats, the biggest Republican gain since 1966.

The next year, 2011, became one in which Democratic public employee unions across the Midwest struggled to survive against newly empowered Republican officials determined to cut the pay, pensions, and bargaining rights of public employees. Republican governors were joined, in turn, by such newly elected Democratic governors as California's Jerry Brown and New York's Andrew Cuomo, both facing deficits and accumulated debt that threatened their states' ability to remain in the bond market.

The flood tide of red ink at every level of government—but most importantly in the states with newly elected Republican governors and legislatures—pits a disproportionately black and Democratic public employee sector, dependent on tax dollars for wages and benefits, against a disproportionately Republican and white constituency of voters who pay relatively higher taxes.

The vulnerability of black Americans to assaults on the government workforce is most apparent in data available for the federal government. The federal workforce, for example, is 17.6 percent African American, while the private sector civilian workforce is only 10 percent black.[35] The percentages of African Americans are highest in just those departments and agencies that are most strongly targeted for cuts by Republicans: Health and Human Services, 19.9 percent black; Housing and Urban Development, 38.3 percent; Equal Employment Opportunity Commission, 42.3 percent; Department of Education, 36.6 percent; Agency for International Development, 28.0 percent.[36] At the state and local levels, the government workforce is 18.5 percent black, as compared to 10.8 percent of the entire workforce, public and private, and 12.9 percent of the general population.[37]

The disproportionate share of government jobs held by African Americans, in combination with the disproportionate percentages of minority recipients of means-tested programs—from food stamps to free/reduced-price school meals to TANF (Temporary Assistance for Needy Families) to Section 8 housing—have proven ideal wedge issues for the GOP to fracture white loyalty to the Democratic Party. This overlay of policy, programs, and race is perhaps the most significant factor in the Democrats' recurrent difficulty in maintaining a biracial coalition.

### Who Loses?

The conflicts arising out of the politics of scarcity are unrelenting. The inescapable question becomes: Who will get the short end of the stick: kids, the elderly, the handicapped, government employees, single women, entrepreneurs, doctors, bankers, CEOs? The list of potential victims goes on.

Congress in 2009 adopted a rule known as PAYGO, requiring either a spending cut or a tax hike to pay for any new government expenditure. PAYGO ensures a zero-sum approach to lawmaking. On August 5, 2010, for example, the Senate won approval of a twenty-six-billion-dollar economic stimulus bill providing money to the states for health care and teachers' salaries while simultaneously slashing food stamps for the poor—reducing the monthly benefit for a family of three by forty-seven dollars. Fifty-seven Democrats voted in favor of the measure.[38] Former senator Blanche Lincoln (D-Ark.), who chaired the Senate Agriculture panel, pointed out that with scarce tax dollars, there was no way to preserve the food stamp money. "We were going to lose those dollars anyway," Lincoln said. "You saw the teachers grab for it."[39]

On Monday, November 15, 2010, Francisco Felix, thirty-two, a Medicaid recipient whose life was threatened by hepatitis C, received a dying friend's offer of her liver. Francisco went to Banner Good Samaritan Medical Center in Phoenix, Arizona, where he was prepared for the transplant operation the next day. On Tuesday, however, the liver was given to another patient. To save money, on October 1, 2010, Arizona had ended coverage of transplants under the state Medicaid program. Felix could not afford the two-hundred-thousand-dollar cost of the operation. The decision amounted to a virtual death sentence. Felix was told in November 2010 that he had a life expectancy of twelve months. Public outrage was intense. In January 2011, ABC News announced: "Two Dead Since Arizona Medicaid Program Slashed Transplant Coverage."[40]

In March 2011, Reuters ran a story about another victim of Arizona governor Jan Brewer's new Medicaid regulation. "She's signing death warrants—that's what she's doing. This is death for me," [said] Douglas Gravagna, forty-four, a heavyset man who needed a heart transplant. Gravagna is one of ninety-eight people who no longer qualify for Medicaid-financed transplants in the ongoing fight over state spending in Arizona.[41] The local Arizona television station KGUN9-TV broadcast local protests: "They're known as the Arizona 98. All of them are in need of a life-saving transplant. On Saturday, with time running out for many of them, the 'Dream of Life Intervention Coalition' staged a silent protest against the state's move to trim Medicaid transplant funding in an effort to reduce the budget deficit."[42]

A fierce political battle erupted, and on April 7, 2011, the Arizona Health Care Cost Containment System announced that Brewer had signed a budget restoring the cuts. As of May 2011, Felix remained alive. Uncertain of his access to medical care under more restrictive financing criteria, Felix was seeking contributions to pay for his operation through the National Transplant Assistance Fund.[43]

Arizona is a case study in how a sudden and steep collapse of the economy has provided fertile ground for anti-Hispanic and anti-immigrant sentiment. The state, which had been one of the most prosperous in the nation, took a particularly severe economic hit in 2008. A slow but steady movement in a progressive direction from 2000 to 2007 came to an abrupt halt. In 2009 the Arizona legislature slashed the budget, aiming spending reductions almost entirely at the heavily Hispanic poor, and in 2010 passed the toughest anti-immigration law in the nation, Senate Bill 1070, the Support Our Law Enforcement and Safe Neighborhoods Act.

The Arizona budget cuts were sponsored by the state's Republican governor and legislature, but Democrats are not immune to these pressures. In New Jersey, Stephen M. Sweeney, the Democratic state senate president and business agent and treasurer of the Ironworkers Local 399, is leading the charge to trim the benefits won by sister public employee unions over the years. "At some point, you reach the limit of your ability to pay," Sweeney declared, echoing the state's Republican governor. In New York, former governor David Paterson, a politician with strong ties to organized labor, threatened to lay off eighty-nine hundred state workers, provoking outrage among former loyalists. "If you told me five years ago that David Paterson would be our enemy, I would have laughed at you," said Danny Donohue, president of New York's Civil Service Employees Association. "He's trying to balance a $9 billion deficit on the backs of public employees."[44]

The fight over basic services is endemic. Phoenix, which cut eleven hundred workers from the city payroll in February 2010, instituted a regressive 2 percent tax on groceries in April 2011 in order to limit cuts in such programs as Meals on Wheels and bus services for seniors.[45]

In East Point, an 80 percent black suburb of Atlanta, sixty-two people were injured when thirty thousand Georgians turned up seeking applications for subsidized low-income Section 8 housing, applications made available by the city for the first time in eight years. The program has no vacancies.[46] The current national budget provides $19.6 billion for Section 8 housing with long waiting lists in every community.[47]

In Newark, New Jersey, an overwhelmingly black and Democratic city has been forced to lay off 16 percent of its police force, a total of 164 officers. Radio station WNYC compared crime rates for the five months after the cuts, December 2010 through April 2011, with rates for the previous year and found that murders were up 54 percent, car thefts 43 percent, robberies 17 percent, and the number of shooting victims by just under 50 percent. While reported crime shot up, the number of arrests fell by 3,400.[48]

To the south, in Camden, a black and Hispanic Democratic base, the mayor and city council have been forced to fire nearly half (46 percent) of the force, putting 168 officers out on the street.[49]

On Monday, January 17, 2011, Dave Seybert, thirty-two, who had served nine years on the Camden police force, gave up his badge and gun. "They shook my hand and told me good luck," he said. "The hardest part was walking out the door."[50]

On May 2, 2011, the Camden County Prosecutor's Office reported a 19 percent increase in violent crime and a 259 percent increase in aggravated assault with firearms after the policy layoffs. Thomas Garrity, Jr., chief of investigations for the prosecutor's office, told the *Philadelphia Inquirer*, "I do know we have the perfect storm that includes a sluggish economy, the proliferation of national gangs, and a reduction of police manpower throughout the county."[51]

## Assault on the Least Economically Secure

The politics of scarcity, then, are inflicting the most severe wounds on Democratic constituencies, especially those living in poverty and dependent on government programs. The political vulnerability of programs serving impoverished minority constituencies is self-evident. There are partisan and strategic reasons for the intensity of the current austerity assault on the least economically secure Democratic populations: from the moment Obama took office, Republicans have deliberately engaged this conflict over diminishing resources, determined to protect the interests of their more middle-class and affluent constituencies. Democrats and liberals, in contrast, had been lulled into complacency by the delusion that the outcomes of the 2006 and 2008 elections marked a Democratic realignment that would be further strengthened by the severe recession.

Instead of a liberal reordering of the electorate, however, the intractable downturn and the inability of the current administration to get the economy back in gear before the November 2010 election produced a sharp shift to the right. Nowhere was that more apparent than among the elderly, a disproportionately white constituency. These voters saw Obama's trillion-dollar health care reform legislation, which included a massive $506 billion cut in Medicare over ten years, as a threat to both Social Security and Medicare.[52] In 2009 and 2010 the administration and the Democratic Congress were seen as transferring scarce tax dollars away from seniors to a younger, poorer, disproportionately minority electorate, not only through expanded health care, but also through the billions spent on extensions of long-term unemployment insurance—which shot up from $35.1 billion in 2007 to $45.3 billion in 2008 to $122.5 billion in 2009 to $160.1 billion in 2010[53]—and through the $787 billion stimulus bill known as the American Recovery and Reinvestment Act of 2009.[54]

Obama foreshadowed the kinds of grueling choices cost-cutting health care reform would impose in an April 14, 2010, interview with David Leonhardt of the *New York Times*. He anticipated the "death panel" controversy that was to erupt over a provision in his bill giving expanded powers to the Medicare Payment Advisory Commission (MedPAC) in determining which medical services for the aged would, or would not, be paid for:

> [W]hen my grandmother got very ill during the campaign, she got cancer; it was determined to be terminal. And about two or three weeks after her diagnosis she fell, broke her hip. It was determined that she might have had a mild stroke, which is what had precipitated the fall. So now she's in the hospital, and the doctor says, "Look, you've got about—maybe you have three months, maybe you have six months, maybe you have nine months to live. Because of the weakness of your heart, if you have an operation on your hip there are certain risks that—you know, your heart can't take it. On the other hand, if you just sit there with your hip like this, you're just going to waste away and your quality of life will be terrible." And she elected to get the hip replacement and was fine for about two weeks after the hip replacement, and then suddenly just—you know, things fell apart. I don't know how much that hip replacement cost. I would have paid out of pocket for that hip replacement just because she's my grandmother. Whether, sort of in the aggregate, society making those decisions to give my grandmother, or everybody else's aging grandparents or parents, a hip replacement when they're terminally ill is a sustainable model, is a

very difficult question. If somebody told me that my grandmother couldn't have a hip replacement and she had to lie there in misery in the waning days of her life—that would be pretty upsetting. So that's where I think you just get into some very difficult moral issues. But that's also a huge driver of cost, right? I mean, the chronically ill and those toward the end of their lives are accounting for potentially 80 percent of the total health care bill out here.[55]

Seniors, who in past elections could be drawn back into the Democratic fold with warnings of Republican plans to privatize and/or cut Social Security and Medicare, in 2009 and 2010 turned against the Democratic Party and the federal government itself. A major April 2010 Pew Center study comparing attitudes from 1997 to 2010 found that voters over sixty-five, who cast one out of every five votes in a presidential year and one out of every four in off-year elections, went from viewing the impact of the federal government on their personal lives as positive, 48–30, in 1997 to negative, 42–33, in March 2010. In 1997, only 34 percent of seniors thought the federal government was in need of "major reform," the lowest level of any age-group. By 2010 the percentage had shot up to 58, the highest of any age-group. By a 50–45 margin, voters over sixty-five in 2010 said federal programs should be cut, the largest antigovernment margin of any age-group.[56]

Analyzing postelection survey data in November 2010, the liberal organization Democracy Corps concluded, "Seniors played an immense role in this result—raising their participation as a share of the electorate to 23 percent and their vote for Republicans by 10 points since 2008. They were clearly spooked by health care reform and the so-called cuts in Medicare."[57]

Republicans learned—after voters demonstrated in the 2006 elections their opposition to George W. Bush's proposal to privatize Social Security—how to avoid this issue. In their pre-2010 election "Pledge to America," House GOP leaders declared:

We will make the decisions that are necessary to protect our entitlement programs for today's seniors and future generations. That means requiring a full accounting of Social Security, Medicare, and Medicaid, setting benchmarks for these programs and reviewing them regularly, and preventing the expansion of unfunded liabilities.[58]

In the trenches of a hard-fought 2010 northeast Mississippi house election, the emerging GOP strategy of capitalizing on the anxieties of older voters was on display. Alan Nunnelee, who went on to beat Democratic incumbent Travis Childers, issued a September 9, 2010, campaign promise that translated what that pledge really means:

> Today I signed two pledges that are important for protecting the seniors of North Mississippi: a pledge to never privatize Social Security, and a pledge to repeal ObamaCare. Our nation has made a solemn, moral promise to our seniors. For their entire lives, the men and women on Social Security today paid into the system as a way to save for their future. . . . [B]ut there's also another issue that is of great concern to our senior citizens: ObamaCare. This Congress jeopardized the financial security of North Mississippi seniors when they passed ObamaCare. ObamaCare cuts Medicare, raises taxes and fees on folks that can't afford it, and makes insurance more expensive. If you say you are standing up for seniors, you have to stand against ObamaCare.[59]

Along similar lines, the 60 Plus Association, a conservative front group seeking to be a counterweight to AARP, ran ads in the districts of eight Democratic incumbents featuring head shots of white-haired voters declaring: "Washington liberals like [then-congresswoman Ann Kirkpatrick, D-Ariz.] aren't listening to Arizona seniors. . . . The Obama/Pelosi health care disaster cuts $500 billion from Medicare, threatens seniors' ability to keep our own doctors, and will hurt the quality of our care. . . . Kirkpatrick pretends she's independent, but when we needed her to stand up for us, Kirkpatrick voted with Pelosi."[60]

After the election, Republicans in the House, including Nunnelee, executed an about-face and backed conversion of Medicare into a voucher program. Key GOP officials and conservative groups aggressively marketed their proposal, arguing that Ryan's budget-cutting plan, which would not go into effect for ten years, was the only way to "save" Medicare from sacrifice, at the hands of Democrats, to Obama's costly health care reform legislation, which would divert funds away from seniors.

Ryan, the prime sponsor of the controversial Medicare voucher proposal, described the choice facing Congress:

Will Medicare become a program in which a board of bureaucrats manages its bankruptcy by denying care to seniors? Or will leaders work together to save and strengthen Medicare by empowering seniors to choose health care plans that work best for them, with less support for the wealthy and more help for the poor and the sick? House Republicans have advanced solutions to save Medicare. Instead of working with us, the leaders of the Democratic Party have opted to play politics with the health security of America's seniors.[61]

Most importantly, conservatives pointed out that the shift to Medicare vouchers, or what they called "premium supports," would affect only those turning sixty-five ten years from now, leaving medical coverage for all currently retired people and for those close to retirement untouched. The Heritage Foundation argued:

> [V]irtually none of the $5.8 trillion in spending reductions in the first decade [of the Republican budget plan] would affect Social Security and Medicare. In fact, seniors would benefit from averting the large tax increases planned in current law and from tax reforms that lower their rates while closing unneeded loopholes. Those currently older than age 55 would be exempt from any future changes to their Social Security and Medicare benefits.[62]

### To Have and Have Not

In effect, the politics of scarcity are changing the composition of traditional haves and have-nots. Once the primary have-not beneficiaries of New Deal and Great Society Democratic programs, the elderly recipients of Social Security and Medicare are now among the haves in that they *have* Social Security and Medicare and are determined to protect those benefits from liberals seeking to redirect tax dollars to pay for health coverage for the younger poor.

From September 1998 to October 2006, the Wall Street Journal/NBC poll found a consistent double-digit advantage for the Democrats on Social Security, ranging from a low of fifteen points in December 2004 to an October 26, 2006, high of twenty-eight points. The next time the WSJ/NBC poll asked the same question, in August 2010, the advantage over the GOP had collapsed to just four points, in effect a statistical tie.[63]

A later poll—conducted just before the 2010 midterm election by the Democratic firm of Lake Research Partners for a nonprofit advocacy organization, Save Our Social Security—found that Republicans had pulled ahead of both President Obama and the Democratic Congress on the question "Who will better handle Social Security?" Respondents chose congressional Republicans over congressional Democrats by a margin of 31–28, and congressional Republicans over Obama by a margin of 33–26.[64]

For more than seventy years, Social Security has been a mainstay of the Democratic Party; it is difficult to overestimate the potential danger to the party if these numbers gain further traction over time.

Although the Republican strategy of strengthening support among older voters by stressing the threat to Medicare and Social Security posed by health care reform worked in 2010, the long-range prospects for the GOP on this issue are mixed. Two top Republicans, House Speaker John Boehner and Budget Committee chair Paul Ryan, are committed to cutting spending on these two popular entitlement programs. "People in Washington assume that Americans understand how big the problem is, but most Americans don't have a clue," Boehner told the *Wall Street Journal* on March 3, 2011. "Once they understand how big the problem is, I think people will be more receptive to what the possible solutions may be." That proposition remains to be seen.

## The Politics of No

The bleak politics of cutbacks, layoffs, debt, deficits, and pay-as-you-go budgeting rules provide a powerful logic to the seemingly simplistic, if risky, Republican strategy of standing in unified opposition to the entire Obama agenda. Republicans are committed to fight any policy that can be viewed as threatening the interests and assets of their constituencies. GOP positions include, for example, protecting the affluent, who have been paying lower taxes under the Bush cuts and fighting any diminution of benefits for those who already have good medical insurance.

The intersection of partisan power and the differing economic outlooks of various demographic groups have produced a pattern worrisome for those seeking progress toward any kind of political consensus.

An exhaustive June 30, 2010, Pew Center report, "How the Great Recession Has Changed Life in America," documents the finding that blacks, Hispanics, and the poor generally took much harder hits over the previous two years than better-off groups.[65]

Some 32 percent of whites have had to reduce their workweeks or take unpaid leaves, compared to 61 percent of blacks and 51 percent of Hispanics. Black unemployment grew by 6.9 points, Hispanic by 6.7, and white by 4.3 points. A later Pew study, released in July 2011, found that inflation-adjusted median wealth fell between 2005 and 2009 by 66 percent, from $18,359 to $6,325, for Hispanic households; by 53 percent, from $12,124 to $5,677, for African American households; and just 16 percent, from $134,992 to $113,149, for white households.[66]

Although whites have had a much easier time weathering the recession, they are substantially more pessimistic about the future than blacks or Hispanics.

Just under one in five whites, 19 percent, believes that the economic changes wrought by the recession have been "major and will prove to be permanent." In contrast, only 12 percent of blacks and Hispanics foresee such a dismal future.

Similarly, 22 percent of Republicans see permanent major changes for the worse, nearly double the 12 percent of Democrats.

Along the same lines, only 59 percent of whites believe "America will always continue to be prosperous and make economic progress," while 81 percent of blacks and 75 percent of Hispanics still believe in this key component of the American dream.

The higher levels of optimism among minorities, despite the bleaker conditions they face, are based, at least in part, on the fact that with Democrats in control of the White House and the Senate, minorities believe their interests are reasonably well represented in the political arena.

Over time, however, a stagnant or eroding economy is likely to undermine optimism across the board, as prospects of a better life become more remote and as efforts of policy makers appear futile. Optimism is the lifeblood of the American political system. The conviction that anyone can get ahead—that everyone has access to upward mobility—has historically trumped concerns over inequality, nurturing tolerance for—and at times faith in—the American hybrid free-enterprise democratic system. The present shape of politics suggests the possibility of a future in which bitterly competing factions come to supplant any clear majority consensus, liberal or conservative.

## The New Normal

The prospect, as some economists put it, of a "new normal"—years of continuing high unemployment and growing deficit pressures—suggests that hostile competition over tax burdens, program benefits, and regulatory decisions will continue.

Compounding domestic hardship, international trends and developments point to new sources of pressure on the American political system. One of the most important of these is the rise in commodity prices, especially of food and oil. The International Monetary Fund warned on March 3, 2011, that structural shifts point toward permanent commodity price hikes: "[T]he world may need to get used to higher food prices . . . the main reasons for rising demand for food reflect structural changes in the global economy that will not be reversed."[67]

The rising prices of food, gas, and other commodities translate directly into higher living costs for families, into larger government deficits, and, more generally, into a heightened sense of downward mobility both in the United States and abroad.

A second, and closely related, phenomenon is climate change, which has the potential to wreak havoc, threatening human lives and—at a stretch—the survival of the species. The *Financial Times* reported on February 2, 2011, on one set of issues relating to climate change:

> [A]s the threat grows of what the environmentalists call "climate chaos," other concerns have become more immediately pressing. Suppressed for a while by the global economic downturn, resource scarcity is re-emerging as an issue. Commodity prices are on the rise again, with oil at $100 a barrel and the cost of food surging because of strong demand growth in emerging economies and disruptions to supply. . . . The danger of more floods, droughts, and hurricanes in a warmer world is one reason to expect a future of increasing commodity price volatility, and increasingly widespread threats of shortages.[68]

In this context, the differing strengths of conservatives and Republicans on one side, and of liberals and Democrats on the other, become highly relevant in determining policy outcomes. Aggressiveness, willingness to use force, a devaluation of empathy, heightened risk tolerance, an acceptance of unequal outcomes, and homage to authority and hierarchy—these attributes can be highly adaptive in a zero-sum or negative-sum competition in which some people will be left behind to lose—and at times to lose badly.

In the short run, the Republican Party brings significant strengths to a struggle over diminishing resources, demonstrating a willingness to go for the kill, a facility in deploying wedge issues, and an aptitude for spotting potential fissures in the opposition. Over the long haul, however, the GOP has often proved to be an inconsistent risk manager, overreaching when victory is at hand and overestimating ideological support from the general public. Given the demographic upheaval unsettling the ground on which it stands, the Republican Party sees the election of 2012 as a last-ditch chance for an overwhelmingly white conservative movement.

For Democrats, the contemporary political struggle represents a crisis. The age of austerity threatens every aspect of the modern liberal state, including but not restricted to civil and citizenship rights, income and food security, health care, the eight-hour workday, the forty-hour week, the minimum wage, workplace safety, clean air, clean water, protection for the aged, and the commitment to reduce poverty.

The stakes could not be higher.

# Chapter Two

# The Moral Underpinnings of Partisan Conflict

Part I

## The White Party

On November 2, 2010, the Republican Party defied the warnings of demographers and political consultants that if it failed to make gains among minority voters, it would be swept away in a Hispanic tidal wave.

Instead, the GOP affirmed its identity as the "white" party. Its leaders and candidates rejected out of hand any compromise on immigration reform to restore ties with Hispanic voters, insisting on a hard-line deportation policy. Republican opposition to taxes and revenue-raising proposals intensified, sharpening the divide between the party and the government-dependent poor. GOP candidates advocated austerity policies targeting programs serving disproportionately large minority populations.

As we have seen, the Republican strategy reaped a massive sixty-three-seat gain in the House in 2010. The percentage of non-Hispanic whites voting for Republican House candidates, 62 percent, set a record. Fully 88.8 percent of all GOP House ballots that year were cast by whites.[1] In the highly polarized elections of 1972 (Nixon-McGovern) and 1984 (Reagan-Mondale), Republican presidential candidates had reached similar margins among white voters, but in House elections, white loyalty to the Democratic Party had never before dropped this low.

The results intensified the struggle between a Republican coalition of the socially and economically dominant and those who identify with them, on one side, and a Democratic alliance of the relatively disadvantaged and those who stand with them, on the other—a struggle over budget cuts and austerity policies replicated in towns, cities, counties, and states across the nation.

The outcome of the 2010 midterms demonstrated to operatives in both parties not only that the solid white-majority strategies of Nixon, Reagan, and both Bushes had a longer half-life than expected, but that these strategies could be transferred from presidential elections to House and Senate contests.

The results delivered a body blow to liberal analysts who had been convinced that the changing demographics of the United States pointed toward an inevitable resurgence of liberalism.

Heading into the 2012 presidential election, the Republicans' strategy received a boost in July 2011 when the Pew Research Center reported that the GOP had made continuing gains among voters. When asked which party they preferred, voter support for Democrats over Republicans fell from a twelve-point edge, 51–39, to just four points, 47–43. Most significant, all the GOP gains were among white voters. In 2008 Republicans had had just a two-point advantage among whites, 46–44; by July 2011 this had shot up to thirteen points, 52–39.

As if that were not enough, the Republican gains were largest among the poorest whites—those with household incomes below $30,000—further weakening Democratic claims of representing the working class. Democratic support also collapsed among young voters, 18–29, undermining Democratic claims to be winning over the next generation of voters. "A seven-point Democratic advantage among whites under age 30 [in 2008] has turned into an 11-point GOP advantage [in 2011]. And a 15-point Democratic advantage among whites earning less than $30,000 annually has swung to a slim four-point Republican edge [in 2011]," Pew reported.[2]

## The Paradoxical Growth of Democratic Constituencies

The Republican strategy represented a major gamble because in fact population trends do support the left. The percentage of Hispanics and single women is growing, while married white Christians (MWC), the core of the Republican Party, are in decline. Married white Christians made up nearly 80 percent of the electorate in the 1950s but are now fast approaching 40 percent.

"The danger posed to the Republican Party by the declining size of its married white Christian base was clearly illustrated by the results of the 2006 midterm election," writes Emory University political scientist Alan Abramowitz. "According to the 2006 national exit poll, married white Christians made up just under half of the midterm electorate and they voted for Republican House candidates over Democratic House candidates by a decisive 62 to 38 percent margin. However, voters who were not married white Christians made up just over half of the electorate, and they voted for Democratic House candidates over Republican House candidates by an even more decisive 68 to 32 percent margin. The result was a big win for the Democrats in the [2006] midterm election."[3]

Each of the key Democratic constituencies continues to grow. The rising strength of the minority vote, which includes blacks, Hispanics, Asian Americans, and others, is illustrated in Figure 2.1.[4]

The work of Emory's Abramowitz, of pollster Stanley Greenberg of

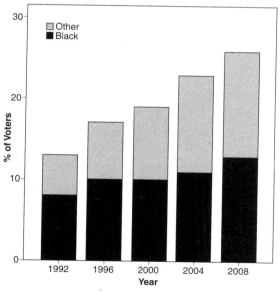

**Nonwhite Share of U.S. Electorate, 1992–2008**

*Source: National Exit Polls*

Figure 2.1

Greenberg Quinlan Rosner Research, and of John Judis and Ruy Teixeira, authors of *The Emerging Democratic Majority*, documents the growth of pro-Democratic constituencies.[5] While liberals delighted in the prospect of a new center-left majority, there was one group that reacted decisively and dramatically to this possibility: Republican Party elites. In the aftermath of the Democratic sweep of the 2006 and 2008 elections, Republicans realized that not only had they lost, but that the emergence of a strengthened left coalition threatened their future as a fully competitive force in American politics and as the upholder of the conservative faith. Abramowitz writes: "The growth of the nonwhite electorate, beginning with African-Americans in the 1960s and 1970s and continuing with Hispanics and Asian-Americans since the 1980s, has had profound consequences for the party system and the electoral process in the United States. Along with liberal whites, nonwhite voters constitute the electoral base of the modern Democratic Party while conservative whites constitute the electoral base of the modern Republican Party."[6]

At the same time, key GOP strategists realized that the white electorate is highly elastic, that white turnout levels and partisan vote margins are acutely responsive to external stimuli, and that voter mobilization is best achieved by tapping into "anger points" and "fear points"—by stressing, in effect, the potential threat posed by the Democratic agenda.[7]

Democrats took control of both houses of Congress in 2006 and of the White House in 2008, quickly enacting legislation designed, in part, to further weaken the conservative movement—most significantly by passing in March 2010 the Patient Protection and Affordable Care Act, a one-trillion-dollar program expanding health coverage to millions of the poor and near poor. If successful, universal health care would vastly enlarge the universe of voters benefiting directly from government support, a constituency Republicans characterize as "government-dependent," those whose allegiance is to expanded government services and thus to the Democratic Party.

### The Republican Counteroffensive

Without missing a beat, Republicans began to gear up for the next battle, the midterm elections of November 2010. The GOP initiated a relentless assault: mob scenes at Democratic town hall meetings, down-the-line opposition in Congress, invoking the specter of a socialist takeover, and raising megadollars for conservative independent expenditure PACs. Republicans were determined to prevent Obama and the Democrats from bringing the conservative era to a close, and their goal was to go for the political kill.

"Our mission statement was to retire Nancy Pelosi," said Texas representative Pete Sessions, who was handpicked in early 2009 to take over the National Republican Congressional Committee (NRCC). "That was the whole mission statement."[8] With the 2010 defeat of the House Democratic majority in hand, the scope of the mission grew: "The single most important thing we want to achieve is for President Obama to be a one-term president," Senate Republican majority leader Mitch McConnell (Ky.) declared.[9]

Not only was the goal to crush the opposition, but the top priority of the Republican campaign agenda was to destroy the signature offspring of the Obama administration and of the insurgent Democratic Party, health care reform. "If all of ObamaCare cannot be immediately repealed, then it is my intention to begin repealing it piece by piece, blocking funding for its implementation and blocking the issuance of the regulations necessary to implement it," declared House Republican whip Eric Cantor (Va.). "It is my intention to use every tool at our disposal to achieve full repeal of ObamaCare."[10]

I n addition to a struggle between haves and have-nots, the contest for power between Democrats and Republicans pits against each other two antithetical value systems; two conflicting concepts of freedom, liberty, fairness, right, and wrong; two mutually exclusive notions of the state, the individual, and the collective good.

The Democratic victory of 2008 brought to the fore the powerful Republican instinct for survival. The attack on the GOP had taken place not only at a moment when Democratic constituencies appeared to have finally gained electoral traction, but in the context of the catastrophic financial collapse of 2008—a collapse that challenged the legitimacy of the free market system and that stood to irreversibly undermine America's position of global dominance—and this at a time when Republicans were at the helm. The political and economic stakes for the winners and losers had been raised to levels unseen since the 1930s and the Great Depression.

How the Republicans recovered from their extraordinary 2008 downfall speaks to the doggedness with which they fought to regain the upper hand

and to the ruthlessness and skill with which they exploited Obama's vulnerabilities and those of his coalition.

## Understanding the Two Coalitions

The conservative rebound in the electorate in 2009 and 2010 emerged out of the struggle between two developing coalitions, one representing the traditional established forces in America and those who identify with them; the other made up of the once-marginalized, seeking entry into the mainstream, and those who identify with the underdog.

In some respects, this partisan configuration has roots dating back to the economically based divisions of the New Deal era. Partisan identification began to change substantially, however, with the emergence of the civil rights, women's rights, and sexual revolutions in the 1960s and 1970s. Economic divisions began to overlap with, and in some cases become subordinate to, competing alliances of racial, ethnic, and sexual identity groups. In the context of the rights revolutions of the decades following the Second World War, many left identity constituencies—including formerly stigmatized, marginalized, and disenfranchised populations—emerged from subordinate or secondary status, often militant and defying explicit and implicit discrimination in law and social custom. Their emergence, over time, had the paradoxical effect of creating counter-identity groupings, including white Christians, those holding traditional values, gun owners, property owners, etc.

The emergence of identity politics and their avatars—blacks, women, gays, members of religious and ethnic minorities—did not eliminate partisan economic conflict. Rather, the fight over government benefits, taxes, and spending programs reemerged in energized fashion in the context of identity group conflicts, escalating hostilities to a new level.

From the 1930s to the early 1960s the toughest political fights were over private sector worker rights and compensation, including minimum wages, workplace safety, the right to form trade unions, and the power of management to hire and fire. Contemporary struggles have shifted emphasis to the tax and spending authority of the government, to the scope of the federal safety net, to the level of domestic spending, to the use of force—in international and domestic affairs—and to securing the nation's borders. Most important, to these disputes have been added the dimensions of race, ethnicity, sexual identity, and gender.

Earlier battles pitted workers against capital, with workers seeking government assistance to rectify the balance of power at the bargaining table. Now the conflicts focused more on competition between, on the one hand, relatively government-dependent populations disproportionately made up of those formerly subject to discrimination (gays, blacks, Hispanics, single women) seeking protection from unrestrained free markets and from majoritarian sociocultural norms and, on the other hand, disproportionately white married Republicans who see themselves as paying the taxes required to finance expanded and downwardly redistributive and culturally subversive government services.

Republicans had not fully recognized the depth and strength of their adversaries until Obama's 2008 victory raised the clear possibility of the eclipse of the contemporary conservative movement. The 2008 election was a striking victory for the left coalition, its so-called downscale wing made up of those in the bottom half of the income distribution and/or those historically barred from exercising authority—those on the periphery of power—joined by two additional segments of the electorate: public employee unions dependent on tax dollars for survival, and middle/upper-income educated voters in creative and/or knowledge-intensive sectors for whom the social, moral, and cultural aspects of progressive politics are decisive.

This left coalition was larger than it initially appeared to be. Greenberg, the Democratic pollster, writing about what he called the Rising American Electorate (RAE), argues that this coalition makes up 52 percent of the *eligible* electorate but cast only 48 percent of the *actual* ballots in 2008.[11]

"Unmarried women, African Americans, Latinos and younger voters share . . . an economic vulnerability that sets them apart even in a country where economic anxiety is more the rule than the exception," Greenberg wrote. "[U]nmarried women are far more interested in affordable healthcare, raising the minimum wage, and pay equity than we see among voters overall. African Americans are 21 points more likely to identify SCHIP (government provided child health care) as extremely important and 25 percent more likely to identify affordable education as extremely important. The youth agenda looks the most like the agenda of the rest of the electorate, but even here, 39 percent identify increased access to student loans and cutting interest rates as extremely important, compared to 29 percent overall. More broadly speaking, these voters seem clearly primed to engage on the healthcare issue in a serious way."[12]

Greenberg also found that among core low-income Democratic voters, an average of 29.6 percent received public assistance, almost seven times the percentage among all other voters, 4.4 percent.[13]

For the Republican Party, the ascendant Democratic coalition represented not only a powerful political adversary but a substantive challenge threatening to transform basic economic policy after three decades of free enterprise, antiregulatory dominance.

This challenge was reflected in a July 2008 Gallup survey asking respondents to categorize themselves as either haves or have-nots. By nearly 2.5 to 1 (64–26), whites consider themselves haves. In contrast, slight pluralities of both blacks and Hispanics see themselves as have-nots (46–45 and 48–40, respectively).[14]

Also notable in light of the repeated accusations from the right that Obama is a "socialist" were the findings of a February 4, 2010, Gallup survey asking respondents whether they had a positive or negative image of socialism. Just 36 percent of Americans view "socialism" positively, and 58 percent have a negative view—not a particularly surprising finding. Looking further at the cross-tabs, however, the survey gets more interesting. By a solid 12 percentage points, 53–41, self-identified Democrats view socialism favorably, as does an even larger share of self-identified liberals, 61–34. Among these segments of the electorate, socialism is not rejected reflexively, according to Gallup. Yet decisive majorities of Republicans and conservatives were found to hold negative views of socialism, by respective margins of 79–17 and 75–20. Gallup reported that by better than two to one, white respondents were critical of socialism, 64–31 negative-positive, while nonwhites were favorable by a 49–40 margin.[15]

For Republicans, these findings suggested the possibility that the political strength of voters whose convictions are similar—on economic and on social/moral/cultural values issues—to those of European Social Democrats was reaching a politically salient level in the United States. With effective organization and mobilization, such voters were, and are, well positioned to set the agenda in the Democratic Party.

It was no wonder, then, that on November 5, 2008, the leaders of the Republican Party reacted strongly when they were defeated not just by another political party but by a party representing a significant economic and ideological challenge.

Between 2008 and 2010 there was a large ideological shift as millions of white, self-identified moderate voters, struggling to survive the economic meltdown, fearful of ballooning government deficits, uncertain of their relationship to the nation's first black president, swung to the right. In the four previous nonpresidential election years—1994, 1998, 2002, and 2006—the conservative bloc had remained relatively stable in size, ranging from 40 to 46 percent of likely voters, averaging 42.5 percent. In 2010, that bloc increased in size by 11.5 percentage points, a huge shift in politics, to 54 percent of the electorate.[16]

Self-described *moderates*, who had made up an average of 40.5 percent of likely voters in the previous four off-year elections, shrank by 13.5 points, a similarly huge shift, to 27 percent. The percentage of self-identified liberals remained relatively constant through these five elections, going from an average of 17 percent during the years 1994 to 2008 to 18 percent in 2010. In effect, moderates moved to the right, augmenting the power of the conservative bloc, which reached an unprecedented size in 2010.[17]

One of the most striking facts about the Republican comeback of 2010 was that the party did not give an ideological inch to its critics. GOP leaders and candidates made no effort to move party philosophy or values toward the center; if anything, the Republican campaigns of 2010 were more consistently conservative in content than in the recent past.

The swing in the electorate between 2008 and 2010 raises a crucial question: What does it mean to be a conservative or a liberal? What does it mean when *swing* voters shift left, as they did in 2006 and 2008, or shift right, as they did in 2010, in order to ally their fortunes with the committed liberal or conservative segment of the electorate?

Understanding the Republican revival of 2010 requires not only the traditional tools of political analysis but also an understanding of the values and convictions—the moral and ideological underpinnings—of contemporary partisan conflict.

A wide range of academic scholarship exploring political belief formation—discussed in detail below—reveals that those who identify themselves as politically conservative, for example, exhibit distinctive values underpinning their worldview and their orientation toward political competition.

Conservatives, argues Philip Tetlock, professor of management and psychology at the Wharton School of the University of Pennsylvania, are less tolerant of compromise; see the world in "us" versus "them" terms; are more willing to use force to gain an advantage; are "more prone to rely on simple (good vs. bad) evaluative rules in interpreting policy issues";[18] are "motivated to punish violators of social norms (e.g., deviations from traditional norms of sexuality or responsible behavior) and to deter free riders."[19]

Some of these conservative values can be discerned in public opinion data. The Pew Research Center for the People & the Press, for instance, provides survey findings on white attitudes and views based on results from a series of polls.

In a September 2010 survey question, Pew asked voters, "If you had to choose, would you rather have a smaller government providing fewer services, or a bigger government providing more services?" White Republican men chose a smaller government by a 92–7 margin and white Republican women made the same choice by an 82–12 margin. Conversely, white Democratic men chose bigger government by a 53–35 margin, and white Democratic women by 56–33. This is a vast ideological gap between Republicans and Democrats of fifty-seven points among white men and forty-nine points among white women.[20]

Along similar lines, Pew asked voters to choose between "Most people who want to get ahead can make it if they're willing to work hard" and "Hard work and determination are no guarantee of success for most people." White Republican men and women both picked "hard work" by decisive margins of 78–21 and 73–24, respectively. White Democratic men and women, in contrast, were far more equivocal, supporting hard work by modest margins of 52–44 and 53–43.[21]

These Pew findings—and those that follow—demonstrate that the differences of opinion between liberals and conservatives are far greater than the differences in opinion between men and women commonly referred to as the gender gap.

Take the case of a key civil rights question in which respondents are asked to choose between two statements: (1) "Our country has made the changes needed to give blacks equal rights with whites," or (2) "Our country needs to continue making changes to give blacks equal rights with whites." Pew found that white Republican men and women are agreed that the country has done what's needed, 70–24 (men) and 63–28 (women); while white Democratic men and women agree with each other but disagree sharply with Republicans: 38–59 (men) and 34–62 (women).[22]

Or take another key issue, immigration: (1) "Immigrants today strengthen our country because of their hard work and talents" or (2) "Immigrants today are a burden on our country because they take our jobs, housing and health care." White Democrats were strongly favorable to immigrants, 63–29 (men), 57–33 (women), while Republicans were hostile, 51–41 (men) and 57–25 (women).[23]

Similarly broad partisan spreads appear repeatedly on such questions as (1) "Business corporations make too much profit" or (2) "Most corporations make a fair and reasonable amount of profit." Responses are also sharply bifurcated on the following questions: "What do you think is more important—to protect the right of Americans to own guns, or to control gun ownership?" "Do you strongly favor, favor, oppose, or strongly oppose allowing gays and lesbians to marry legally?" and "Do you think the U.S. made the right decision or the wrong decision in using military force in Iraq?"[24]

The Pew questions are designed to test opinion on public policy issues. The strength of the Pew surveys and other comparable, well-designed polls is that the sample is carefully selected to be representative either of the general public or of all voters. The limitation of such surveys is that they are not designed to reveal more subtle distinctions that can be equally or more significant.

The less easily answered question—what liberal and conservative really mean—has been explored by a team of academic researchers collaborating at a Web site—www.YourMorals.org—designed to test a variety of theories about the connection between views on morality and politics. Jonathan Haidt and Nicholas Winter of the University of Virginia and Ravi Iyer of the University of Southern California have collected and systematized very large numbers of responses to questions designed to elicit new information about political values orientation. Haidt et al. have ranked responses to a set of online public opinion surveys to show where self-described liberal/moderates differ most sharply from conservative/moderates. The strength of the YourMorals.org surveys lies in the large number of respondents; the weakness grows out of the fact that the participants are self-selected, and represent well-educated elites on the left, right, and center, with little representation of the poor, working class, or lower middle class.[25]

The findings published by Haidt et al. powerfully reinforce the paradigm of two roughly equivalent political coalitions: the first, a coalition of those in the top half of the social and economic hierarchy on the right; the second, a coalition on the left composed of relatively disadvantaged voters in alliance with relatively well-educated, well-off, culturally liberal professionals ("information workers," "symbol analysts," "creatives," "knowledge workers," etc.).[26] The Haidt et al. data shed new light on what it means, across a gamut of issues, when someone says he or she is a liberal or a conservative.[27]

What kinds of questions and values statements provoke the sharpest divide between left and right? The team looked at responses to 107 questions and found that the most divisive questions included those in the following areas:[28]

### 1. War, Peace, Violence, Empathy with the World:

On key questions and statements in this category, liberals scored high, conservatives low: "I believe peace is extremely important"; "Understanding, appreciation, and protection for the welfare of all people and for nature"; "One of the worst things a person could do is hurt a defenseless animal"; "How close do you feel to people all over the world?" On other key questions in this area, conservatives scored high, and liberals low: "War is sometimes the best way to solve a conflict"; "There is nothing wrong in getting back at someone who has hurt you."

### 2. Crime and Punishment; Morality Elasticity; Authority:

Again, on some questions in this category, liberals scored high, conservatives low: "I believe that offenders should be provided with counseling to aid in their rehabilitation"; "What is ethical varies from one situation and society to another."

On other questions, conservatives scored high and liberals low: "People should not do things that are disgusting, even if no one is harmed"; "Respect for authority is something all children need to learn"; "I believe that 'an eye for an eye' is the correct philosophy behind punishing offenders"; "The 'old-fashioned ways' and 'old-fashioned values' still show the best way to live"; "It feels wrong when . . . a person commits a crime and goes unpunished."

*3. The Poor, Redistribution, Fairness:*

Liberal high, conservative low: "It feels wrong when . . . an employee who needs their job is fired"; "I think it's morally wrong that rich children inherit a lot of money while poor children inherit nothing"; "I often have tender, concerned feelings for people less fortunate than me."

Conservative high, liberal low: "[I place a high value on] safety, harmony, and stability of society, of relationships, and of self"; "[It's desirable when] employees [who] contribute more to the success of the company receive a larger share"; "[I value] social status and prestige, control or dominance over people and resources."

*4. Morals, Hedonism, Self-Fulfillment, Hierarchy:*

Liberals high, conservatives low: "I see myself as someone who . . . is original, comes up with new ideas"; "Pleasure or sensuous gratification for oneself"; "What is ethical varies from one situation and society to another."

Conservative high, liberal low: "If certain groups stayed in their place, we would have fewer problems"; "People should be loyal to their family members, even when they have done something wrong"; "Respect, commitment, and acceptance of the customs that traditional culture provide"; "[I favor] restraint of actions, inclinations, and impulses likely to upset or harm others and violate social expectations or norms."

Through their survey, Haidt, Winter, and Iyer were seeking to address the following issues: (1) "the fact that white men appear to be leaving the Democratic party at fairly high rates and [that] it would be useful to pinpoint the variables that lead some white men to desert the Democratic party while others remain" and (2) "what causes some white men to gravitate toward the Republican Party and not others?"[29]

Facets of the ideological and moral schism between left and right are illustrated in Figure 2.2[30] and Figure 2.3,[31] constructed from survey results available at the Web site www.Polipsych.com, where liberal/moderate white males are contrasted with conservative white males.

Each individual question in Figure 2.2 and Figure 2.3 reveals how profound the chasm is on values questions between liberals and conservatives. Generally, not only do liberals place high importance on peace, mutual understanding, and empathy for those who have difficulty prevailing in competition, but they also demonstrate concern for equality of outcome, while conservatives place pointedly low or negative importance on such values.[32] On the other side, conservatives believe that the use of force is a legitimate method of conflict resolution across a range of domains, from war to law enforcement to the discipline of children.[33] Conservatives are more likely to believe in an "eye for an eye," are more likely to respect received tradition, and are overwhelmingly committed to the proposition that individuals are responsible for their own economic condition—all views rejected by liberals.[34]

### Adjectives and Ideology

From a different vantage point—taking data from American National Election Studies (ANES) surveys conducted between 1972 and 2004, the University of Virginia's Nicholas Winter analyzed the words respondents used to describe the two political parties. In "Masculine Republicans and Feminine Democrats: Gender and Americans' Explicit and Implicit Images of the Political Parties," Winter categorized words respondents volunteered as stereotypically "male" or "female":

> [M]asculine men are thought to be *active, independent,* and *decisive;* feminine women are thought to be *compassionate, devoted to others, emotional,* and *kind.* These core traits are linked with a range of other features, including other traits (masculine men are *aggressive, practical, tough, hardworking,* and *hierarchical;* feminine women are *gentle, submissive, soft, ladylike,* and *egalitarian*); physical characteristics (masculine men are *big, strong,* and *muscular;* feminine women are *small, weak,* and *soft spoken*).[35]

---

Data in Figures 2.2 and 2.3 are presented in terms of effect size. Effect Size (ES) is a statistical measure used by social scientists. If ES is below 0.1, it is considered trivial; if ES is between 0.1 and 0.3, it is considered small; ES between 0.3 and 0.5 is considered moderate; and ES greater than 0.5 is large. ES for all of the examples in Figures 2.2 and 2.3 are large, ranging from 0.5 to 2.01.

☐   < 0.1 = trivial effect
☐   0.1 – 0.3 = small effect
☐   0.3 – 0.5 = moderate effect
☐   > 0.5 = large difference effect

| Sample Question | Number of People | Effect Size (lib-con) | Liberal-Moderate | Conservative-Moderate |
|---|---|---|---|---|
| The 20 questions fromYourMorals.org to which liberal white U.S. males responded most affirmatively, compared to answers given by conservative white U.S. males, as measured by effect size: | | | | |
| I believe peace is extremely important. | 1409 | 1.42 | +0.57 | −0.85 |
| I believe that offenders should be provided with counseling to aid in their rehabilitation. | 1583 | 1.27 | +0.39 | −0.87 |
| Understanding, appreciation, and protection for the welfare of all people and for nature are extremely important. | 2753 | 1.21 | +0.43 | −0.78 |
| What is ethical varies from one situation and society to another. | 2163 | 1.09 | +0.16 | −0.94 |
| It feels wrong when an employee who needs his/her job is fired. | 1098 | 1.06 | +0.45 | −0.61 |
| I think it's morally wrong that rich children inherit a lot of money while poor children inherit nothing. | 31089 | 1.05 | +0.53 | −0.53 |
| I feel close to people all over the world. | 3746 | 0.93 | +0.35 | −0.57 |
| I often feel a sense of oneness with the natural world around me. | 701 | 0.92 | +0.26 | −0.67 |
| One of the worst things a person can do is to hurt a defenseless animal. | 31089 | 0.88 | +0.47 | −0.41 |
| People's biological makeup influences their talents and personality. | 431 | 0.81 | +0.08 | −0.73 |
| How desirable is it to investigate each employee's needs, and then adjust bonuses up or down to reflect each individual's level of need? | 747 | 0.62 | +0.26 | −0.36 |
| I see myself as someone who is original, who comes up with new ideas. | 6575 | 0.60 | +0.30 | −0.30 |
| It is never necessary to sacrifice the welfare of others. | 2163 | 0.59 | +0.26 | −0.33 |
| When perceiving beauty in a work of art, I feel emotional. | 1442 | 0.56 | +0.20 | −0.36 |
| There are times in my life when I've experienced strong feelings of love for all people, not just the specific people I'm close to. | 860 | 0.50 | +0.20 | −0.30 |
| How desirable is it for to all employees to get an equal share? | 747 | 0.48 | +0.08 | −0.39 |
| The notion of thinking abstractly is appealing to me. | 2861 | 0.41 | +0.26 | −0.15 |
| Excitement, novelty, and challenge in life are extremely important. | 2753 | 0.38 | +0.04 | −0.37 |
| Independent thought and action—choosing, creating, exploring—are extremely important. | 2753 | 0.38 | +0.02 | −0.35 |
| Please describe your highest educational level: | 29092 | 0.12 | +0.10 | −0.04 |

*Figure 2.2*

| The 20 questions from YourMorals.org to which conservative white U.S. males responded most affirmatively, compared to answers given by liberal white U.S. males, as measured by effective size: | | | | |
|---|---|---|---|---|
| Sample Question | Number of People | Effect Size (lib-con) | Liberal-Moderate | Conservative-Moderate |
| It annoys me when other people perform better than I do. | 898 | **−0.64** | −0.22 | +0.42 |
| [You would need to pay me a lot to] make a disrespectful hand gesture to [my] boss, teacher, or professor. | 4877 | **−0.67** | −0.38 | +0.28 |
| Safety, harmony, and stability of society, of relationships, and of self are extremely important. | 2753 | **−0.67** | −0.42 | +0.25 |
| [You would need to pay me a lot to] renounce [my] citizenship and become a citizen of another country. | 4877 | **−0.79** | −0.38 | +0.41 |
| I spend time trying to grow in my understanding of my faith. | 1671 | **−0.79** | −0.21 | +0.58 |
| In case of uncertainty, I prefer to make an immediate decision, whatever it may be. | 718 | **−0.83** | −0.28 | +0.55 |
| [You would need to pay me a lot to] get a blood transfusion of 1 pint of disease-free, compatible blood from a convicted child molester. | 4877 | **−0.84** | −0.44 | +0.40 |
| It feels wrong when a person commits a crime and goes unpunished. | 1098 | **−0.85** | −0.32 | +0.54 |
| Restraint of actions, inclinations, and impulses likely to upset or harm others and violate social expectations or norms are extremely important. | 2753 | **−0.91** | −0.51 | +0.40 |
| I feel close to people in [my] country. | 3746 | **−0.95** | −0.28 | +0.67 |
| Respect, commitment, and acceptance of the customs that traditional culture provide are extremely important. | 2753 | **−0.97** | −0.48 | +0.48 |
| People have complete control over the decisions they make. | 431 | **−1.01** | −0.44 | +0.56 |
| Most people spend too much time in unprofitable amusements. | 208 | **−1.12** | −0.27 | +0.85 |
| People should be loyal to their family members, even when they have done something wrong. | 31089 | **−1.15** | −0.57 | +0.59 |
| I believe that "an eye for an eye" is the correct philosophy behind punishing offenders. | 1583 | **−1.26** | −0.59 | +0.67 |
| Respect for authority is something all children need to learn. | 31089 | **−1.35** | −0.65 | +0.70 |
| War is sometimes the best way to solve a conflict. | 1409 | **−1.48** | −0.62 | +0.86 |
| People should not do things that are disgusting, even if no one is harmed. | 31089 | **−1.48** | −0.61 | +0.88 |
| If certain groups stayed in their place, we would have fewer problems. | 1635 | **−1.51** | −0.62 | +0.89 |
| The "old-fashioned ways" and "old-fashioned values" still show the best way to live. | 1512 | **−2.01** | −0.60 | +1.41 |

*Figure 2.3*

Winter found that in describing what they like about each of the two parties, voters used more words and phrases that Winter coded as "masculine" in describing the GOP than in describing the Democrats, by an overwhelming ratio of 7 to 1. Conversely, voters used more words and phrases Winter coded as "feminine" to describe the Democrats than they used for Republicans, again by a strong ratio of 5.7 to 1.[36]

At the same time, Winter wrote, polls showed:

Republicans are thought to handle better such issues as defense, dealing with terrorism, and controlling crime and drugs; these are precisely the sorts of issues that Americans associate with men or with masculine traits. Conversely, Democratic-owned issues include education, health care, helping the poor, protecting the environment, and promoting peace; these are all also associated with women or with feminine traits.[37]

In summary, Winter found:

During the past three decades Americans have come to view the parties increasingly in gendered terms of masculinity and femininity. Utilizing three decades of American National Election Studies data . . . this paper demonstrates empirically that these connections between party images and gender stereotypes have been forged at the explicit level of the traits that Americans associate with each party, and also at the implicit level of unconscious cognitive connections between gender and party stereotypes. These connections between the parties and masculinity and femininity have important implications for citizens' political cognition and for the study of American political behavior.[38]

Even as the two parties have increasingly reflected gender-stereotypes, millions of women remain loyal to the GOP and millions of men are deeply committed Democrats. Aggression, competitiveness, risk-taking, support for hierarchy, and tough stands on law and order characterize both male and female Republicans. Similarly, compassion, empathy, aversion to violence, and support for progressive redistribution can be found among both Democratic men and women.

James Sidanius, professor of psychology and African and African American studies at Harvard and a founder of the field of social dominance theory (SDT),[39] which seeks to explain social hierarchy (more on this in Chapter Three), provided this portrait of white male Democrats:

[E]verything we know about ideological gender differences would lead us to believe that they [white male Democrats] should be younger; better-educated; not be members of the "working-class"; relatively dove-like in their war attitudes; politically & socially liberal; have relatively low levels of aggression, authoritarianism, social dominance orientation [SDO], individualism, competitiveness, and testosterone; have relatively high levels of altruism and empathy; tend to be single and without children; live in the North East and West Coasts; and not live in the Southeast.[40]

Throughout the cold war and in the aftermath of the 9/11 terrorist attacks, Republicans capitalized on perceptions of the GOP as better equipped to handle issues of national security than Democrats. In 1984, for example, the Reagan-Bush campaign ran the now-famous commercial "The Bear"[41] to raise doubts about the credentials of the Democratic candidate that year, Walter Mondale. The ad ran as follows: "There is a bear in the woods. For some people, the bear is easy to see. Others don't see it at all. Some people say the bear is tame. Others say it is vicious and dangerous. Since no one can really be sure who's right, isn't it smart to be as strong as the bear—if there is a bear?" A man with a gun appears and the bear takes a step back.[42]

In 2004 the Bush-Cheney campaign ran a similar wolves ad both to burnish its candidate's stature in the war on terrorism and to question John Kerry's capacity and determination to ensure the safety of the nation.[43] Echoes of the bear ad are striking: As a pack of wolves, gathered in a dark forest, rises up from a resting position and begins to move toward the camera, the narrator says, "In an increasingly dangerous world, even after the first terrorist attack on America, John Kerry and the liberals in Congress voted to slash America's intelligence budget by $6 billion. Cuts so deep they would have weakened America's defenses. And weakness attracts those who are waiting to do America harm."[44]

The broader question is: What is it about the Republican Party that leads to the success of the wolves and bear ads, and why is it that the Democratic

Party has a history of leaving itself vulnerable to the manipulation of such wedge issues?

What is behind the Republican resolve to reject the kinds of ideological compromise necessary to make inroads among minority voters? And why does the Republican Party hold firm to the conservative social agenda when the country as a whole is moving in a more socially liberal direction?

The research of Haidt, Winter, Iyer, and Sidanius reveals the largely unexplored psychological underpinnings of ideological and partisan conflict. The well-documented rise of polarization over the past three decades suggests that the psychological differences these scholars have targeted for study are intensifying and gaining in salience.

The next chapter will examine how the two parties are driven by deeply embedded values and belief systems to respond in characteristic ways to sharpened competition over scarce resources when zero-sum or negative-sum choices are required.

# Chapter Three

# The Moral Underpinnings of Partisan Conflict

## Part II

### A Willingness to Inflict Harm

In the winter of 2010–2011, New England and New York experienced some of the harshest weather on record. In Burlington, Vermont, 121.4 inches of snow fell, and in Syracuse, New York, 173.5 inches. Across the Frost Belt, the cold was relentless, and so were the heating bills. U.S. Energy Information Administration officials reported that the cost of heating oil had risen ninety-three dollars a gallon from the year before. The number of people struggling to pay for natural gas, propane, and oil swelled as millions lost their jobs. On February 17, 2011, New Hampshire representative Charles Bass pleaded with House colleagues to restore fifty million dollars in federal funds to the Low Income Home Energy Assistance Program. "Winters in the Northeast are long and hard," Bass said. "It's been a tough year."[1]

Bass was not trying to increase spending on the program, which serves poor families across the country. He wanted to pare back a $303 million cut called for by the Republican House leadership. His pleas fell on deaf ears as the newly elected Republican Congress voted, 322–104, to kill his amendment.[2]

The next day, as the House continued deliberations on HR1—the appropriations bill calling for a total of sixty-one billion dollars in cuts to the FY 2011 federal budget—Representative Ted Poe of Texas took the floor with an amendment to bar the Environmental Protection Agency (EPA) from further attempts to regulate greenhouse gas emissions.

"Probably no Member of Congress represents more refineries than I do in Southeast Texas, and the regulatory process, the overregulation of the EPA coming in and trying to now regulate the State of Texas regarding greenhouse gases is a detriment to the industry," Poe told colleagues. "We're in the midst of a massive economic downturn, and the last thing we need to do is to shoot ourselves in the foot with unnecessary, expensive new regulations that are on business and industry."

Jay Inslee, Democrat from Washington State, took the lead in attacking Poe's amendment. The prohibition, Inslee said, would stall antipollution industries in the United States, giving China and other countries the opportunity to surge ahead in the field. Then Inslee made a more emotional case for voting no: "Anyone who has ever seen a child gasping for breath due to a persistent asthma problem . . . should be adamantly opposed to this amendment, because it would strip the legal right and obligation of Uncle Sam to protect our children's right to breathe."

Inslee's argument was ignored by the Republican House, which proceeded to vote 249 to 117 to bar the EPA from regulating the pollutants. The margin in support of Poe among Republican members was 236 to 2.[3]

In one case, deficit cutting trumped the danger that poor children, the elderly, and the disabled might be forced to live without heat in subzero temperatures. In the other, refusing to regulate pollutants trumped concern for the 8.9 percent of children in the United States who struggle for breath as they suffer from respiratory diseases.

These examples demonstrate the willingness of conservatives first to create a negative-sum confrontation—in this case, legislation calling for sixty-one billion dollars in cuts—and then to impose the cost on the most vulnerable: the poor in the North and children living near refineries.

Conservatives, in other words, are willing to inflict harm.

## Republican Party Discipline

In addition to a willingness to inflict harm, Republicans are disciplined in the pursuit of their agenda. In 1993 and 2009, when Democrats controlled the White House and both branches of Congress, the Republican minority formed a solid phalanx determined to oppose first Clinton and then Obama at every step. In contrast, during the Democrats' parallel moments—2001, part of 2002, 2003, and 2004—when they were in the minority in both branches of Congress, George W. Bush walked all over them, winning approval of tax cuts heavily tilted in favor of the affluent, the invasion of Iraq, energy legislation, a pro-pharmaceutical industry prescription drug program, and free trade bills.

Republicans "consistently display more unity when it matters, and more willingness to bend legislative procedures to achieve outcomes—for example, the use of reconciliation* on the tax cuts in 2001/02. Democrats have more trouble keeping their troops together," notes American Enterprise Institute congressional scholar Norman Ornstein.[4] Stephen Ansolabehere of the Government Department at Harvard makes a similar observation: "The evidence is that the GOP in Congress has held together more cohesively than the Democrats, and that has been true for a very long time, regardless of their status as minority or majority party."[5] Along similar lines, Yale political scientist David Mayhew argues that "without unity, it gets more difficult to wage a tough, determined fight. The Congressional Republicans have been remarkably unified in confrontations. . . . The Democrats haven't been."[6] Columbia political scientist Robert Erikson amplifies the point: "The Democrats [in Congress] are too timid to take their case to the court of public opinion, as if ordinary folk would reject their arguments in favor of what the Democrats see as simplistic but clever Republican slogans. Why fight when you think you will lose? Republicans seem to believe they can prevail with public opinion."[7]

Erikson's point was driven home in late 2010, when Democrats, with solid public support, sought to end the Bush tax cuts for the wealthy, a step that would have raised $143.1 billion in FY 2011 and 2012. Republicans fought tooth and nail to protect families making more than $250,000 in taxable income. At that time, Congressional Democrats and the Obama administration caved in, and Republicans emerged as victors.[8]

In 2011, when Republicans regained majority control of the House, they immediately changed the pay-as-you-go, or PAYGO, rule, which required that any spending increase or tax cut be fully financed by other spending cuts or tax hikes. The PAYGO rule had wide bipartisan support among fiscal conservatives.

---

* Reconciliation is a legislative process of the U.S. Senate intended to allow consideration of a contentious budget bill with debate limited to twenty hours under Senate rules.

On January 5, 2011, the newly elected Republican-controlled House voted to approve a more adversarial rule known as CUTGO, or cut-as-you-go, taking the GOP's antitax ideology a giant step further. While Democrats under PAYGO had treated new spending and tax cuts as raising the deficit and thus requiring compensatory tax hikes and/or spending cuts, the GOP exempted tax cuts altogether from such requirements. In effect, under CUTGO, tax cuts can be enacted without restraint. Spending increases, in contrast, require slashed spending in other areas and can no longer be compensated for with tax hikes.[9]

### The Moral Spectrum

When it comes to partisan confrontation, Democrats and Republicans are, arguably, different breeds. As Jonathan Haidt of the University of Virginia writes, "[T]hink of the moral mind as being like an audio equalizer, with five slider switches for different parts of the moral spectrum. Democrats generally use a much smaller part of the spectrum than do Republicans. The resulting music may sound beautiful to other Democrats, but it sounds thin and incomplete to many of the swing voters that left the party in the 1980s, and whom the Democrats must recapture if they want to produce a lasting political realignment."[10]

A 41 percent plurality of Republicans surveyed in a USA Today-Gallup poll shortly after the November 2010 election said that political leaders should stand firm in their beliefs even if little gets done, compared to just 18 percent of Democrats. Nearly three-fifths of Democrats, 59 percent, said leaders should be willing to compromise to get things done, compared to just 31 percent of Republicans.[11]

A similar Wall Street Journal/NBC poll conducted in early December 2010 found that Democrats believe that elected officials should "make compromises to gain consensus on legislation," as opposed to "stick[ing] to their positions even if this means not being able to gain consensus," by a margin of 63–29, while Republicans were split, 47–47.[12]

These differences are more than skin deep and become significant in political fights over scarce resources. The evidence presented below suggests that greater Republican resistance to accommodation can have serious consequences: austerity policies adopted by Congress—as well as by state and local governing bodies (which are bound by law to maintain balanced budgets)—will fall heavily on domestic spending, especially on programs and services for the disadvantaged and the poor—i.e., Democratic voters.

Not only are the disadvantaged less well equipped to press their case, insofar as power correlates with cash, but their primary defenders, contemporary liberals, often flinch in warfare over resources. Scarcity seems to play to the psychological and competitive strengths of conservatives, reinforcing their hierarchical and authoritarian preferences, while increasing the likelihood that those on the left will compromise and concede on matters large and small.

### The Politics of Loss Allocation

Toward the close of the Jimmy Carter administration, in the spring of 1980, energy prices were skyrocketing, inflation and interest rates were in the double digits, and unemployment was high. In this crisis atmosphere, MIT economist Lester Thurow wrote his best-selling book *The Zero-Sum Society*, arguing that it was imperative, at that moment of austerity, to adopt new policies to deal with energy shortages and stagflation, the unprecedented combination of inflation and unemployment.

The problem in developing solutions to the country's major problems, according to Thurow, was that virtually every policy initiative involved a zero-sum proposition in which there had to be a loser for each winner. This posed what he described as the dilemma of "loss allocation . . . precisely what our political process is least capable of doing. When there are economic gains to be allocated, our political process can allocate them. When there are large economic losses to be allocated, our political process is paralyzed."[13]

Thurow was writing before our current political polarization had taken root and produced a more oppositional and ideologically coherent Republican Party. As polarization intensified over the next three decades, the GOP, from its leadership to its voters, became more consistently conservative with moderates steadily leaving or being forced out.[14]

As the center of gravity in the GOP moved right, and as the party became more internally consistent, it proved ready and willing to allocate losses, as long as the losses were imposed on others—ideally on Democratic constituencies.

## Politics and Personality

As noted in the previous chapter, political scientists and scholars from a range of disciplines have begun to study the moral and ideological—sometimes called psycho-ideological—underpinnings of partisan conflict.

Chapter Two (pages 45–53) presented research on the differing views of liberals and conservatives in four general areas:

- War, peace, violence, empathy with the world
- Crime and punishment; moral elasticity; authority
- The poor, redistribution, fairness
- Morals, hedonism, self-fulfillment, hierarchy

Here our focus is more specifically on those values differences between liberals and conservatives that are particularly relevant to their approaches to resource competition under conditions of scarcity.

Dana Carney of Columbia University, John Jost of New York University, Samuel Gosling of the University of Texas, and Jeff Potter of Atof, Inc., in their 2008 paper "The Secret Lives of Liberals and Conservatives: Personality Profiles, Interaction Styles, and the Things They Leave Behind," published in the journal *Political Psychology*,[15] theorize that there are certain personality traits associated with liberal or left-wing orientations and conservative or right-wing orientations, as described in Figure 3.1.[16]

Carney et al. argue that although

> skeptics continue to doubt that most people are "ideological," evidence suggests that meaningful left-right differences do exist and that they may be rooted in basic personality dispositions. . . . We obtained consistent and converging evidence that personality differences between liberals and conservatives are robust, replicable, and behaviorally significant. . . . In general, liberals are more open-minded, creative, curious, and seeking, whereas conservatives are more orderly, conventional, and better organized.[17]

Carney's team describes conservatism "as an ideological belief system that is significantly (but not completely) related to motivational concerns having to do with the psychological management of uncertainty and fear. . . . Similarly, concerns with fear and threat may be linked to the sec-

---

**Personality Traits Theorized to Be Associated with Liberal (or Left-Wing) and Conservative (or Right-Wing) Orientation, 1930–2007**

**Liberal/Left-Wing**

Slovenly, ambiguous, indifferent, eccentric, sensitive, individualistic; open, tolerant, flexible; life-loving, free, unpredictable; creative, imaginative, curious; expressive, enthusiastic; excited, sensation-seeking; desire for novelty, diversity; uncontrolled, impulsive; complex, nuanced; open-minded; open to experience.

**Conservative/Right-Wing**

Definite, persistent, tenacious; tough, masculine, firm; reliable, trustworthy, fiathful, loyal; stable, consistent; rigid, intolerant; conventional, ordinary; obedient, conformist; fearful, threatened; xenophobic, prejudiced; orderly, organized; parsimonious, thrifty, stingy; clean, sterile; obstinate, stubborn; aggressive, angry, vengeful; careful, practical, methodical; withdrawn, reserved; stern, cold, mechanical; anxious, suspicious, obsessive; self-controlled; restrained, inhibited; concerned with rules, norms; moralistic; simple, decisive; closed-minded; conscientious.

---

*Figure 3.1*

ond core dimension of conservatism, *endorsement of inequality*"[18] (emphasis added).

Working along parallel lines, Harvard professor of psychology James Sidanius and colleagues, in the context of their work on social dominance theory (SDT) (see page 52), have developed a measure of what they describe as social dominance orientation (SDO). Sidanius and his associates use a sixteen-question survey to place respondents on a scale of high to low SDO. Those high in SDO gave favorable responses to the first eight statements and negative responses to questions nine through sixteen:[19]

1. Some groups of people are just more worthy than others.
2. In getting what your group wants, it is sometimes necessary to use force against other groups.
3. It's OK if some groups have more of a chance in life than others.
4. To get ahead in life, it is sometimes necessary to step on other groups.
5. If certain groups of people stayed in their place, we would have fewer problems.
6. It's probably a good thing that certain groups are at the top and other groups are at the bottom.

7. Inferior groups should stay in their place.
8. Sometimes other groups must be kept in their place.
9. It would be good if all groups could be equal.
10. Group equality should be our ideal.
11. All groups should be given an equal chance in life.
12. We should do what we can to equalize conditions for different groups.
13. We should increase social equality.
14. We would have fewer problems if we treated different groups more equally.
15. We should strive to make incomes more equal.
16. No one group should dominate in society.

Sidanius et al. found that SDO is higher among whites than among African Americans; is negatively related to empathy, openness, and agreeableness; and is positively linked to aggressivity, vindictiveness, coldness, tough-mindedness, and a belief that "the world is a zero-sum game." In addition, those ranking high on an SDO scale "will use others to get ahead . . . they believe that harming people is legitimate, are observably disagreeable, cold, and vindictive, are low in benevolence, and do not hesitate to humiliate others. Their dog-eat-dog mentality leads them to support economic competition and war over social welfare programs . . . people high in SDO tend to be callous, confident, and cruel."[20]

In a separate set of studies, published in the paper "Social Dominance Orientation: A Personality Variable Predicting Social and Political Attitudes," Sidanius and colleagues found that "Republican political party preference correlated positively and significantly with SDO in six out of six samples."[21]

While Carney, Jost, Sidanius, et al. describe conservatives in terms that are arguably pejorative, the University of Virginia's Jonathan Haidt (see Chapter Two) and Jesse Graham of the University of Southern California contend that liberal scholars may be restricting their definition of morality by failing to acknowledge values and principles important to conservatives.

Haidt and Graham submit that conservatives are concerned not only with the welfare and rights of the individual but also with the institutions of family, patriotism, loyalty to one's group, and recognition of the legitimacy of hierarchy and order as beneficial to the larger society. As a result, according to Haidt and Graham, conservatives will sometimes take what they see as moral stands—attacking abortion and divorce as undermining the

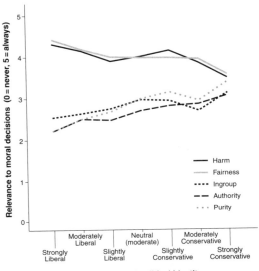

*Figure 3.2*

family—that liberals may well see as immoral incursions on the autonomy of individuals, especially women.

Haidt and his colleagues, in their paper "Liberals and Conservatives Rely on Different Sets of Moral Foundations," graph five "moralities"—see Figure 3.2[22]—(1) harm/care (strong empathy for those that are suffering and care for the most vulnerable); (2) fairness/reciprocity (life, liberty, and justice for all); (3) in-group/loyalty (tribalism, patriotism, nationalism); (4) authority/respect (mechanisms for managing social rank, tempered by the obligation of superiors to protect and provide for subordinates); and (5) purity/sanctity (related to the evolution of disgust, that makes us see carnality as degrading and renunciation as noble)—to show how liberals give priority to only the first two, harm/care and fairness/reciprocity, while conservatives give roughly equal weight to all five.[23]

## Why the Electorate Elects Republicans

In interpreting their data, Haidt and Graham write:

> [J]ustice and related virtues . . . make up half of the moral world for liberals, while justice-related concerns make up only one fifth of the

moral world for conservatives. Conservatives have many moral concerns that liberals simply do not recognize as moral concerns. When conservatives talk about virtues and policies based on the in-group/loyalty, authority/respect, and purity/sanctity foundations, liberals hear talk about theta waves [i.e., from outer space]. For this reason, liberals often find it hard to understand why so many of their fellow citizens do not rally around the cause of social justice, and why many Western nations have elected conservative governments in recent years.[24]

Haidt and Graham look at the issue of harm not from the viewpoint that conservatives are more willing to inflict it but from the other end of the telescope, that liberals place a higher value than conservatives on avoiding inflicting harm.

This distinction is crucial. There is a strong tendency in the social sciences to demonize Republicans and the right. The result is often a caricature rather than an accurate portrayal of conservatism and the values it represents. Without an accurate portrait of conservatism, the outcome of elections in which majorities periodically back conservative candidates cannot be fully understood.

Recognizing the danger that "behavioral research . . . runs the risk of becoming an extension of the political struggle between left and right," two other researchers, Philip Tetlock of the Wharton School, and Gregory Mitchell of the University of Virginia Law School, have tried to look objectively at "flattering and unflattering cognitive and motivational characterizations of liberals and conservatives" with the aim of producing a more balanced view of the competing value systems of left and right.

Four excerpts from their research paper "Liberal and Conservative Approaches to Justice: Conflicting Psychological Portraits" are instructive:[25]

*1. Flattering liberal portrait:*

They [liberals] do not equate downtrodden or impoverished status with inherent unworthiness or inability. . . . In a nutshell, liberals are less selfish and more empathic and tolerant than conservatives. Their fear of aiding the undeserving is outweighed by their fear of not helping the truly needy. . . . Liberals do not need to bolster their self-esteem by living in a stratified society in which they can claim superiority over this or that group. . . . Finally, liberals do not blame the victim or make defensive attributions. . . . Liberals acknowledge that fate can be capricious and that bad things happen to good people.

## 2. *Flattering conservative portrait:*

Conservatives realize the importance of incentives and that no, or little, aid is often the best help of all. The conservative response to social problems avoids the simplistic first response of treating the symptom by creating a new and expensive government program . . . conservatives are more integratively complex than liberals because they understand how often well-intentioned political reforms have unintended consequences or perverse effects. . . . Finally, conservatives understand how free markets work, [they] recognize that the invisible hand of free market competition leads in the long term to incentives to produce goods at levels of quality and quantity that satisfy effective demand for those goods.

## 3. *Unflattering liberal portrait:*

They practice, in effect, a kind of social homeopathic medicine that treats symptoms rather than underlying causes. . . . They fail to take into account the growing burden on the economy and the perverse incentives that dependency on public programs creates. . . . Liberals not only exaggerate the efficacy of government; they underestimate the creativity of the free market. Many liberals mindlessly condemn capitalism as a culture of greed and ignore the power of the market to stimulate hard work, investment and entrepreneurship. . . . [Liberalism] is a reflection of the widespread "psychology of dependency" in which government, by transference, takes on the role of nurturant, powerful parent.

## 4. *Unflattering conservative portrait:*

[C]onservatives do not understand how prevalent situational constraints on achievement are and thus commit the fundamental attribution error when they hold the poor responsible for poverty. . . . [C]onservatives are too prone to engage in zero-sum thinking, either I keep my money or the government takes it. They fail to appreciate the possibility of positive-sum resolutions of societal conflicts. . . . Conservatives cling to the comforting moral illusion that there is a sharp distinction between allowing people to suffer and making people suffer. Finally, conservatives fail to recognize that even if each transaction in a free market meets their standards of fairness, the cumulative result could be colossally unfair. Some people will acquire enormous power over others. . . . [C]onservatism and compassion are antithetical.[26]

The competing value systems of liberals and conservatives are further illuminated by American National Election Studies poll data that support research finding that conservatives and Republicans are more willing than liberals or Democrats to endorse free market solutions even when high costs are imposed on those less able to compete. ANES asked in 2004 and 2008 whether the government has an obligation to provide its citizens a good job and decent standard of living. Democrats and liberals agreed that government has the obligation by 40.5–26.5 and 47.5–24.5 margins respectively. In contrast, Republicans and conservatives said people should get ahead on their own by margins of 63.5–15 and 68–14, respectively.[27]

These findings demonstrate the danger of demonizing the left or right. Instead, a balanced approach to the strengths and weaknesses of each position—recognizing the salience of Tetlock and Mitchell's "flattering" and "unflattering" characterizations—is essential to understanding how it is possible for the electorate to shift back and forth from election to election.

At the state and federal levels, Republicans justify budget cuts in basic health and welfare programs by positing that the poor are responsible for their condition; emphasizing the costs of social welfare policies and the tax burdens that such benefit programs impose on the middle class; alleging that the consequences of denied food stamps or medical care can be absorbed in the larger scheme of things; asserting that market forces provide better solutions than government "handouts"; and believing that requiring people to shoulder hardship has salutary effects.

Under conditions of scarcity, a significant number of "discipline"-oriented Americans will be drawn to the hard-edged doctrines of conservatism, providing support to the Tea Party and the moral orientation of the current Republican House. Conditions of scarcity work to the advantage of conservatives, undermining the willingness of voters to sacrifice—pay higher taxes—for the less fortunate.

In contrast, periods of economic growth work to the advantage of those on the left, who are more committed to values of nurturance and care. These voters feel the suffering of others; their compassion is intensified by the sight of the jobless and homeless and hopeless. They believe that a helping hand is morally appropriate and benefits the larger polity. Democrats depend on such voters for core support. In times of plenty, voters in the center can find themselves sympathetic to this position.

For both left and right, packaging is crucial—placing political ideology and public policy in the most "flattering" light—to use the Tetlock-Mitchell template. In the 2000 election, for example, the concept of compassionate conservatism was key to George W. Bush's victory. Similarly, Democrat Bill Clinton's 1992 promise to "end welfare as we know it," to press for "more empowerment and less entitlement," to seek a "government that is leaner, not meaner; that expands opportunity, not bureaucracy" was designed to win wary independent voters. Along the same lines, during the 2008 campaign, Obama, seeking to reframe "unflattering" stereotypes of Democrats, supported the death penalty and the right to bear arms,[28] announced his approval of a House-passed intelligence surveillance law,[29] and urged absentee fathers to "realize that what makes you a man is not the ability to have a child—it's the courage to raise one."[30]

### The Polarizing Effects of Scarcity

In many ways, the themes explored in this chapter go to the heart of the problem of loss allocation posed by MIT economist Lester Thurow. Republicans are willing to allocate losses in ways that harm their adversaries, if the outcomes favor their own interests and are consistent with conservative value systems. Large numbers of voters—indeed, intermittent majorities—appear to agree with GOP values when decisions about loss allocation must be made, even though these values are anathema to the disadvantaged and to ideological liberals.

Values clashes of this nature are stark—and result in the contemporary phenomenon of acute political polarization. Conditions of scarcity magnify and intensify the conflicts underlying polarization. The electorate is now divided into two roughly equal but ideologically antithetical blocs. The swing segment of the electorate—i.e., those who have "an unstable attachment to the major political parties," according to analyst Mark Gersh,[31] those who switch their votes from Republican to Democrat, and back again, from one election to another—is very small, ranging from just 5 or 6 percent, according to estimates by former Republican strategist Matt Dowd,[32] to 10 percent, according to political analysts Alan Abramowitz and Bill Bishop.[33] In many elections this 5 to 10 percent slice of the electorate proves crucial to the electoral outcome. The candidate who successfully identifies and mobilizes the key movable segments of the electorate—swing voters—often proves to be the winner.

In 2008, for example, Obama's core constituency of blacks, "netroots," creatives, single women, young voters, and Hispanics was augmented by a sizable number of white swing voters who were put off by Bush himself, by the Iraq War, and by the financial collapse of September 2008—as well as by John McCain's weak campaign and his choice of Sarah Palin as running mate. Two years later many of these same swing voters, angered by an ongoing recession, continuing unemployment, ballooning deficits, and the perceived distributional impact of health care reform, swept House Democrats out of office.

## An Economic History of Polarization

Contemporary polarization began to take root in the conflicts of the 1960s during the rights revolutions—civil rights, women's rights, reproductive rights, gay rights, welfare rights, rights for the mentally ill, the rights of non-Christian religious minorities, etc. Many of these rights were fought for by groups that had been previously stigmatized, marginalized, or disenfranchised on the basis of traits and ascriptive attributes (e.g., race, sex, ethnicity, gender, and sexual orientation), leading to the prominence, on the left, of what came to be known as identity politics.

This dynamic was described by Lester Thurow in 1980:

> In the past, political and economic power was distributed in such a
> way that substantial economic losses could be imposed on parts of
> the population if the establishment decided that it was in the general
> interest. Economic losses were allocated to particular powerless

groups rather than spread across the population. These groups are no longer willing to accept losses and are able to raise substantially the costs for those who wish to impose losses upon them. With the civil rights, poverty, Black power, and women's liberation movements, many of the groups that have in the past absorbed economic losses have become militant. They are no longer willing to accept losses without a political fight. The success of their militancy and civil disobedience sets an example that spreads to other groups representing the environment, neighborhoods, and regions. All minority groups have gone through a learning process.[34]

Thurow added that "there are American winners and American losers. Some incomes go up . . . but others go down. Individuals do not sacrifice equally. Some gain; some lose. A program to raise the occupational position of women and minorities automatically lowers the occupational position of white men."[35] The resulting politics become a more explicitly and equal struggle for resources—and an increasingly bitter one.

By the late 1970s resource competition had ratcheted up with millions of newly empowered and assertive contenders, including new immigrants in the aftermath of liberalized immigration legislation in 1965.

The rights revolution in effect intensified competition for jobs, college admissions, and promotions, as well as for such less tangible benefits as status, deference, and authority. Growing numbers of minorities and women entered the marketplace just as the sustained expansion of the 1960s faltered and as the economy entered a severe recession in 1973. From 1947 to 1973 median family income (in inflation-adjusted 2001 dollars) doubled from $20,042 to $41,590. Then it stopped. For the next ten years, from 1974 to 1983, median family income stagnated, averaging $41,744 a year.[36]

At the same time, the rate of productivity growth dropped sharply. From 1947 to 1973, productivity had grown by a healthy 2.8 percent a year. Between 1973 and 1979 it dropped precipitously to an anemic 1.1 percent.[37] As if this were not enough, the steady growth in manufacturing jobs, many of them unionized, that had been the entry point for so many into the middle class came to a halt. In 1947 there were 18.5 million goods-producing or manufacturing jobs, and by 1973 there were 24.8 million. Over the next decade the average number of manufacturing jobs stayed flat at 24.5 million while the population increased by 21.9 million.[38]

The 1970s were also a decade of hyperinflation, producing growing anxiety that elected and appointed officials were unable to manage the economy. The Federal Reserve Bank of St. Louis published the following description of the condition of the U.S. economy in the 1970s:

> For nearly 30 years after the Great Depression, the financial sector experienced an era of relative profitability and little stress. That began to change in the late 1960s and early 1970s with the increases in the level and volatility of the rate of inflation, the advent of the electronic age and new competition, and the increasing internationalization of the world's economies. The average annual rate of inflation rose from less than 2 percent in 1950–1965, to about 4.5 percent in 1966–1973, to nearly 9.5 percent in 1974–1981; in that last period the rate was also very volatile, ranging from about 6 percent to almost 14 percent. As the level and volatility of inflation increased, so did the level and volatility of interest rates. Faced with higher levels of inflation, lenders demanded higher interest rates since the dollars with which they would be repaid in the future would be able to purchase less than the dollars they were lending. These higher, more volatile interest rates increased the general level of risk.[39]

In fact, by the end of the Carter administration, in 1979 and 1980, inflation was in the double digits, 11.3 percent and 13.5 percent respectively.[40] Prices were increasing at two to three times the rate that Americans had become accustomed to. The prime interest rate, which dictates the cost of consumer loans and mortgages, was even worse, reaching 20 percent on April 2, 1980, Carter's last year in office.[41]

Americans were also used to "normal" unemployment rates of less than 5 percent. From 1964 to 1973 the average was 4.6 percent. But for the decade after that, the unemployment rate averaged 7.4 percent, remaining at a level that in the past had been considered recessionary.[42]

The competitive forces that exploded in the 1970s went far beyond the nation's borders. Suddenly American manufacturers of cars, steel, and other products that had enjoyed a favorable international balance of trade status throughout the post–World War II years discovered that they were being outproduced and underpriced by foreign companies. The manufacturing balance of trade, for the first time since 1946, turned negative in 1971, minus $2.62 trillion, and nose-dived to $31.1 trillion in 1978 and $33.9 trillion in 1979.[43]

Corporate America realized the economic consequences of global competition well ahead of organized labor. Without public announcement, business abrogated what had been a cooperative arrangement with trade unions, an arrangement in which owners profited from steadily rising productivity and from new markets abroad, while workers won wage hikes and expanded fringe benefits. In the 1970s, the relationship abruptly turned not just adversarial but hostile. Corporations not only played hardball at the bargaining table but began drives to decertify unions and move facilities to right-to-work southern states or to low-wage locations beyond U.S. borders.

For nonunion employees—from office assistants to middle and upper management—the heightened levels of competition meant the end of lifetime employment and job security. These hypercompetitive trends have continued without remission into the present.

The interaction between the emerging rights revolution, which was essentially redistributive in nature, and a period of exacerbated economic hardship drove the shift from bipartisanship and consensus to political polarization.

Among the first signs of this political transformation was the passage in 1978 of California's Proposition 13, severely restricting the ability of the state and local governments to raise new revenues and setting in motion what became a national antitax movement. That same year the Republicans picked up fifteen House seats, and one of the new victors was Newt Gingrich.

Political polarization did not find full political expression, however, until the election of 1980, with the nomination and election of the first explicitly conservative president since Herbert Hoover. The 1980 contest marked the emergence of the gender gap as millions of formerly Democratic white men jumped ship to cast ballots for the GOP.

And the man who ascended to the White House, Ronald Reagan, was ready and willing to conduct an assault on the liberal welfare state and the people dependent on it.

Reagan's two terms were marked by a sustained attack on affirmative action—that is, race- and gender-based preferences in hiring, firing, and job promotion, as well as in college and university admissions.[44] The president appointed William Bradford Reynolds, an outspoken critic of affirmative action, to head the Civil Rights Division of the Justice Department; he cut the budgets of the Equal Employment Opportunity Commission and the Office of Federal Contract Compliance programs. Reynolds filed suit challenging existing court orders requiring cities from Birmingham to Chicago to hire specific numbers of black and Hispanic police and firefighters. The largest spending cuts during the Reagan years were made in means-tested programs serving heavily African American populations, staffed, in many cases, by black personnel. These programs included Aid to Families with Dependent Children (welfare), food stamps, and both the Social Services Block Grant and the Community Services Block Grant programs.

In 1981 Reagan successfully pressured a Democratic-controlled Congress to enact the Gramm-Latta budget reconciliation bill—a direct assault on the domestic "safety net" that Democrats had carefully constructed over the previous fifty years.[45] Gramm-Latta called for major spending reductions—$145 billion over three years in 1981 dollars—cuts in food stamps, child nutrition, subsidized housing, federal workers' pay and pensions, and, not least, welfare benefits. The measure was denounced by House Speaker Thomas P. "Tip" O'Neill, Jr., as "a deliberate effort to transfer wealth from the struggling families of this country and award that wealth to those that are already wealthy," but O'Neill lost the vote by a margin of 215–211 to a combination of Republicans and conservative southern Democrats.[46] The measure was a salvo in what became a sustained drive to "defund the left"—i.e., to inflict harm on the Democratic Party and its constituents by cutting off their life support, federal dollars.

Gramm-Latta, incorporating President Reagan's tax reduction and spending reform plans, marked a striking departure from past Republican approaches, under Presidents Dwight Eisenhower and Richard Nixon, to dealing with the welfare state. Both presidents had been fundamentally accommodationist, if not, in some instances, expansionist in their approaches to big government. One of Reagan's major legacies is that such accommodation is now—in 2011—considered treasonous within the GOP.

## Cut to the Bone

Fifteen years after passing Gramm-Latta, Republican majorities in the House and Senate tore another major hole in the domestic safety net, ending welfare as an entitlement. The 1996 Personal Responsibility and Work Opportunity Reconciliation Act (aka Welfare Reform) set a five-year limit on the receipt of aid and required work participation. The legislative assault, which got its original impetus during the 1992 presidential campaign with Bill Clinton's promise to "end welfare as we know it," split Democrats while receiving overwhelming Republican backing. The budget and tax bill did not stop there: food stamp benefits were cut; legal immigrants were barred from participation unless they could prove that they had worked for a total of ten years without receiving benefits, and the eligibility of children for SSI (Supplemental Security Income for the disabled) was sharply curtailed. The measure won approval with the near-unanimous support of Republicans—230 to 2 in the House, and 53 to 0 in the Senate—while Democrats were split—98 to 97 in the House, and 25 to 21 in the Senate.[47]

Republicans voiced no qualms about cutting off what had been a basic source of income for millions of poor people. From 1996 to 2010 the welfare caseload dropped from 4.6 million families to substantially less than half that, 1.9 million.[48]

This willingness to slice domestic spending to the bone, spending aimed at Democratic priorities, was put on display once again immediately after Republicans took over the House in 2011. Although later rejected by the Democratic-controlled Senate, the first bill passed by the newly elected Republican House—the Full-Year Appropriations Act of 2011—cut spending in FY 2011 by sixty-one billion dollars. The programs that got hit made up a Republican enemies list. Every cent of federal money flowing to Planned Parenthood was eliminated, and the bill prohibited paying federal employees to implement health care reform.

The list of targeted programs included $1.1 billion cut from public housing construction spending; $1 billion from the Corporation for National and Community Service; $86 million from the Corporation for Public Broadcasting; $50 million from the National Labor Relations Board; $100 million in grants for organizations serving Hispanics; $85 million for historically black colleges; $5 billion from the Department of Education, ranging from Title I grants to schools in poor neighborhoods ($693.5 million) to math and sciences programs ($180.5 million); $390.3 million from the low-income energy assistance program; $1.1 billion from Head Start; $1.6 billion from the National Institutes of Health; $317.5 million from family planning programs; $100 million from community health centers; $2.9 billion from the Department of Labor, including $108.5 million from a program to reintegrate ex-offenders; $100 million from a dislocated worker assistance program; $525 million from community service employment for older Americans; $2.7 billion from Environmental Protection Agency programs; $121.8 million from the White House budget; $470.1 million from the Legal Services Corporation; and $747.2 million from the Supplemental Nutrition program for Women, Infants and Children (WIC).[49]

## Democrats Cave in, Republicans Overreach

Just as the Republican Party has demonstrated exceptional levels of unity since 1980, so the Democratic coalition has a record of fracturing when under pressure. Dissident House Democrats, most of them from the South, were critical to the 1981 passage of the Gramm-Latta bill. Tax cuts favoring the wealthy were enacted under both Reagan and George W. Bush with just enough Democratic support to allow Republicans to call the measures bipartisan. In early 2011, as eighty-four newly elected Republican members of Congress, most with Tea Party backing, demanded massive reductions in federal spending, the House voted on a series of short-term continuing appropriations to prevent a government shutdown. The Republican interim bills calling for major cuts passed only because they received substantial Democratic support. On March 15, 2011, for example, the House approved a three-week appropriation that cut spending by six billion dollars. Eighty-five Democrats voted in favor while 104 voted no.[50]

There are many reasons for the internal conflicts within the Democratic coalition, but one of them is the reality that a coalition two-thirds of which is drawn from the ranks of the disadvantaged has more to lose than its opponents in a life-and-death contest. I have argued previously along these lines:

> First, the GOP is the party of the socially and economically dominant and of those who identify with the dominant. It is the party of the affluent, of CEOs, of the managerial elite, of successful entrepreneurs, of viable small businesses. It is the party of those blue- and

white-collar workers with a record of holding their own in market competition, the party of more stable families, and of those belonging to ascendant rather than to waning religious communities. In 2004, 87.5 percent of citizens who voted Republican in the presidential election were white.

The Democratic Party, conversely, is the party of the so-called "subdominant" and of those who identify with the subdominant, including those upper-income voters who have taken the side of the insurgents in the sexual, women's rights, and civil rights revolutions. Roughly two-thirds of the Democratic Party's adherents are Americans who struggle to survive in an increasingly brutal competitive environment. The party is also the representative of organized labor and of the leadership of old-line religious denominations—institutions in decline.

In a struggle between two numerically equal forces, the side more broadly skilled in economic combat, whose constituents control more resources—the side more accustomed to the rigors of the market, more practiced in the arts of commerce and marketing; the side with greater access to corporate power, the side more adept at risk management, the side with the means to repeatedly assemble and sustain long-lasting, powerful coalitions, the side that has revealed ruthless proficiency in winning and in shaping American institutions to its purposes—the side that has behind it most of those at the helm of the financial, technological, commercial, and information revolutions—this side has had a substantial long-term advantage.[51]

Republicans themselves, however, do not come to partisan conflict with an unblemished list of assets. The right regularly overreaches. Relatively recent examples include the decision of the Republican House under Newt Gingrich to twice close down government, in November and December 1995. House GOP leaders mistakenly assumed that the public would support them, even as polls showed that voters opposed such disruptions. The House leadership additionally failed to take into account the sharp decline in public hostility toward government after the 1995 bombing of the Oklahoma City federal building and the alarming emergence of secret antigovernment militia movements in Texas, Michigan, Montana, Arizona, and a number of other states.

Gingrich has consistently embodied an excessive propensity for risk. In 2006, he told journalist Ronald Brownstein, "If you think you are the subordinate wolf, you spend your time cultivating the dominant wolf. If you think you are capable of becoming the dominant wolf, you spend a lot of your energy beating the dominant wolf."[52]

Recklessness was manifest in the decision by the House Republican leadership in 1998 to impeach President Clinton. Many of the top Republicans spearheading the drive to expel the president from the White House on the ground that he was having an extramarital affair with intern Monica Lewinsky were themselves having, or had had, soon-to-be-publicized extramarital affairs: Gingrich with House aide Callista Bisek;[53] Bob Livingston, in line to become House Speaker, with four different women;[54] and House Judiciary chairman Henry Hyde with a married Illinois woman, Cherie Snodgrass.[55]

Another instance of Republican overreach was George W. Bush's decision to invade Iraq in 2003 without the backing of the UN or of key allies, in the face of opposition from China, Germany, France, Belgium, Austria, Mexico, Canada, Brazil, India, Russia, Turkey, Vietnam, and Bangladesh, among others. Bush conducted the post-9/11 invasion lacking adequate preparation for reconstruction and adopted policies in Iraq that weakened the civilian infrastructure and strengthened the opposition.

The invasion of Iraq in turn forced the transfer of manpower and other resources away from Afghanistan, which the United States had also attacked in the aftermath of 9/11, but with broader international and domestic support. The overcommitment of American military forces fueled the revival of the Taliban and Al Qaeda in Afghanistan and in neighboring regions and has led to prolonged and costly American military involvement in the Middle East that is likely to leave unfulfilled expectations and animosity in its wake.

The Congressional Research Service (CRS), a legislative branch agency within the Library of Congress,[56] reported in September 2010 that Congress had authorized a total of "$1.121 trillion for military operations, base security, reconstruction, foreign aid, embassy costs, and veterans' health care for operations initiated since the 9/11 attacks: Operation Enduring Freedom, Afghanistan and other counter terror operations; Operation Noble Eagle, providing enhanced security at military bases; and Operation Iraqi Freedom."[57]

Joseph Stiglitz, a Nobel laureate in economics, and Linda Bilmes of Harvard's Kennedy School, have published an exhaustive study of the wars in Afghanistan and Iraq, *The Three Trillion Dollar War: The True Cost of the Iraq Conflict*. They have estimated the total cost of U.S. military operations in those countries—factoring in, among other things, the long-term care of injured soldiers—at more than twice the figure given by the CRS: the three trillion dollars cited in the title.[58]

On the domestic front, Bush's unyielding free market, antiregulatory ideology contributed substantially to a period of breathtaking financial brinksmanship and fatally flawed risk management marked by the explosive growth of bonds comprising all or parts of subprime mortgages, credit default swaps, collateralized debt obligations, and the engineering of complex derivatives and other exotic financial instruments. Those banks and financial interests that made huge profits during the run-up to the crash toppled the world into a global economic castastrophe, which became the proximate cause of the ongoing worldwide crisis of scarcity.

Insofar as the September 2008 "trillion-dollar meltdown" crested on George W. Bush's watch, the Republican Party paid a steep price in the November 2008 election. Democrats, however, were soon forced to pick up the baton. Obama inherited an economy in terminal distress. Eight days before his January 20, 2009, inauguration, Obama was compelled to ask Congress to advance $350 billion in bailout money. By Obama's eighth week in office, the stock market had lost half its peak value. By June 1, 2009, General Motors and Chrysler had filed for bankruptcy and, to prevent dissolution, required a $35 million government infusion. "I was angry at first, then I cried, then I got angry again," said Don Skidmore, the president of United Automobile Workers Local 735. "I'm hurt for the people."[59]

In the first year of Obama's presidency, the United States hemorrhaged jobs: 651,000 in February 2009, 724,000 in March, 539,000 in April—8 million lost by the fourth quarter of 2009. The wars in Iraq and Afghanistan continued; the Obama White House requested a total of $664 billion for defense in FY 2010. Credit for businesses and for ordinary Americans froze as housing prices spiraled downward. Obama's signature achievement, passage of the Patient Protection and Affordable Care Act, was so controversial and poorly understood that public opinion began to move decisively against him.

The Republican Party was eager to leverage every opportunity to splinter the left. In a demonstration of the GOP's willingness to push the envelope, the Republican Governors' Association released a Web video in April 2010 designed to go viral. The video first shows Obama declaring, "Yes, we can . . ." and a placard flashes, "ignore the will of the people." Again, Obama says, "Yes, we can . . ." and the words "corrupt your representatives" flash on-screen. The video then shifts to black Democratic congressman Alcee Hastings of Florida* chairing a House committee, declaring, "Ain't no rules around here, we make them up as we go along." Next comes a clip of Nancy Pelosi saying, "We have to pass the bill so we can find out what's in it." Then Al Sharpton, the African American activist, appears on-screen boasting, "The American people overwhelmingly voted for socialism when they elected President Obama." That sequence culminates in a photo of a Fidel Castro quote: "Passage of Obama's health care is a miracle." The video shifts to House Republican leader John Boehner warning: "Certainly the government can't continue to spend money we don't have," followed by Obama appearing to answer, "Yes, we can." Pictures of slums appear on-screen while three unseen narrators intone, "We suffer from a fiscal cancer. . . . This will leave us far worse off in the future than if we acted today," and "We've killed off what made us a great nation," followed by Obama, again appearing to answer: "Yes, we can."

By November 2010 voters were more than willing to entrust governance to the GOP once again. Republicans picked up sixty-three seats in the House and six in the Senate.

Voters had rejected the Republican Party and its record of risk management in the congressional midterms of 2006 and in the presidential election of 2008. Those two elections demonstrated that the Democratic coalition of the "economically and socially subdominant"—Stan Greenberg's Rising American Electorate—can and will at times defeat the coalition of the so-called dominant. Still, the RAE took a beating in 2010.

The crucial question now is: Can a left coalition—made up of an alliance of the economically and socially disadvantaged and their better-off socioculturally liberal champions—compete effectively at a time of austerity

---

*Hastings was impeached as a sitting judge in 1988.

to retain what it has and make inroads on terrain currently held by the GOP? Put another way: Will middle-class and moderate voters shun the party of the needy when resources, especially tax dollars, are in short supply? Or will enough of these voters identify with the less fortunate as many of them endure their own run of bad luck?

The next two chapters will explore aspects of American politics that touch on this question.

# Chapter Four

## The Economics of Immigration

On February 10, 2011, the House State and Federal Affairs Committee of the Kansas legislature was holding a hearing on immigration issues when Republican state representative Connie O'Brien from Tonganoxie, just west of Kansas City, told an anecdote.

She recalled standing in line with her son, who was registering for classes at Kansas City (Kan.) Community College and having difficulty paying tuition. In front of them was a female student who appeared to be foreign. "My son, who's a Kansas resident, born here, raised here, didn't qualify for any financial aid," O'Brien said. "Yet this girl was going to get financial aid. . . . My son was kind of upset about it because he works and pays for his own schooling and his books and everything and he didn't think that was fair. We didn't ask the girl what nationality she was, we didn't think that was proper. But we could tell by looking at her that she was not originally from this country."

Another committee member, Democrat Sean Gatewood from Topeka, asked, "Can you expand on how you could tell that they were illegal?"

"Well, she wasn't black," O'Brien replied. "She wasn't Asian. And she had the olive complexion."[1]

Within a month another Kansas legislator, Republican state representative Virgil Peck of Tyro, Kansas, called and raised O'Brien. Peck was listening to a witness before the Appropriations Committee describe the effectiveness of shooting wild hogs from a helicopter as a way to deal with the problem of feral swine, when a thought occurred to him: "Looks like to me, if shooting these immigrating feral hogs works, maybe we have found a cure to our illegal immigration problem."[2]

Animosity toward the wave of illegal immigrants entering this country over the past three decades reached new heights with the onset of the financial collapse in late 2007. This rising anger stood in contrast with the opening years of the first decade of this century, when there was a strong possibility that Congress would agree to a fundamental reform of the law to grant a "path to citizenship" to many of the millions of undocumented aliens now firmly ensconced here with jobs and families. President George W. Bush was a strong proponent of the proposal, along with most Democrats and a sprinkling of influential Republicans in the House and Senate. At the local level, states as diverse as Texas, California, New York, Utah, Illinois, Washington, Nebraska, New Mexico, Oklahoma, and even rock-ribbed conservative Kansas passed laws early in the first half of the decade giving the children of illegal immigrants the benefits of in-state tuition rates at state colleges and universities.

By the end of the decade, however, prospects for enactment of liberal immigration measures were nil. In the aftermath of the financial collapse that began in December 2007, the tone of the debate over immigration reached a new level of harshness as the balance of power shifted to the opposition on the right:

- "Mothers killed. Children executed. The tactics of vicious Central American gangs, now on U.S. soil. Pushing drugs. Raping kids. Destroying lives. Thanks to gutless politicians who refuse to defend our borders." *Tom Trancredo television ad in his 2010 bid to become governor of Colorado.*[3]
- "It is not being cold-hearted to acknowledge that every dollar spent on illegal immigrants is one dollar less that's spent on our own children, our own senior citizens and for all those who entered this society who played by the rules, who paid their taxes and expect their government to watch out for their needs before it bestows privileges and scarce resources on illegals." *Republican representative Dana Rohrabacher of California on the House floor, December 8, 2010.*[4]

- On March 7, 2008, Republican congressman Steve King of Iowa declared on a local radio station: "I don't want to disparage anyone because of their race, their ethnicity, their name, whatever the religion of their father might have been. I'll just say this, that when you think about the optics of a Barack Obama potentially getting elected president of the United States, I mean, what does this look like to the rest of the world? What does this look like to the world of Islam? And I will tell you that if he is elected president, then the radical Islamists, the al Qaeda and the radical Islamists and their supporters will be dancing in the streets in greater numbers than they did on September 11th. . . . They'll be dancing in the streets because of his middle name. They'll be dancing in the streets because of who his father was. . . . There will be dancing in the streets if he's elected president and that has a chilling effect on how difficult it will be to ever win this global war on terror."[5]

In hard times, few, if any, issues are as effective as immigration in forcing to the surface the hard edges of conservatism: hostility to outsiders seen as a drain on tax revenues, a siege mentality, a hypertrophied fear of "corrupting forces," the perception of newcomers as adversaries and as "disease-carrying aliens."

### Getting Cold Feet

Arizona is the epicenter of the battle over immigration. There is no better evidence of the ascendance of anti-immigration forces by 2010–2011 than the 180-degree policy turn of Arizona senator John McCain, a politician who once took pride in his maverick status and willingness to defy conservative orthodoxy. As recently as May 25, 2006, McCain stood apart from many in his party as a proud cosponsor with Edward M. Kennedy of legislation that aimed to give many of the eleven to twelve million illegal immigrants in the country a path to citizenship.

The McCain-Kennedy bill would, McCain declared,

provide for a new, temporary worker program to enable foreign workers to work legally in this country when there are jobs that American workers won't fill. And, it will acknowledge and address in a humanitarian and compassionate way the current undocumented population. . . . Why not say to those undocumented workers who are working the jobs that the rest of us refuse, come out from the shadows, earn your citizenship in this country. You broke the law to come here, so you must go to the back of the line, pay a fine, stay employed, learn our language, pay your taxes, obey our laws, and earn the right to be an American.[6]

Then came the fight for the Republican presidential nomination. In the second half of 2007, McCain's pro-immigration stance was proving a clear liability, severely damaging his bid. "As McCain's town hall meetings developed into shouting matches over immigration, the candidate let his frustrations show through," wrote John Heilemann and Mark Halperin in their book *Game Change.* "The issue had more than injured McCain politically. It had thoroughly crippled his already lame and halting fund-raising."[7]

By the end of 2007 McCain had shifted, although not in a complete about-face, in a move designed to placate anti-immigration forces: before immigration reform could be considered, America's borders had to be made impenetrable. "I understand why you would call it a, quote, shift," McCain told reporters in Simpsonville, South Carolina, on November 3, 2007. "I say it is a lesson learned about what the American people's priorities are. And their priority is to secure the borders."[8]

For pro-immigration forces, McCain's altered stance was a clear signal that one of their strongest allies, especially important because he was a Republican, was getting cold feet. If McCain had cold feet in 2008, two years later he was in full retreat. McCain faced what he thought would be a tough 2010 primary challenge by anti-immigrant former representative J. D. Hayworth. More important, Arizona itself had become a bastion of opposition to immigration.

On April 19, 2010, McCain stunned his early allies in the immigrant advocacy community by endorsing legislation, then moving through the state legislature, that gave police the power to demand papers from anyone suspected of being in the country illegally and to arrest anyone without sufficient documentation.

"I think it's a very important step forward," McCain declared in describing the legislation. "I can fully understand why the legislature would want to act." The onetime champion of immigrant rights went on FOX News to tell Bill O'Reilly: "The state of Arizona is acting and doing what it feels it needs to do in light of the fact that the federal government is not fulfilling its fundamental responsibility—to secure our borders."[9]

Frank Sharry, executive director of America's Voice, was incredulous: "He risked his political career for immigration reform, and now he is compromising his principles to fight for his political life."[10]

After the 2010 election, McCain voted against the DREAM (Development, Relief and Education for Alien Minors) Act,* a measure he had sponsored two years earlier. The bill provided an avenue to citizenship for undocumented aliens who serve in the armed forces or who have attended college for at least two years. McCain had been a leading cosponsor and strong proponent of this exact same legislation for three years running—2005, 2006, and 2007.

For advocates of immigration reform legislation, McCain's switch was the canary in the mine shaft, a clear signal that virtually the entire Republican Party had made a crucial decision to stand firm against liberalization.

The transformation of John McCain was the most dramatic of the conversions on the Republican side of the aisle, but he is not alone. Pro-immigrant Republicans have changed their position, been defeated in primaries, or been marginalized by their colleagues. Under intense pressure from a stridently conservative primary electorate, the GOP has become the anti-immigrant party. Its own constituents—most important, voters in primaries—will not support a pro-immigrant candidate, as McCain discovered.

## A Perfect Wedge Issue

The Republican Party has found that in a time of scarcity, immigration is an effective wedge issue, a lever to break the partisan loyalty of moderate white Democrats fearful that immigrants will consume tax dollars for the education of their children, for treatment in public hospitals, for receipt of food stamps, and for other public benefits. An auxiliary concern that the Republican Party deftly manipulates is that the immigrant population will transform political and cultural norms—a concern often voiced as a threat to the notion, now appropriated by the right, of "American exceptionalism."

---

*A law providing undocumented aliens, brought to the United States as children, the opportunity to earn conditional permanent residency upon completion of two years in the military or two years of college.

Those conservatives and Republicans who have dehumanized immigrants clearly have breached the boundaries of decency. Only somewhat less blatantly, the anti-immigration campaign does violence to America's history as a nation of immigrants.

At an operational level, however, Democrats cannot afford to turn to the right on immigration for three reasons: first, it would be morally repugnant to core constituencies; second, the party cannot credibly compete with the GOP on immigrant bashing; third, the Hispanic electorate has grown to become a crucial part of the Democratic base. Just as, at a purely expedient level, Republicans cannot renounce the Christian right, Democrats cannot abandon either Hispanics or blacks.

For Democrats, the immigration issue requires a more nuanced strategic approach than it does for Republicans. At the moment, in such states as Arizona, Nevada, and Texas, anti-immigration positions can gain majority support. In time, however, these stands are increasingly likely to become a liability as the Hispanic share of the electorate grows and as older, more conservative whites die off. The immediate problem for Democrats is that the Great Recession produced an intensification of anti-immigrant views that have fueled, for the moment, the GOP and the Tea Party. The history of the immigration issue in California offers the Democrats their best hope.

In 1994 Republican governor Pete Wilson made effective use of Proposition 187, an anti-immigrant referendum, to win reelection. At the time California was considered competitive for Republicans in presidential elections. By the 1990s, however, the increase in the size of the Hispanic electorate was a key factor in flipping California into the Democratic column, and the state is now considered a Democratic bastion.

## Crime

In much of the rest of the nation, however, immigration is, and will continue to be, problematic for Democrats. In Arizona, for example, a Republican state that as recently as 2006 was moving in a Democratic direction, the immigration issue halted Democratic gains in their tracks in 2010. Arizona's 350-mile border with Mexico has become a major source of fear. There were a total of 217, 318 apprehensions of illegal immigrants crossing into Arizona in 2010, and over the past six years the number of dead bodies found in the Arizona desert has ranged from a low of 187 to a high of 283.[11]

While the flow of illegal immigrants has slowed dramatically since the start of the recession, anti-immigration Republicans had solid voter concerns to work with. Serious criminal activity on the border, primarily drug smuggling, has escalated. In February 2011 the U.S. Immigration and Customs Enforcement announced that a cooperative program with Mexico called the Alliance to Combat Transnational Threats had, since September 2009, resulted in the seizure of more than 1.6 million pounds of marijuana, 3,800 pounds of cocaine, and 1,000 pounds of methamphetamine; more than thirteen million dollars in undeclared U.S. currency and 268 weapons; and the denial of entry of fourteen thousand aliens with criminal backgrounds or other disqualifying information.[12]

### Jobs

On the jobs front, the Pew Hispanic Center, a fundamentally liberal institution, has found, for example, that corporations laid off disproportionately more native-born workers than immigrants (foreign born) and, at least during the first year of the recovery, hired proportionately more foreign- than native-born Americans.

"In the year following the official end of the Great Recession in June 2009, foreign-born workers gained 656,000 jobs while native-born workers lost 1.2 million," the Pew study found. "As a result, the unemployment rate for immigrant workers fell 0.6 percentage points during this period (from 9.3 percent to 8.7 percent) while for native-born workers it rose 0.5 percentage points (from 9.2 percent to 9.7 percent)." In addition, another key measure, labor force participation—the share of the working-age population working or actively looking for jobs—grew a modest 0.2 percent for foreign born, from 68 to 68.2 percent, while the native-born participation rate fell 0.8 points, from 65.3 to 64.5 percent.

These figures reinforce claims by anti-immigrant forces that newcomers take jobs away from citizens. At the same time, the trends provide some support to liberal claims that corporations have exploited the recession to lay off native-born workers and have taken advantage of the recovery to hire, at lower pay, foreign-born workers. The Pew report found that foreign-born workers experienced a 4.5 percent drop in their pay, while native-born workers experienced less than a 1 percent drop.[13]

The Pew data demonstrate that there are two sides to the immigration debate. Both sides have shown a powerful inclination to ignore information damaging to their positions. Liberal proponents of immigration reform calling for a path to citizenship neglect the costs of this option at their peril. Opponents of legalization, at the same time, have refused to deal with the crucial role of immigrants, legal and illegal, in the economy, and the contribution their payroll taxes make toward keeping Social Security and Medicare afloat as the native white population ages and retires from the workforce.

Not only are immigrants now one-seventh of the population and one-sixth of the workforce, but their education and skill levels have been rising. In 1980, just under 20 percent of immigrants between the ages of twenty-five and sixty-four had college degrees, while 40 percent had not finished high school. In 2010, 30 percent of immigrants had at least a college degree, while the percentage of those without high school diplomas dropped to 28 percent, according to the Brookings Institution.[14]

T he scarcity-driven escalation of anti-immigrant sentiment has clearly worked to the political advantage of the GOP. There are additional findings that the GOP and its more affluent constituents benefit in other ways from growing numbers of legal and illegal immigrants.

In their book *Polarized America*, three political scientists, Nolan McCarty of Princeton, Howard Rosenthal of New York University, and Keith T. Poole of the University of California San Diego, found several striking correlations.[15] The first, and least surprising, is that there is a correlation of political polarization—measured by the percent of House votes in which majorities of the two parties vote in direct opposition to each other—with the increase in income inequality since the mid-1970s, as measured by the Gini Index. A society that scores 0.0 on the Gini scale has perfect equality in income distribution: every working member of the society earns an equal income. The higher the number over 0, the higher the inequality, and the score of 1.0 (or 100) indicates total inequality where only one person corners all the income.[16] As the Gini Index goes up, so does polarization. This relationship is illustrated in Figure 4.1.[17]

One reason the Gini Index goes up, the authors of *Polarized America* contend, is that increased immigration enlarges the population of the poor, since immigrants, especially those from Mexico particularly and Latin America generally, receive low wages and thus drive down wages for workingmen and -women overall.

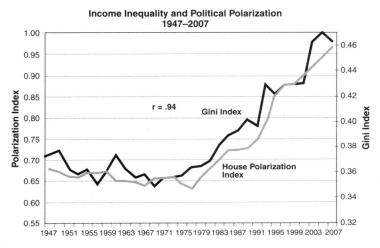

*Figure 4.1*

The relationship between polarization and immigration, as measured by the percentage in the population of foreign born, is illustrated in Figure 4.2[18] by the line tracing the polarization of House votes and the dots showing the percent of the U.S. population that is foreign born.

There is a clear advantage that flows to the political right as a result of these dynamics: insofar as the two parties are roughly split along a have vs. a

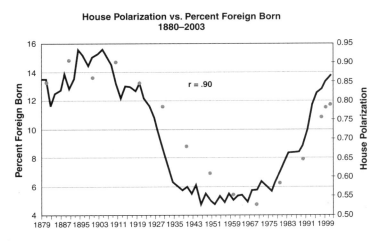

*Figure 4.2*

have-not axis, rising numbers of poorly paid immigrants increase the share of the have-not population that does not vote and is therefore politically powerless, tilting the advantage to the haves.

While there is a strong correlation between levels of immigration and polarization, this does not constitute evidence of causality. One explanation is that the rise of immigration, starting with the enactment of liberalized legislation in 1965,[19] is a part of the broader rights revolution that over time has encompassed African Americans, women, defendant rights, and, not least, beneficiaries of the right to sexual privacy. These developments have contributed to a population sharply divided on hot-button issues and have contributed to the contemporary trend toward polarization.

### The State that Sold the Capitol Building

By 2008 the Mountain West states had become ground zero in the partisan battleground. The inhabitants of Colorado, Nevada, and even Arizona were showing clear signs that voting for a Democrat for president was no longer outside the realm of possibility. Obama won Colorado and Nevada and, with the help of the Hispanic vote, could well have been competitive in Arizona except for the fact that it was McCain's home state and he carried it, 54–45 percent.

Arizona, starting in the 1990s, had rolled the economic dice, cutting income, sales, and property taxes, gambling that the state's phenomenal rate of growth and commercial development would produce a steady revenue stream. For years the risk-taking paid off. Immigrants flooded into the state, housing sprang up, and work was easy to find.

Growth in turn fueled support for expansive state programs and a modest political shift to the left. In 2000 the overwhelmingly white Arizona electorate decisively—903,134 to 532,317—approved Proposition 204, extending Medicaid coverage to all adults below the federal poverty level ($16,700 for a family of four in 2000). The measure made 253,184 uninsured Arizonans, all of them poor and a plurality of them Hispanic, eligible for coverage.[20] The governor's office, which had been controlled by Republicans all through the 1990s, was taken over by Democrat Janet Napolitano in 2002.

Despite warnings of a rising voter backlash, Napolitano in 2005 vetoed three anti-immigration bills, one denying in-state tuition and day care for illegals, another making English the official state language, and a third empowering local police to enforce federal immigration laws.[21] There was no backlash: in 2006, Napolitano won reelection in a landslide, crushing her Republican opponent, conservative activist Len Munsil, 959,830 to 543,528, or 62.58 percent to 35.44 percent.

At the start of 2007 Arizona was basking in optimism. On January 4, 2007, in her second inaugural address, Napolitano proudly boasted, "Arizona is now, officially, the fastest growing state in the nation. Nevada, step aside."

> Only four years ago, this state was mired in deficit. We had neglected the most vulnerable among us—our children and the elderly. When I stood here four years ago, I said these words: "[G]enerations to come will not remember us for how we balanced the budget. . . . Instead, they will remember how we educated our children, how we protected our seniors, how we built a new economy, and how we made this wonderful state an even better place to live." . . . [Now there is] a New Arizona: one in which innovation, pride and strength have allowed us to address many of the challenges that faced us four years ago, and to build on what we have begun.[22]

By March 2007 it looked as if Arizona's risk-taking had paid off. The state was basking in a $1.7 billion surplus. "Overall, the employment revisions point to a state that remains very healthy. Almost all sectors are growing," reported Elliott D. Pollack & Company, a real estate and economic consulting firm. "[I]n 2006 more jobs were created in Arizona than ever before. . . . About 1 in every 20 jobs created in the U.S. in 2006 was created in Arizona."[23]

Then it fell apart. At the end of 2007 the Arizona economy went south. Less than three years after Napolitano's optimistic inaugural address, Arizona was no longer the fastest-growing state. Dependent on continuing population growth and an expanding home-building industry, the "Great Recession hit Arizona hard," wrote Marshal J. Vest, forecasting director for the University of Arizona.

> From the third quarter of 2007 through year-end 2009, Arizona lost one in every nine jobs. Unemployment topped 9 percent, up from 3.5 percent only two years earlier. Population recorded the smallest numerical increase in 20 years (and the smallest percentage increase

in at least 50 years). During 2009, personal income in current dollars declined—for the first time ever. State tax receipts, which are based on sales taxes and income taxes, fell by nearly one-third. In recent rankings among states, Arizona has fallen near the bottom or even last on measure after measure.[24]

Now Arizona became famous as the state that sold its capitol building in a desperate bid for cash.

Bad news was unrelenting. The state next became the focus of national attention when it decided to stop paying the cost of transplant operations for poor people, effectively condemning to death very sick and very poor men and women. As of October 1, 2010, the state Medicaid program ended coverage of lung transplants, heart transplants for nonischemic cardiomyopathy, pancreatic transplants, some bone marrow transplants, and liver transplants for patients infected with hepatitis C.

During the first three months of reduced coverage, from October 1 to December 31, 2010, two patients died: one whose name was withheld needed a new liver; the other, Mark Price, a thirty-seven-year-old with leukemia, needed a bone marrow transplant.[25]

Few states were as vulnerable to the destructive financial forces that swept the nation as Arizona, which had bet the future on the housing boom. By November 2010 the state's home foreclosure rate was the second highest in the nation, with 1 out of every 210 households foreclosed on, worse than Florida and Michigan and exceeded only by Nevada.[26] From April 2007 to July 2010 the state unemployment rate tripled, from 3.5 to 10 percent.[27]

As the state's finances nose-dived, Arizona, which had been a case study in the expansive politics of growth, became a poster child for the politics of austerity. By FY 2010 what had been a $1.1 billion surplus in 2006 had turned into a $1.7 billion deficit. Desperate for cash, the state sold off twenty buildings, including not only the capitol but also the legislative chambers, and leased them back. More drastically, the Republican governor and Republican state legislature began cutting programs for the poor, most infamously the removal of 310,000 adults from Medicaid and the termination of Kids Care, a health care program for 47,000 low-income children.[28]

On January 15, 2010, newly elected governor Janice K. Brewer officially declared that the halcyon days of only a few years earlier, "a period of unprecedented growth and prosperity . . . those days of expanded government services are over."[29]

In this environment of shortage and want, in the winter and spring of 2010, the issue of illegal immigration rose to the top of the governor's priorities. In fact the flow of illegal immigrants entering the state had slowed considerably. Border apprehensions fell by 57 percent, from 499,851 in 2004 to 217,318 in 2010.[30] More important, the incidence of crime had begun to drop sharply. In the first part of the decade the number of violent crimes was generally in the 29,000 range, reaching a high of 30,833 in 2006. After that, violent crime steadily declined, falling to 26,094 in 2009, the lowest level in ten years.[31]

By these two measures, declining numbers of violent crime and falling crime rates overall, concern over illegal immigration should have diminished in 2010. In practice just the opposite occurred. The immigration issue of 2010 was the Arizona bill known as SB1070, a proposal sponsored by the state senate president, Russell Pearce, Republican of Mesa. The measure empowers Arizona law enforcement officers to determine the immigration and citizenship status of any person whenever a "reasonable suspicion exists that the person is an alien who is unlawfully present in the United States."[32]

Local police, in other words, are instructed to enforce federal immigration law, and once an officer determines that someone is in the country illegally, that person is arrested and turned over to federal authorities.

When Jan Brewer faced the question of whether to veto the legislation, her political future was on the line. If she had vetoed the legislation, she would have lost the 2010 Republican primary. Instead, she signed the measure and became a hero to the right.

The measure provoked a national furor; it had widespread popular support in Arizona and across the country but was bitterly opposed by Hispanic advocacy groups and by the Obama administration. The White House immediately initiated court action to block its implementation.

## Revolt of the Middle-Class Voter

What had changed in Arizona to give anti-immigration forces so much momentum? The simple answer: economic collapse. Here is a state where in 2000 voters had decisively approved the major expansion of Medicaid by

a landslide margin.[33] The Arizona electorate in 2000 was decisively majority white, but a majority of the beneficiaries of this expansive policy were
minorities. Of the 1.58 million Arizonans living beneath the poverty line,
775,100 (49 percent) were Hispanic; 81,000, or just over 5 percent, were
black; 212,200, or just over 13 percent, were classified as "other"; and the rest,
512,500, or just over 32 percent, were white.[34]

In early 2010, with the state in severe recession, the political mood had
shifted 180 degrees. Not only did Governor Brewer, with strong support from
the legislature, cut money for health care and sign the immigration law, but
she fought for and won federal approval to gut the 2000 liberalization of
Medicaid and to cut from the Medicaid rolls 250,000 childless adults living
at or below the poverty level.[35]

The political/economic climate of Arizona is reflected in Figures 4.3,[36]
4.4,[37] and 4.5.[38]

Prosperity and growth, as Arizona demonstrated in the early and mid-
2000s, encourage a spirit of generosity. Austerity, budget cuts, and the threat
of tax hikes do just the opposite: middle-class voters want to preserve and
protect what they have; needy constituencies, like the majority-minority
poor and the thousands of illegal immigrants in Arizona, become, under
the pressure of exacerbated resource competition, a drain, a burden, a cost.

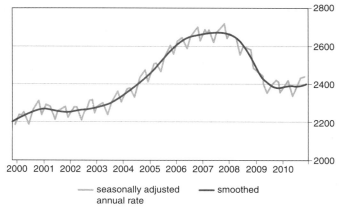

**Total Non-farm Employment — Arizona**

———— seasonally adjusted    ———— smoothed
annual rate

Source: Economic and Business Research, University of Arizona;
U.S. Bureau of Labor Statistics, Current Employment Statistics

*Figure 4.3*

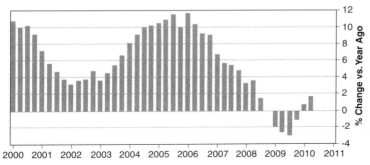

*Source: U.S. Bureau of Economic Analysis, Regional Economic Accounts*

*Figure 4.4*

There has been widespread criticism of the Republican anti-immigration initiatives in Arizona, voiced on editorial pages, by advocacy groups, and by leaders of the Democratic Party. Looked at from a purely political point of view, however, not only has the GOP stance helped mobilize voters in the party's behalf, but the deep hostility to immigrants has worked in Arizona to help extend the life of the white majority.

In 2010, the census found that there were at least 600,000 more Hispan-

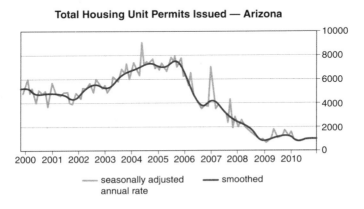

*Source: Economic and Business Research, University of Arizona; U.S. Bureau of Labor Statistics, Current Employment Statistics*

*Figure 4.5*

ics in the country than had been anticipated in earlier studies. Most states with large Hispanic populations were at, or over, predicted levels: New Jersey at 1.56 million, 4.6 percent over predictions; California at 14.01 million, 0.7 over; Illinois at 2.03 million, 1.1 over; Nevada right at the predicted number, 717,000; North Carolina over by 7.2 percent at 800,000; Pennsylvania over by 7.5 percent at 720,000; Texas over by 0.9 percent at 9.46 million; and Virginia over by 6.7 percent at 632,000.

Arizona, the cauldron of hard-core anti-immigration politics, stood out as the major exception: at the time of the 2010 census, there were 1.9 million Latinos there, 8.6 percent *fewer* than had been predicted.[39] Tom Rex, associate director of the Center for Competitiveness and Prosperity Research at Arizona State University, said, "The only conclusion I could reach was that the immigration laws seemed to have driven more people out because it couldn't just be the economy."[40] In other words, the Republican strategy of hostility to immigrants demonstrably worked to drive them away.

In early 2011 an unexpected development occurred in the Arizona legislature: the state senate actually rejected a collection of anti-immigrant bills, confirming the importance of scarcity in driving the immigration issue.

On February 21, 2011, Arizona State Senate President Pearce had upped the ante, introducing SB1611, which required recipients of all public benefits to show proof of legality and sign a sworn statement subject to perjury; granted citizens the right to sue state agencies they believed were providing benefits to illegals; denied bail to anyone accused of a felony who was suspected of being in the country illegally; required all students enrolling in public and private schools to show proof of legal status; and subjected any illegal immigrant driving in Arizona to thirty days in jail and confiscation of the vehicle.[41] The pending legislation immediately provoked angry demonstrations in front of the state capitol building as immigrant rights advocates and backers of the anti-immigrant legislation hurled epithets at each other while hearings on the measure were taking place inside.

On March 18, 2011, less than a month after SB1611 was introduced, the state senate voted to kill the bill along with four others, including one that would have required hospitals to confirm the legal status of all patients and to report those suspected of being in the country illegally.[42]

A major factor in the legislative vote was the emergence of strong opposition to this new, controversial immigration legislation from Arizona's business community, which had been stung by a sharp decline in the state's tourism industry. "When Arizona goes it alone on this issue, unintended consequences inevitably occur," sixty in-state CEOs wrote legislators. "Last year, boycotts were called against our state's business community, adversely impacting our already-struggling economy and costing us jobs. Arizona-based businesses saw contracts cancelled or were turned away from bidding. Sales outside of the state declined."[43]

Equally important, the Arizona economy had begun a modest but steady recovery, easing the hostility provoked by declining jobs, tax dollars, homeownership, and virtually all the material goods sought by all Americans.

State employment, which fell from 2.68 million in June 2007 to 2.36 million in September 2010, a loss of 320,000 jobs, had begun to very slowly edge back up, reaching 2.38 million in January 2011.[44] From June 2010 to December 2010 retail sales grew rapidly from $5.4 billion to $7.5 billion.[45] Total personal income, which reached $226 billion in the second quarter of 2008, fell to $218 billion in the third quarter of 2009 but, by the third quarter of 2010, had risen to $225.4 billion, almost back to the 2008 high.[46]

Just as when the economy collapsed, anti-immigration sentiments soared, when the economy eased, so too did the drive to get tough.

## The White Voter Strategy—a Strategy for Success or Oblivion

Immigration policy has become a highly partisan issue. A solid 56–27 majority of Democrats supported the Justice Department suit against the draconian April 2010 Arizona anti-immigrant law while Republicans overwhelmingly opposed it, 79–11, according to Gallup.[47] In the December 8, 2010, House vote on the pro-immigrant DREAM Act, Democrats voted 208–38 in favor, while Republicans were opposed by a 160–8 margin. In the Senate, Democrats supported the legislation by 52–5, while Republicans were in opposition by a 36–3 margin. (Because of filibuster rules, 60 votes were required, so the bill did not pass.)

In political terms, the Republican anti-immigrant stance represents a major gamble that the GOP can continue to win as a white party despite the growing strength of the minority vote.

In substantive terms, the Republican position has major consequences for the country. It is a repudiation of the view that immigration is crucial:

(1) for the economic health of the nation, supplying at the high end the technical expertise crucial to innovation and at the low end workers willing to perform essential jobs rejected by U.S. citizens, and (2) at another level, supplying young workers who pay Social Security and Medicare payroll taxes that help address the dependency ratio, filling the growing gap as the white population gets older.[48]

For whites with a conservative bent, the shift to a majority-minority nation will strengthen the already widely held view that programs benefiting the poor are transferring their taxpayer dollars to minority recipients, from whites first to blacks and now to "browns." The antipathy to transfer programs will be reinforced by the already strong view among conservative white voters that immigration and Hispanic expansion are radically changing what it means to "be an American." This perspective gave strength and resonance to the Tea Party declaration "Take Back Our Country" during the election of 2010.[49]

The political calculation is straightforward. Driven largely by the growth of the Hispanic electorate, minorities have gained sufficient strength that it is increasingly dangerous to disregard them. These next two charts, Figure 4.6 from the U.S. Census,[50] the other, Figure 4.7,[51] put together by Emory political scientist Alan Abramowitz, clearly demonstrate the trends:

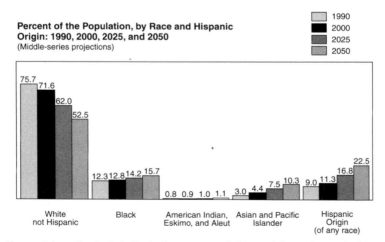

*Figure 4.6 shows the steady decline in the percentage of whites and the steady growth of the minority population.*

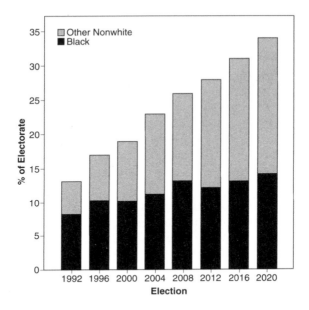

*Source: Exit poll data for 1992–2008; author's projections for 2012–2020*

*Figure 4.7 shows the steady growth of the minority share of the electorate.*

African Americans generally cast nine out of ten votes for Democratic presidential candidates, and Hispanics a little more than six out of ten; thus these trends all suggest that the forty-plus-year Republican strategy of depending disproportionately on white votes will at some point run out of gas.

The election of 2010 demonstrated, however, that that moment may not have arrived yet.

Just as the minority vote is crucial for the Democrats, so the white vote is key to the Republican future. In presidential elections from 1972 to 1988 Republicans carried white voters by landslide margins averaging 21.8 percentage points. In 1994, when the GOP took over the House for the first time in forty years, Republican candidates won the white vote by a solid 16 percentage points, 58–42. In the presidential elections of 2000, 2004, and 2008, however, as the Democrats were becoming more competitive, Republican margins among whites dropped to an average of 12.3 percentage points.[52]

The 2010 House contests, however, showed that it was possible for the Republican Party to once again achieve the huge white margins of the seventies and eighties. The GOP took over the House with a record-setting twenty-four-point white margin, 62–38, dwarfing the eight-point, 54–46 white margin in 2008 House races, and six times the size of the four-point, 52–48 white margin in 2006.

In fact the Republican House vote margin among whites in 2010 was higher than in any House election since 1968, when exit polling began, even counting the previous landslide year, 1994, when GOP candidates carried the white vote by sixteen points, 58–42.

### Anti-Immigration Politics—an International Trend

America is not alone is seeing the growing strength of the anti-immigrant right and a decline in the strength of the left. In the aftermath of the global financial meltdown of 2008, a parallel shift was emerging across Europe. In September 2010 the Sweden Democrats (Sverigedemokraterna, SD), whose platform calls for a 90 percent reduction in legal immigration, for the first time broke the 4 percent threshold in national elections to qualify for twenty seats in Parliament (Riksdag) with 5.7 percent of the total. At the same time, the once-dominant Social Democrats have been relegated, for the second election in a row, to minority party status, winning just 30.9 percent of the vote.[53]

Sweden in turn has plenty of company.[54] In the 2009 Bulgarian election, the anti-Roma (Gypsy) nationalist political party, Ataka, won 9.4 percent of the vote to become the fourth-largest political party in the country. In Hungary's April 2010 elections, the Jobbik Party, which calls for placing Roma in "public order protection" camps, won forty-seven seats, the first time it has gained entry to parliament.

In both France and Britain, mainstream conservative party leaders are preempting hard-right challenges. In Britain newly elected Tory prime minister David Cameron is committed to setting a permanent cap on migrants from outside the European Union. French president Nicolas Sarkozy, backed by the UMP (Union pour un Mouvement Populaire), has called for the repatriation of Roma and the cancellation of citizenship for foreign-born convicted criminals.

In June 2010 voters in the Netherlands turned the once-fringe Party for Freedom, PVV (Partij voor de Vrijheid) into the third strongest in the nation, and polls later in the year showed that it had enough support to become the strongest of all parties.

The success of the nationalist and anti-immigrant True Finn Party—support shot up from just 4.1 percent in 2007 to 19.1 percent on April 17, 2011—threatens Finland's continued support for European Union bailouts of Greece, Portugal, and Ireland. In Switzerland, famed as a neutral country that has integrated four national language/cultural communities (French, Italian, German, and Romansh), the right-populist Schweizerische Volkspartei (SVP) won more votes than any other party. Its starkly racist posters can be found everywhere (see Figures 4.8, 4.9, and 4.10).

*Figure 4.8. "STOP! Yes to the Minaret Ban."* (Supporting a referendum to prohibit construction of any new minarets atop Swiss mosques)

*Figure 4.9. "Create Security."* (By deporting "black sheep" foreigners)

*Figure 4.10. "Stop Mass Naturalization. Yes to the Naturalization Initiative."* (Make Swiss citizenship much more difficult for foreign residents to obtain)

In an attempt to preempt extremist parties from capitalizing on fears about immigrants, especially Muslims, Britain's Cameron, Germany's Angela Merkel, and other center-right leaders have renounced multiculturalism and called for policies effectively requiring newcomers to accept the customs, laws, and democratic principles of their adopted countries.

"Under the doctrine of state multiculturalism, we have encouraged different cultures to live separate lives, apart from each other and apart from the mainstream," Cameron told a Conservative Party gathering on February 5, 2011.

> So, when a white person holds objectionable views, racist views for instance, we rightly condemn them. But when equally unacceptable views or practices come from someone who isn't white, we've been too cautious frankly—frankly, even fearful—to stand up to them. The failure, for instance, of some to confront the horrors of forced marriage, the practice where some young girls are bullied and sometimes taken abroad to marry someone when they don't want to, is a case in point. This hands-off tolerance has only served to reinforce the sense that not enough is shared. And this all leaves some young Muslims feeling rootless. And the search for something to belong to

and something to believe in can lead them to this extremist ideology. Now for sure, they don't turn into terrorists overnight, but what we see—and what we see in so many European countries—is a process of radicalization.[55]

The scope and intensity of anti-immigration views here and abroad were apparent in an August 2010 poll conducted by the *Financial Times* of the United States, Britain, Germany, France, Spain, and Italy. The survey, which asked about immigration generally, not illegal immigration, found that "[m]ajorities in four of the countries and pluralities in the other two believe that immigration makes it harder to find new jobs. Majorities in three countries and over 40 percent in the other three believe it has a bad effect on education. Majorities in four of the countries and 40 percent or more in the other two think it has a bad effect on health care services."

Perhaps most strikingly, when asked whether immigration makes their country better, worse, or makes no difference, majorities or pluralities in every country said worse: 64 percent in Britain, 60 percent in Spain, 57 percent in Italy, 49 percent in the United States, 44 percent in Germany, and 43 percent in France. High percentages of American (57), British (57), Spanish (67), and Italian (60) respondents said immigration makes it harder to find jobs. Similarly, 63 percent of American, 66 percent of British, 60 percent of French, and 54 percent of Spanish respondents said immigration is making the provision of health services worse.[56]

The opposition to immigration in Norway, a wealthy nation with low levels of inequality and a strong tradition of tolerance, was brought home on July 22, 2011, when Norwegian right-wing extremist Anders Behring Breivik slaughtered ninety-three people in Oslo and on the nearby island of Utoya, many of them teenage summer campers, in what Breivik claimed was a protest against the Labor Party's support of immigration. A survey released July 7, two weeks before the violence, showed that a majority of Norwegians, 53.7 percent of 1,380 people surveyed, supported a halt to immigration.[57]

## The Coming Minority America

On August 14, 2008, as the United States' financial system was on course for a crash, the U.S. Census Bureau announced that non-Hispanic whites would become a minority in the United States in 2042, eight years earlier than had been predicted. By 2050, whites would make up only 46 percent of the population.

The figures were striking. According to the U.S. Census Bureau, from 2008 to 2050, minorities would grow from 34 to 54 percent, reaching a total of 235.7 million. The non-Hispanic, single-race white population will, in effect, stagnate, with a much lower birthrate and a much higher percentage dying of old age. Overall, the non-Hispanic white population is predicted to increase by less than 5 million, from 199.8 million to 203.3 million in 2050. The number of Hispanics will nearly triple, from 46.7 million to 132.8 million; while the number of African Americans will grow from 41.1 million to 65.7 million, from 14 to 15 percent; the number of Asian Americans will grow from 15.5 million to 40.6 million, from 5.1 to 9.2 percent.[58]

For a political party that has chosen a strategy banking on mobilizing white voters—the attempt to boost turnout and margins among Anglo voters to levels that could sustain an election day majority for the next decade or so—the issue of immigration has become an ideal tool to appeal directly to the white electorate at a time of political conflict over scare resources.

The Republican Party has formally adopted opposition to any path toward legalized status or citizenship for undocumented immigrants as part of its platform. The formal agenda adopted at the 2008 GOP convention declares:

> Border security is essential to national security. In an age of terrorism, drug cartels, and criminal gangs, allowing millions of unidentified persons to enter and remain in this country poses grave risks to the sovereignty of the United States and the security of its people. . . . The rule of law means guaranteeing to law enforcement the tools and coordination to deport criminal aliens without delay—and correcting court decisions that have made deportation so difficult. It means . . . the denial of federal funds for self-described sanctuary cities, which stand in open defiance of the federal and state statutes that expressly prohibit such sanctuary policies, and which endanger the lives of U.S. citizens. . . . We oppose amnesty. The rule of law suffers if government policies encourage or reward illegal activity. . . . In our multiethnic nation, everyone—immigrants and native born alike—must embrace our core values of liberty, equality, meritocracy, and respect for human dignity and the rights

of women. The American people's rejection of en masse legaliza-
tions is especially appropriate given the federal government's past
failures to enforce the law. . . . We support English as the official
language in our nation.[59]

The GOP platform is a declaration that the party will not give an inch in
its commitment to deport eleven million illegal immigrants. While viewed by
the Republican Party as criminals, undocumented migrants are, to millions
of voting Hispanics, neighbors, relatives, friends, fellow workers, parishio-
ners, and, in a surprising number of cases, pastors. The Republican Party's
"white" strategy amounts, in this case, to an overt rejection of Hispanics.

### Manpower and Brainpower

The ascendance of anti-immigrant views in American politics has crowded
out the argument that immigrants, including a majority of those currently
in the country illegally, are essential for sustained national growth, providing the manpower necessary for both the manufacturing and service sectors and the brainpower crucial to the high-tech community. This is not
to say there are no costs. There are Americans who lose jobs; programmers
and other information technology specialists have, in some cases, seen their
wages undercut; and there is rising gang crime.

In the case of the debate over H-1B visas for skilled workers—needed
particularly by high-tech firms—the opposition to immigration has been
dominated by Democrats, in contrast to the overwhelmingly Republican
opposition to immigration reform providing a path to citizenship for the
millions of illegal immigrants currently in the country.

Democrats support low- and semiskilled immigrants in part for humanitarian reasons and in part because unions are seeking to organize Hispanic service, construction, and health care workers. More highly skilled
H-1B visa holders are not targets of union organizing. Many businesses,
however, are seeking to expand the ranks of highly skilled, but less expensive, information technology workers to fill key posts, and Republicans have
generally been supportive of these efforts.

Although over the top in many respects, magazine publisher and former

Republican presidential candidate Steve Forbes makes a strong and credible case that immigration is essential to the future success of the nation: "Removing caps on the H-1B program that permits crucial scientists and engineers to come here for six years is imperative. The quota is now set at a ridiculously low 65,000. Let market forces dictate the number. At a time of rising pressure from India, China, and central and Eastern Europe, we can use all the bright, ambitious talent we can attract."[60]

Some of the strongest pro-immigration arguments have been made in behalf of the H-1B visa program for foreign nationals with scientific expertise. One prominent specialist in the field, Vivek Wadhwa, senior research associate at Harvard Law School and director of research at the Center for Entrepreneurship and Research Commercialization at Duke University, has studied patent applications at the World Intellectual Property Organization and has found that "in 2006, 24.2 percent of U.S.-originated international patent applications were authored or co-authored by foreign nationals residing in the U.S. These immigrant non-citizens, as we called them, are typically foreign graduate students completing their PhDs, green card holders awaiting citizenship, and employees of multinationals on temporary visas. *This percentage had increased from 7.8 percent in 1988*—and this count *doesn't include immigrants who had become citizens* [italics added]."[61]

In fact 48 percent of Ph.D.'s in science and engineering awarded by American universities in 2006 went to students who had been born outside the United States.[62] More than half, 52 percent, of the Silicon Valley firms founded in the decade 1995–2005 were started by immigrants, according to Wadhwa. With the adoption of new bureaucratic rules governing H-1B visas, however, Wadhwa writes:

> There are now hundreds of thousands of highly educated and skilled workers who also could be starting companies that are stuck in "immigration limbo." . . . Immigrant professionals have helped open foreign markets; identified overseas sources of talent and innovation; and pioneered long-distance partnerships. Far from being zero-sum, this process continues to expand economic opportunities for both Silicon Valley and its collaborators.[63]

In a globalized economy, placing tight restrictions on highly skilled immigrants is self-defeating, depriving the United States of talent it has frequently recruited and trained. Forcing an exodus of expertise to other countries penalizes the United States in terms of innovation, productivity, and expanded employment and forces the nation to increase imports and to borrow to finance such imports.

## Fear: The Driver of American Politics

One of the central problems created by the politics of austerity is that reasoned debates over not only immigration but a host of other issues—from the deficit to entitlement spending to U.S. foreign policy—are trumped by fear. The national turn against immigration is part of a larger pattern of a potentially self-destructive politics. Such politics, and the anxiety that fuels them, will be explored in subsequent chapters.

# Chapter Five

# Race

## Race and the Wake County Public School Wars

On Tuesday, March 2, 2010, a meeting of the Wake County School Board in Raleigh, North Carolina, became ground zero in the ongoing battle between the Tea Party and the NAACP.

In this fast-growing county, both sides said they wanted the same thing: quality public education. But the path each chose to achieve that goal put them on course for a head-on collision.

A strong majority of whites who voted in the November 3, 2009, school board election wanted to end a program that was using socioeconomic status as a factor in assigning students to schools, a program that had mixed middle-class (i.e., white) students with poor (i.e., black and Hispanic) students. Insofar as low-income status is widely regarded as a proxy for racial and ethnic minorities, African American parents and civil rights leaders were outraged at the prospect of a return to schools subject to de facto segregation.

The issue provoking battle was the nationally recognized and widely respected Wake County busing plan adopted in 2000. The plan had set a goal of limiting to 40 percent the proportion of students at any one school who were beneficiaries of the free or reduced-price school lunch program. Blacks sought to preserve the plan, which gave them access to better-quality schools; whites sought to end it.

The Wake County confrontation had been brewing for years, but it initially broke out into the open in 2008, just as the country began to struggle with the severe recession, lost tax revenues, foreclosures, plummeting home values, unemployment, and mounting pessimism.

Garner, North Carolina, a rapidly growing, majority-white suburb just south of Raleigh, was at the forefront of the antibusing drive in Wake County. In 2008, Garner aldermen refused to authorize construction of two new county schools, absent a guarantee from the school board that very few poor children would be bused in. "We as a community don't want more Southeast Raleigh students coming to Garner, with all due respect to them," Mayor Ronnie Williams told the *Raleigh News & Observer*.[1] Southeast Raleigh is heavily poor, black, and Hispanic.

That year the Wake County school system—encompassing the city of Raleigh, where most African Americans and Hispanics live, and eleven rapidly growing, predominantly white suburban communities—was fast approaching a tipping point: the once solidly white majority of students in the public school system was on the verge of becoming a minority. From 1987 to 2010 the number of Latino students shot up from 295 to 20,909, a 7,100 percent increase.[2] And on November 24, 2010, the *Raleigh News & Observer*[3] announced that the percentage of white students in Wake County schools had fallen to 49.5 percent. These data are illustrated in Figure 5.1.[4]

At the same time, however, the county's voters—the population over eighteen—remained decisively white. Non-Hispanic whites were the majority of the county population—64.2 percent[5]—and, more important, of its registered voters—71.9 percent.[6]

The solidly white voting majority in turn controlled the election of the school board and the Wake County Board of Commissioners, two boards empowered to set policy for the now majority-minority school system.

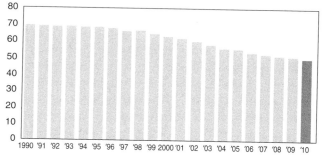

**Percentage of White Students Attending Wake County's Public Schools**

*Source: Wake County Public School System*

*Figure 5.1*

This racial split—a majority-white county with a majority African American, Hispanic, and Asian public school student body—emerged just as the county budget was running into the red. Despite three rate increases, property taxes showed zero growth in FY 2010. Real estate sales, which had grown from $5.2 billion in 1990 to $11.4 billion in 2008, fell to $10.4 billion in 2009. Foreclosure filings grew from 3,478 in 2005 to 5,179 in 2009. The unemployment rate grew from 5.0 percent in July 2008 to 9.1 percent in July 2009.[7]

In other words, Wake County was facing both diminishing resources—a loss of jobs, home equity, and tax revenues—and a racially explosive struggle over a key public good, access to quality public education.

In the October 6, 2009, school board election, with four of the nine seats at stake, the antibusing Republican–Tea Party slate swept all four seats, giving the conservatives, who already had one incumbent, a five to four majority.

School board meetings promptly became embattled. Angry blacks and their liberal white allies accused the new Republican majority of racism. At a March 2, 2010, school board hearing on busing, many in the audience shouted their disapproval of the new conservative majority. The Republican chair of the board, Ron Margiotta, unaware that his voice was being recorded, turned to a colleague and said, "Here come the animals out of their cages."[8]

Not to be outdone, NAACP attorney Al McSurely countered: "[Margiotta] doesn't even have a college degree. . . . They've got clowns running this school board." The Reverend William Barber, North Carolina NAACP chairman, poured more gasoline on the fire, declaring, "This is not a Mafia meeting." The two leaders of the antibusing school board majority were Italian American, Margiotta and John Tedesco.[9]

Just nine months later, on November 3, 2010, the antibusing alliance of the Republican Party and the Tea Party swept all four contests for seats on the County Board of Commissioners to win a four to three majority. The board approves the school budget. With the two boards under their control, conservatives were fully empowered to set school busing policy.

On December 6, 2010, the new County Board met for the first time. At the contentious six-hour-and-forty-five-minute meeting, the commissioners voted, four to three, to join the school board in renouncing busing.[10] The previous Democratic-majority board had passed, on April 19, 2010, a resolution endorsing the county's busing program, formally declaring the board's "deep concern over any attempt to re-segregate Wake's public schools by either race or socioeconomic status." The disputed resolution read, in part:

### Resolution Regarding Re-Segregation of Wake's Public Schools

Whereas, it has been widely established that schools with concentrated populations of low income students have low academic achievement levels; and

Whereas, high poverty schools have lower levels of qualified, experienced teachers; and

Whereas, it is difficult and costly to improve the performance of such schools; and

Whereas, middle class parents will locate or move to other areas to avoid such schools; and . . .

Whereas, middle class flight will adversely impact economic development, job creation and property values in the City of Raleigh and Eastern Wake County; and

Whereas, the City of Raleigh and Wake County merged their public school systems over thirty years ago to avoid the problems noted above; and

Whereas, this merger has aided in the growth and economic vibrancy of both areas.

Be it resolved that the City Council of Raleigh and the Wake County Board of Commissioners hereby express their deep concern over any attempt to re-segregate Wake's public schools by either race or socioeconomic status.[11]

The new board voted, four to three, to rescind the resolution, effectively clearing the way for the county school board to kill the busing plan. It did so despite the threat of lost accreditation and despite the objections of former president Bill Clinton, who went out of his way to praise the busing program—"Based on decades of evidence that with really poor people who come from families under stress or from broken homes, if they spend time in stable environments with lots of supportive adults, turns out they're just as smart as everybody else and they do just as well as everybody else"[12]—and Secretary of Education Arne Duncan, who wrote in the *Washington Post*, "In an increasingly diverse society like ours, racial isolation is not a positive outcome for children of any color or background. . . . This is no time to go backward."[13]

The power shift in Wake County was part of the conservative wave that swept the nation in 2009 and 2010, following the sharp economic downturn that began in late 2007. Even though the income-based busing policy of Wake County had received widespread praise, locally and nationally, the inflammatory combination of race and an economy in acute decline produced a voter revolt in the area's white suburbs. The powerful national movement to the right was fueled by local struggles over schools; deficit-plagued state, city, and county budgets; and the forced adoption of austerity measures.

Leaders of the antibusing forces in Wake County contended that the practice weakened the performance of all students, white, black, and Hispanic. Income-based busing "sounds like a noble idea," said newly elected board member John Tedesco. "But it was terrible for kids and for the community. We took our eye off the prize—academic achievement for all kids—and put it on trying to meet quotas in a balancing act."[14]

In the last five years Wake County test scores and graduation rates dropped every year, and the racial achievement gap widened, said Tedesco. Low-income students, he argued, suffered most. "We were classifying kids by group, and labeling low-income kids 'at risk' just because of the money in their parents' pockets," he said. "We've actually dumbed these kids down." Wake County's test scores and SAT scores are still better than those of most other North Carolina districts, according to Tedesco, but, he argued, as home to the renowned Research Triangle, the county has one of the most highly educated workforces in America. "The academic success we do have is attributable to our demographics, not our busing program," said Tedesco.[15]

In controversial and sharply disputed claims, Tedesco contended that busing has provoked cultural division, not unity. While the county's overall poverty rate is about 10 percent, 30 percent of the students in the public schools are from families whose incomes fall below the federal poverty line, because the affluent are fleeing to private schools, says Tedesco. The national average for opting out of public schools is about 8.5 percent, he said. "Our rate has doubled in 10 years to almost 18 percent. Guess who's left behind?"[16]

From the vantage point of many white suburban voters, not only were white students the new minority, but their disproportionately affluent, homeowning, property tax–paying parents were carrying the bulk of the costs of transporting students from neighborhood schools to facilities an hour or more away. In addition, the financially strapped school system was exploring new ways to tap parents' wallets through fees for sports, parking, and, adding insult to injury, busing to schools.

Some of Tedesco's claims have been flatly disputed by supporters of Wake County's economic diversity program. Neil Riemann, who runs a Web site called WakeReassignment.com, argues that Tedesco is claiming a 30 percent poverty rate on the basis of the percentage of students in the free lunch program, 31.2 percent in 2009–2010. But this is not an accurate measure of the percentage of students from poverty-level families, says Riemann: free lunches are available to students from families at up to 185 percent of poverty level. In addition, Riemann cites state data showing that the number of Wake County students going to private school or getting home schooled increased by just over one percentage point from 13.29 percent in 2000–2001 to 14.45 percent in 2009–2010.[17]

More important, African American and Latino parents saw that with the end of busing, students who struggle the most would be packed together without good teachers, in the most run-down neighborhoods. The white-driven pressure to abandon the integration plan reflects in turn the purposeful isolation of minorities from the mainstream of American society.

Underlying busing is an explosive issue for many parents who resist economic integration; such integration plans put black and Hispanic students into the same schools with white students who average higher scores on standardized tests. In 2010, Advocates for Children's Services (ACS), a special statewide project of Legal Aid of North Carolina, published a report—"The Racial Achievement Gap in the Wake County Public School System"—by two Legal Aid attorneys, Jason Langberg and Cary Brege. The report argues that in Wake County "African American students' rates of proficiency range from 23 percent to 45 percent lower than Caucasian students. Latino students' rates of proficiency on state standardized tests range from 9 percent to 45 percent lower than Caucasian students. When considering [*sic*] the reading and math portions of the SAT, African American students score 211 points lower than Caucasian students. Latino students score 99 points lower than Caucasian students."[18]

In addition, the Legal Aid study contends that in the 2007–2008 school year, the student body was 26.5 percent African American, but "African American students received 64.0 percent of the total short-term suspensions and 72.3 percent of the total long-term suspensions."[19]

The Wake County Legal Aid report goes on to say:

> Large percentages of African American and Latino students in the WCPSS [Wake County Public School System] are not receiving their fundamental constitutional right to the equal opportunity to receive a sound basic education, as demonstrated by various measures of achievement. . . . Shockingly, during the 2008–2009 school year, fewer than half of all WCPSS African American and Latino students in grades three through eight could read and do math at a proficient level. During that same year, only 59 percent of African American high school students and 66 percent of Latino high school students were proficient on all of their standardized end-of-course tests.[20]

In a complaint to the federal Department of Education charging violations of the Civil Rights Act of 1964, the NAACP argued, along similar lines, that in Wake County schools in 2008–2009 "only 45.2 percent of African American students in grades three through eight were proficient in reading and math on their end-of-grade exams, compared to 86.4 percent of Caucasian students (a 41.2 percentage point gap). Only 58.5 percent of high school African American students were proficient on all of their end-of-course exams, compared to 91.0 percent of Caucasian students (a 32.5 percentage point gap). During that same year, 47.9 percent of high school dropouts in the WCPSS were African American, whereas only 27.8 percent were Caucasian (a 20.1 percentage point gap). Finally, in the 2008–2009 school year, the four-year cohort graduation for African American students in the WCPSS was 63.4 percent, while the rate for Caucasian students was 89.4 percent (a 26.0 percentage point gap)."[21]

Strikingly, the same facts are used by both sides in the ongoing battle over integration in Wake County, a battle that is replicated across the country. The very different interpretation of findings about Wake County school performance on the part of pro- and antibusing forces are reflected in the virulent comments posted on the *Raleigh News & Observer* Web site following stories about busing and the racial makeup of the Wake County school system. From someone identifying himself as "mike27513": "The Plan of Forced Busing and Massive Immigration of Illegals have destroyed the school system. . . . Enjoy the Second rate system you have created, just like Detroit, Washington DC, Newark and other 'Fine' school systems."[22]

From "nancync": "White flight began long ago in the direction of home schooling as well as private and charter schools. . . . People are tired of their kids falling through the cracks of the public education system."[23]

From "gingerlynn": "Come to a PTSA or parent meeting night at school and look at the demographics of the parents that are there. We had a fund raising event at a 'majority minority' school a few weeks ago. There was one Indian parent there, one Asian, and the rest white. When the parent support vacates the schools, they will become Los Angeles."[24]

### Irreconcilable Differences?

The Wake County busing fight is a microcosmic reflection of a deep and in many respects irreconcilable conflict between such traditional civil rights groups as the NAACP and the Tea Party, a conflict heightened as austerity measures are increasingly imposed.

Nationwide the view of many Tea Party members on the issue of racial discrimination was clear in a poll published in November 2010 by the non-partisan Public Religion Research Institute in Washington, D.C. The survey, conducted from November 3 to November 7, 2010, found that solid majorities of Tea Party supporters (61 percent) and Republicans (56 percent) agreed with the statement that "today, discrimination against whites is as big a problem as discrimination against Blacks and other minorities." In the overall sample, 44 percent agreed and 54 percent disagreed.[25]

On July 13, 2010, delegates to the NAACP convention in Kansas City unanimously approved a resolution condemning "extremist elements" within the Tea Party movement and called on leaders of the conservative movement to repudiate members who used racist language in their signs and speeches.

Benjamin Todd Jealous, NAACP president, denounced "the Tea Party's continued tolerance for bigotry and bigoted statements. The time has come for them to accept the responsibility that comes with influence and make clear there is no place for racism and anti-Semitism, homophobia and other forms of bigotry in their movement."[26]

The NAACP released to the press some striking photos of Tea Party demonstrators (see Figures 5.2 and 5.3).

The Tea Party immediately fired back, with the St. Louis Tea Party Coalition declaring:

> Whereas, it is a hallmark of America that we settle our disputes civilly and avoid the gutter tactic of attempting to silence opponents by inflammatory name-calling, and
>
> Whereas the very term "racist" has diminished meaning due to its overuse by political partisans including members of the NAACP, and . . .
>
> Whereas, the NAACP does its entire membership a grave disservice by hypocritically engaging in the very conduct it purports to oppose,
>
> Now therefore be it resolved that the St. Louis Tea Party condemns the NAACP for lowering itself to the dishonorable position of a partisan political attack dog organization.[27]

On the one hand, the Tea Party gives voice to a broadly based worldview, a commitment to a highly restricted role for government, and a strong

*Figure 5.2*

*Figure 5.3*

emphasis on the economic and property rights of the individual. These positions can simultaneously signal support for antiblack policies in the form of "coded rhetoric"—just as advocacy of constitutionally granted "states' rights" served as a proxy for Jim Crow, and arguably still does—most notably as used by the Tea Party and by Texas governor Rick Perry.[28] Both "We support states' rights for those powers not expressly stated in the Constitution" and "[We] oppose government intervention into the operations of private business" are statements affirming limited government, on principle, and they are also statements rejecting the role of the federal government in enforcing civil rights.[29]

Phrases from the "Tea Party Patriots Mission Statement and Core Values" similarly carry double meanings.[30] "Fiscal responsibility by government honors and respects the freedom of the individual to spend the money that is the fruit of their own labor" can be construed, on the one hand, as an expression of a so-called American ethos related to concepts of self-reliance and individualism; on the other hand, the phrase can be heard as a rejection of U.S. social policy aimed at protecting the income and health security of disadvantaged American families.

onversely, the NAACP was not functioning as a "partisan political attack dog." The organization has its own political agenda and correctly sees the Tea Party as a direct threat to the broader civil rights movement. An active, interventionist federal government is a crucial linchpin in the battle for equality, in the view of the NAACP and virtually all other civil rights groups. National politics have polarized citizens into two warring camps over the role of government in civil rights enforcement. A key element of this polarization is race, and—as we saw in the previous chapter—immigration.

*Tea Party Nationalism*, a report issued by the NAACP at the same Kansas City convention, condemns the Tea Party's tolerance for racism and documents, for example, the clear overlap between Tea Party activism and Republican opposition to liberalized immigration policies.[31] Of the fifty-one members of the House Tea Party Caucus, forty-two were also members of the House Immigration Reform Caucus in Congress, "the most steadfast opponents to any reform legislation that would include a pathway to citizenship for those without proper papers," the NAACP report noted. In addition, thirty-nine of the Tea Party Caucus members were sponsors of the Birthright Citizenship Act of 2009 that would end citizenship for children born in the United States to undocumented immigrant parents.

In effect, the escalating intensity of Republican hostility to government has sharpened racial conflict. To conservatives, government intervention of almost every sort represents a threat to individual freedom. Policies designed to correct past injustice, from affirmative action to minority set-asides, are in turn seen by such voters as making competition for jobs, college admission, and contracts unfair, tilting the playing field against whites.

There are many ways to views these trends. Political scientists Michael Tesler and David Sears, both of UCLA and authors of "President Obama and the Growing Polarization of Partisan Attachments by Racial Attitudes and Race"—a paper presented in 2010 to the American Political Science Association—reported a sharp increase in the correlation between Republican identification and *conservative* responses to the following four assertions, agreeing with 1 and 4, disagreeing with 2 and 3:[32]

1) Irish, Italian, Jewish and many other minorities overcame prejudice and worked their way up. Blacks should do the same without any special favors; (2) generations of slavery and discrimination have created conditions that make it difficult for Blacks to work their way out of the lower class; (3) over the past few years, Blacks

have gotten less than they deserve; (4) it's really a matter of some people not trying hard enough; if Blacks would only try harder they could be just as well off as whites.[33]

A sample of Tea Party signs and slogans reflects the broad conservative stance that, for civil rights advocates, amounts to unregenerate racism: "Taxation Equals Slavery," "Marx Lenin Stalin Obama Pelosi Reid," "No Taxes for Tyranny," "I'll Keep My Freedom, My Guns, My Money—You Keep 'The Change.'"

The Tea Party Patriots' "Mission Statement" in turn lays out its case against redistributive taxes and spending policies:

> Fiscal Responsibility by government honors and respects the freedom of the individual to spend the money that is the fruit of their [*sic*] own labor. . . . A free market is the economic consequence of personal liberty. The founders believed that personal and economic freedom were indivisible, as do we. Our current government's interference distorts the free market and inhibits the pursuit of individual and economic liberty. Therefore, we support a return to the free market principles on which this nation was founded and oppose government intervention into the operations of private business.[34]

Most African Americans, as well as many white Democrats, have a sharply different view: instead of threatening individual liberty, government activism has opened the door to freedom and opportunity. Federal spending programs, federal antidiscrimination policies, federal civil rights laws, federal regulatory decisions, and federal court rulings have been and are crucial to the achievement of equality. From this point of view, the Republican–Tea Party agenda is regressive in that it would set back not only black advancement but advancement by those who have ascriptive traits—attributes such as gender, race, ethnicity, and class origin—that cannot be erased and that would have formerly subjected them to rank discrimination.[35]

### One Person's Freedom Is Another's Tyranny?

The consequences of the conservative agenda for blacks and Hispanics were explored in detail by the Boston-based group United for a Fair Economy in a report titled "State of the Dream 2011: Austerity for Whom?"[36]

As Figure 5.4[37] demonstrates, the retention of low tax rates on dividend and interest income, a key demand by the GOP, overwhelmingly benefits whites as opposed to blacks and Hispanics (per person).

Similarly, as shown in Figure 5.5,[38] the drive to reduce the size of the government workforce at the state, local, and federal levels, along with government pay freezes and pension cutbacks, falls far more heavily on blacks, who are more dependent on government employment than are whites.

The divide between the civil rights movement and the Tea Party reflects the broader conflict of material interest between non-Hispanic whites and Americans of color, a conflict that has become increasingly hostile in a time of austerity.

This hostility is most apparent in spending cuts targeted at programs serving the poor. Such cuts were instigated at every level of government—federal, state, and local—beginning in 2008. Poverty is, and has been, a much more serious problem for blacks and Hispanics than for whites. A 2009 U.S. Census report found that the percentage of people living beneath the poverty line—defined as an income of $21,756 for a family of four—was 9.4 percent for non-Hispanic whites, less than half the 25.6 percent rate for blacks and the 25.3 percent rate for Hispanics.[39]

The consequences can be seen in Figure 5.6,[40] which shows the distri-

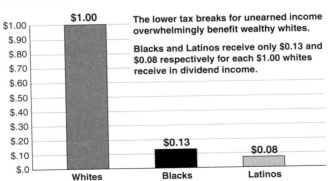

**Value of Dividend Income of Blacks & Latinos Compared to Whites, 2008**

The lower tax breaks for unearned income overwhelmingly benefit wealthy whites.

Blacks and Latinos receive only $0.13 and $0.08 respectively for each $1.00 whites receive in dividend income.

Source: Original analysis of mean dividend income provided by Litinomics using Survey of Income and Program Participation (SIPP) data, combining 5 waves (Dec. 2008 through April 2010), filtering for individuals 18 or over, resident population of the United States (excluding persons living in institutions and military barracks).

*Figure 5.4*

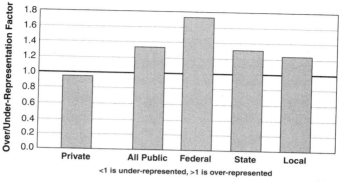

**Representation of Blacks to Overall Workforce in Public and Private Sector, 2005–2009**

Source: Unpublished Center for Economic and Policy Research analysis of the Current Population Survey Outgoing Rotation Group, 5-year average ending 2009

*Figure 5.5*

**Race of TANF Recipients**

Families receiving Temporary Assistance for Needy Families (TANF), by ethnicity or race, fiscal year 2003

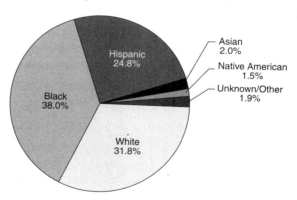

Note: Hispanic may be of any race.

Source: "TANF Seventh Annual Report to Congress," December 2006, Administration for Children and Families

*Figure 5.6*

bution by race and ethnicity of beneficiaries of Temporary Assistance for Needy Families (TANF), which replaced Aid to Families with Dependent Children (AFDC) under the 1996 Welfare Reform Act.

Minorities are relatively more reliant not only on means-tested programs like TANF but also on such universal programs as Social Security and Medicare—*universal* because they are structured to provide benefits to everyone over the age of sixty-five.

As Figure 5.7[41] shows, 45.6 percent of white seniors are dependent on Social Security for 80 percent or more of their entire income, compared to 59.1 percent of blacks and 64.8 percent of Hispanics. In other words, any attempt to reduce or slow the rate of growth in Social Security payments will be felt substantially more acutely by blacks and Hispanics than by whites.

For nearly eighty years, since Franklin Roosevelt signed the Social Security Act into law on August 14, 1935, conservatives and Republican strategists have been itching to break the linkage that the program created between the elderly and government, a linkage many on the right view as making seniors dependent on government and, with that, dependent on the Democratic Party. That itch grew stronger with the enactment of Medicare thirty years later in 1965, a key aspect of Lyndon Johnson's civil rights–oriented Great Society initiatives.

**Percentage of Seniors Reliant on Social Security for More Than 80% of Income, by Race**

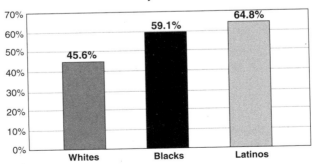

Source: UFE analysis of data from Miriam King, Steven Ruggles, J. Trent Alexander, Sarah Flood, Katie Genadek, Matthew B. Schroeder, Brandon Trampe, and Rebecca Vick, Integrated Public Use Microdata Series, Current Population Survey: Version 3.0. *[Machine-readable database]*, University of Minnesota, 2010, <http://cps.ipums.org/cps/index.shtml>.

*Figure 5.7*

### "Government Dependency"

By 2010 "government dependency"—and its racially freighted connotations—had become a premier target of Republican rhetoric. William W. Beach, director of the conservative Heritage Foundation's Center for Data Analysis, argued in a March 11, 2010, *Washington Times* op-ed that America was approaching "a tipping point":

> Last week, Heritage published a new Index of Dependence on Government. For the seventh year running, it shows Americans' growing dependence on government for such necessities as food, shelter, health care and retirement income—once the province of civil society, not big government. Some 60.8 million Americans now depend on the government for their daily housing, food and health care. That doesn't count federal employees. . . . Nearly 80 million baby boomers are about to begin relying more on government, as the number of retirees doubles. They'll be eligible to collect from Social Security and from Medicare or Medicaid. These programs, which already make up 41 percent of federal spending, will account for nearly 62 percent in 20 years as 10,000 baby boomers a day retire. . . . It's time to take skyrocketing Social Security, Medicare and Medicaid spending off auto-pilot. . . . America is closing in on a tipping point that imperils our form of self-government. Now it's up to Americans to decide what to do about that rendezvous.[42]

An entitlement, as the U.S. government defines it, "legally obligates the United States to make payments to any person who meets the eligibility requirements established in the statute that creates the entitlement."[43] Entitlement reform lends itself to multiple interpretations, some relatively neutral, others with strong moral and ideological connotations. Government entitlement programs are what most Americans, like citizens in other advanced industrialized countries, depend on to insure themselves against illness, misfortune, and old age. In the United States, entitlement programs include Social Security, Medicare, Medicaid, most Veterans Affairs programs, federal employee and military retirement plans, unemployment compensation, food stamps, and agricultural price supports.

More than half, 58 percent, of all federal government spending is on entitlements, as Figure 5.8[44] demonstrates.

At the same time, *entitlement* carries with it a connotation ideally suited to the conservative agenda, which takes as its central objective the cessation of the downward redistribution of wealth and a reduction in the size and scope of the federal government. The *Wall Street Journal*, for example, on its editorial page attacked the Obama administration's health care reform bill as a key component of the Democratic Party's "cradle-to-grave entitlement citadel."[45] Along similar lines, a popular Tea Party slogan is "You Are Not Entitled to What I Have Earned" (see Figure 5.9).[46]

The word *entitlement* has now taken its place in the pantheon of coded political rhetoric. The Republican coalition has proved, over the past forty-five years, that voters can be reached by code words or coded phrases that signal conservative values and interests and that, in target audiences, access or tap

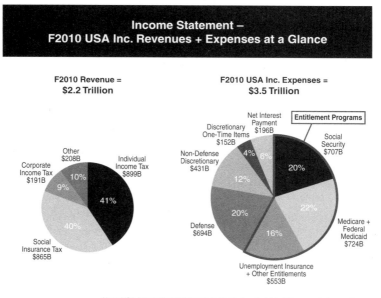

*Figure 5.8*

*Figure 5.9*

"anger points." Such words and phrases as *the culture of life, the Ten Command-ments, activist judges, the death tax, tax relief, school prayer, marriage between a man and a woman,* and even *Harvard* have reliably signaled support, to those sensitive to such cues, for a larger conservative package.[47]

Entitlement, in addition to conveying value-neutral information on a *right* based in law, now signals or cues a set of partisan commitments and a conservative political identity. A Google search of the word *entitlement* links it, repeatedly, to every conservative talk show host and to every lead-ing Republican politician—from Rush Limbaugh to Glenn Beck to Sena-tor Rand Paul (R-Ky.) to Senator Jim DeMint (R-SC) to Representative Paul Ryan (R-Wis.) to Senator Marco Rubio (R.-Fla.) to Republican New Jersey governor Chris Christie, as well as to a broadly dispersed population of right-wing pundits, Tea Party officials, and supporters. *Entitlement reform* as a catchphrase has two political advantages: first, it softens what are in fact draconian cuts in federal benefits aimed at the poor and disabled, children, and the elderly; secondly, insofar as it refers to a government-granted *right,* it appeals to a conservative hostility to the catalog, over the past fifty years, of government-sanctioned *rights* of all kinds, collectively known as the rights revolution—civil rights, gay rights, abortion rights, prisoners' rights, criminal defendants' rights, the right to sexual privacy, and so forth.

The coded meanings of *entitlement, government, rights,* and *poverty* have by now become so familiar to many Republican voters that conservative politicians whose positions are abundantly clear do not have to explicitly use these words. Representative Michele Bachmann (R-Minn.), leader of the Congressional Tea Party Caucus, speaking to a gathering of the Constitutional Coalition in St. Louis in February 2011 demonstrated her mastery of ellipsis: "So, what you have to do, is keep faith with the people that are already in the system, that don't have any other options, we have to keep faith with them. But basically what we have to do is wean everybody else off. . . . And wean everybody off because we have to take those unfunded net liabilities off our bank sheet. . . ."[48]

Others continue to hammer on the word *entitlement.* Sarah Palin told Bill O'Reilly on March 4, 2011, "Oh yes, entitlement programs have to be reformed. You know, they're going to eat our lunch."[49]

The New Boston Tea Party is more direct: "After 45 years, the time has come to dismantle the entitlement system. . . . Fraud is pervasive, the locusts are eating or should we say devouring the productive output of the hard working taxpayer. . . . We know many will be thrown out in the cold, but this needs to be done. . . . [The] free lunch is over."[50]

On February 13, 2011, House Speaker John Boehner said on *Meet the Press*: "[N]obody wants to touch the third rail of American politics, entitlement spending: Social Security, Medicare, Medicaid. We have to deal with it . . . we're going to deal with the entitlement problem. . . . You'll see the House this week move to cut spending by over $100 billion. . . . Republicans will not punt. Everything is on the table."[51]

Eric Cantor, the majority leader, told Capitol Hill reporters on February 14, 2011, "Yes, we will include entitlement reform provisions in our budget, again, unlike the President, and unlike Harry Reid who doesn't even admit there needs to be any reform of Social Security. We are going to lead."[52]

Rush Limbaugh on March 23, 2011, slammed entitlements using *poverty* and *government* as code words:

A story here from the *Asbury Park Press*: New Jersey's burgeoning numbers of poor and nearly poor show the need for government

to "provide more help, more care and more protection" to its suffering residents, according to a report on poverty issued Tuesday.
The report, made public by the Poverty Research Institute of Legal
Services of New Jersey[,] says that nearly 2 million residents—more
than the combined populations of Boston, Baltimore, Cincinnati
and Pittsburgh—are either in poverty or hovering on the edge of
the federal threshold for poverty. So what they're saying is that we
have three whole cities' worth of poor people in New Jersey, in one
state. I'm struck here. Who do you think is hardest hit here? That's
right, children, women—he-he-he—the elderly, African-Americans,
Hispanics, and single mothers. The coalition of the screwed.
These are the people that are constantly suffering the most in
America, the coalition of the screwed: women, children, the elderly,
African-Americans, Hispanics, and single mothers. Now, just stop
for a second and think about a culture that embraces, supports, and
encourages strong families with a father and mother and see if you
find them in the midst of the coalition of the screwed. I mean I hate
to be so blunt about it. . . . [53]

Without our grasping the racial/ethnic salience of entitlement reform,
the full import of the issue, in terms of political mobilization for the right,
can be easily overlooked.

### Supplemental Security Income, SSDI Unemployment Compensation, and the Minimum Wage

The same racial and ethnic issues that emerged in the debate over entitlement reform apply in the case of unemployment compensation. In February
2010, with unemployment above 9 percent, not only were the out of work
disproportionately African American, but those out of work for twenty-six
weeks, as well as those out of work for a full year, were even more disproportionately black, as shown in Figure 5.10.[54]

The same issues surface in the case of the recurring debate between liberals in Congress seeking to raise the minimum wage and conservatives who
oppose any hikes. In racial and ethnic terms, disproportionately larger percentages of blacks and Hispanics are in minimum wage jobs than are whites.
Blacks are 11.2 percent of the total workforce, but 18.7 percent of those earn-

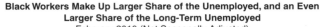

**Black Workers Make Up Larger Share of the Unemployed, and an Even Larger Share of the Long-Term Unemployed**
February 2010 (Not Seasonally Adjusted)

| | Labor force | Unemployed | Unemployed for 27+ weeks | Unemployed for 52+ weeks |
|---|---|---|---|---|
| Other | 7.1% | 6.7% | 6.9% | 7.4% |
| Black | 11.5% | 17.8% | 20.3% | 22.1% |
| White | 81.5% | 75.5% | 72.8% | 70.5% |

Source: JEC Majority Staff Calculations based on unpublished data from the Bureau of Labor Statistics, Current Population Survey

*Figure 5.10*

ing just the minimum wage; Hispanics are 14.4 percent of the workforce, but 19.3 percent of those at the bottom of the wage ladder.[55]

Here is Glenn Beck in a 2009 broadcast on the minimum wage:

> Hey, if you are making minimum wage, I've got some good news: Your life is about to change. Yes, it's time to celebrate; you just got a raise—from $6.55 an hour, all the way to $7.25 an hour. What will you do with all that extra money? Retire? Buy a boat? Here's the One Thing: Increasing minimum wage is like hugging a polar bear. It looks all cute and cuddly, so you give it a shot. But then it rips your throat out. Liberal rags like the *New York Times* are all for the increase: "The raise is badly needed," they say. But they also say it doesn't go far enough; it needs to be even higher. President Obama agrees with that assessment. . . .[56]

Conservatives, and Tea Party members in particular, are angry over what they see as the "undeserving" poor, especially racial or ethnic minorities, "gaming the system" to qualify for benefits. Against such people Beck posits employers—"evil profit-driven trolls," he calls them, with heavy irony—who struggle to be productive and profitable in the face of government mandates and interference.

One target of right-wing outrage is the Supplemental Security Income (SSI) program, overseen by the Social Security Administration, which provides monthly income benefits to disabled adults and children who meet poverty thresholds and who are disabled or blind.

In 2007, the most recent year for which data on the race of SSI recipients is available, the program was 51.4 percent white and moving steadily toward becoming a majority-minority program. That year, 35.8 percent of recipients were black and 10.9 percent Hispanic.

SSI has been growing rapidly, from 6.69 million recipients in 2001 at an annual cost of $28.7 billion, to 8.06 million in July 2011, at an estimated cost of $46 billion. More than half the recipients qualify for benefits because of a mental disorder.[57] Children can qualify for benefits if they are diagnosed with attention deficit hyperactivity disorder (ADHD), attention deficit disorder (ADD), autism, depression, mental retardation, or learning disabilities.[58]

A second rapidly growing program, Social Security Disability Insurance (SSDI), is also a target of the right.

As joblessness remains high, and as the out-of-work lose eligibility for unemployment compensation, millions of men and women are seeking to qualify for SSDI, which is not means tested—although recipients cannot earn significant outside income.

The program, which is financed by employer and employee payroll taxes channeled into the Federal Disability Insurance Trust Fund, covers workers who are judged by the Social Security Administration to be unable to perform paid work, for mental or physical reasons. The average annual payment is $12,800, and after two years recipients are also eligible for Medicare.

In 2007 there were 8.7 million men and women on SSDI at a cost of $95.9 billion. By 2010 the number of beneficiaries had risen to 10.0 million and the cost to $124.2 billion. In 2011, the number was expected by the Social Security Administration to reach 10.4 million and the cost $129.3 billion.[59]

## It Is Not Really That Big a Problem . . .

As austerity measures work their way into every facet of American life, discord between haves and have-nots grows. On a key ANES polling question—"Some people feel that the government in Washington should see to it that every person has a job and a good standard of living. . . . Others think the government should just let each person get ahead on his/their own. Where do you stand?"—whites in 2008 chose "let each person get ahead on his own" by a 50–20 margin, while African Americans took the opposing position, contending that government should ensure a job and good standard of living by a 54–22 margin.[60]

The gulf between blacks and a plurality of whites was dramatically reflected in their respective assessments of the Obama administration's health care reform legislation. Throughout 2009 the Pew Research Center found black support for the legislation twice as strong as white backing, with 58 percent of African Americans favorable by October 2009, compared to just 30 percent of whites.[61]

As we have seen, Tea Party members and supporters have emerged as a driving force within the Republican Party, pressing for the adoption of major spending cuts more effectively, in the aftermath of the 2010 election, than the Christian right in previous decades. And the key area where Tea Party supporters stand out is their position on issues of race and immigration.

The Public Religion Research Institute found in a survey published in November 2010 that 37 percent of all voters believe the government "has paid too much attention to the problems of blacks and other minorities." In addition, the institute found that 64 percent of Tea Party members and supporters agree that "It is not really that big a problem if some have more chances in life than others," compared to 41 percent of all those surveyed. In addition, 64 percent of the Tea Partiers believe "immigrants are a burden on the country," compared to 48 percent of all respondents.[62]

Hard-edged comments about the poor and minorities have become commonplace among Tea Party whites. In 2010, for example, the Tea Party backed Carl Paladino, who ran for the Republican gubernatorial nomination in New York. Paladino explicitly proposed turning little-used state prisons into housing for welfare recipients:

> Instead of handing out the welfare checks, we'll teach people how to earn their check. We'll teach them personal hygiene, the personal things they don't get when they come from dysfunctional homes. . . . These [prisons] are beautiful properties with basketball courts, bathroom facilities, toilet facilities. Many young people would love to get the hell out of cities. . . . You have to teach them

basic things—taking care of themselves, physical fitness. In their dysfunctional environment, they never learned these things.[63]

The most striking thing about the Paladino candidacy was that, in a state where the Republican Party had nominated and elected such figures as Jacob Javits, Nelson Rockefeller, Theodore Roosevelt, and Fiorello La Guardia, in 2010 it nominated Paladino to be its gubernatorial standard-bearer. He did not win the general election, but his primary victory reflects the ideological upheaval of a former mainstay of the moderate wing of the GOP.

In the contemporary polarized era, Paladino's offhand remarks are no longer exceptional. Public discourse has changed radically. When, for example, the *Washington Post*—published in one of the more liberal areas of the country—ran a story on January 11, 2011, on the Wake County busing controversy, the paper's Web site was flooded with vituperative comments from readers.[64] The first one was from "sero11," who wrote: "If Blacks had any sense, they'd work hard and raise their offspring responsibly. When will society realize this integration nonsense don't hunt no more? Let's stop wasting precious tax money down a rat hole. If Black society can't make it on its own by now, it's their own fault. They keep breeding and white society keeps paying and making excuses. How pathetic. Sorry but you know this is the truth."

"sero11" was by no means the exception. Within thirty-seven seconds, "fastaire" wrote: "This social engineering nonsense has to end. Why is it that liberals believe that the only way a low income kid can succeed academically is if they sit next to some white or other minority middle class kid in the classroom all day? It's insulting. Kids should go to the schools in the areas where they live not be bused for miles to meet some socialist's dream classroom. What's next, forcing middle class whites or middle class minorities to take lower income kids into there [sic] homes during the school year for a better home learning environment?"

The antibusing comments were not left unchallenged. "Broadwayjoe" wrote: "Now will the mainstream media finally call out the Tea Party as a racist, anti-Semitic hate group, a successor to the Dixiecrats and the segregationist parties of the 50s and 60s?"; "calif-joe": "Every day the tea baggers reveal themselves more, the shooting in Arizona and their reaction, now this confirms what everyone knew already, they are racist, violent and regressive, I feel sorry for the good people of North Carolina."

Cumulatively, these findings demonstrate that when have vs. have-not conflicts become exacerbated, as they do in times of scarcity, they translate, in many respects, into conflicts between a disproportionately black and Hispanic have-not coalition and a disproportionately white coalition of haves.

On a broader scale, the ideological gulf between Democrats, with their large component of blacks, Hispanics, and other ethnic minorities—37.1 percent in all—and white conservative Republicans is vast. There is a chasm between the two on concepts of the basic role of government, the courts, the individual, and the collective. African Americans, on the one hand, and Republicans aligned with the Tea Party, on the other, are engaged in escalating conflict: what one side considers crucial to liberty amounts to submission to tyranny and second-class citizenship in the eyes of the other; each side claims the moral high ground.

It is this kind of thinking that leads to the new coarseness and brutality characteristic of contemporary politics—the subject of the next chapter.

# Chapter Six

# Brutality, Coarseness, and the Fracture of American Politics

A central pillar of contemporary Republican ideology is: never raise taxes on the affluent. It is the GOP's Berlin Wall; no member of the party can cross over without risking sanctions.

Other conservative principles proved disposable when politically opportune. Balanced budgets went out the window during the Reagan and George W. Bush administrations, both of which produced a flood tide of red ink. Congressional special interest earmarks grew by 285 percent after Republicans took over the House and Senate in 1995.[1] The animosity of the right to entitlement programs briefly and expediently vanished in 2003, when the Republican House and Senate enacted the prescription drug bill, the Medicare Prescription Drug, Improvement, and Modernization Act, a successful move to take what had been a Democratic issue off the table at a ten-year cost to taxpayers of $549.2 billion.

These violations of conservative orthodoxy stand in contrast to the far more consistent refusal to raise taxes on those in the upper brackets. This stance was enshrined in the rules of the Republican-controlled House in 2011, and the policy has a hard-nosed enforcer in Grover Norquist, an influential Republican Party activist who founded Americans for Tax Reform in 1985.

Norquist, an exceptionally talented self-promoter, has pressured decisive majorities of House and Senate Republicans, most Republican presidential candidates, and hundreds of state and local elected Republicans to sign a pledge "to the American people" that reads, "I will: ONE, oppose any and all efforts to increase the marginal income tax rates for individuals and/or businesses; and TWO, oppose any net reduction or elimination of deductions and credits, unless matched dollar for dollar by further reducing tax rates."[2]

Cloaked in principle—"The government's power to control one's life derives from its power to tax. We believe that power should be minimized"[3]—the pledge has proved to be an ideal vehicle to protect the interests of middle class and affluent taxpayers against the so-called liberal agenda of transferring income and other resources to the less fortunate. The pledge is, additionally, a powerful weapon in support of the larger conservative strategy of "starving the beast" and cutting off liberal access to revenue to pay for downwardly redistributive social programs.

And most important, the pledge specifically focuses on income taxes, which are disproportionately paid by those in the upper half of the income distribution, as opposed to either Social Security/Medicare payroll taxes or sales taxes, which constitute a much larger share of money earned by low-wage earners than by the rich.

The beneficiaries of income tax cuts—the better off, whom Norquist is interested in protecting—are evident in Figure 6.1[4] from the Urban Institute and Brookings Institution Tax Policy Center. The figure shows that 89.9 percent of those making less than twenty thousand dollars pay no income tax. Among the affluent making more than one hundred thousand dollars, just 2 percent pay no income tax. In other words, an income tax cut or tax hike

| Percentage of Tax Units with Zero or Negative Federal Tax Liability by Cash Income Level, 2010 | | |
|---|---|---|
| Cash Income Level | Percentage of Total | No Income Tax |
| Less than $20,000 | 29.7% | 89.9% |
| $20,000–$50,000 | 31.5% | 48.2% |
| $50,000–$100,000 | 22.7% | 12.5% |
| More than $100,000 | 16.2% | 2.0% |
| All tax units | 100.0% | 45.0% |
| Source: Urban-Brookings Tax Policy Center Microsimulation Model (version 0509-4) | | |

Figure 6.1

has little or no relevance for those on the bottom but has major consequences for those on the top.

The adoption of an uncompromising stance against any income tax increase and support for almost any cut in income tax rates are, then, a policy position inherently benefiting those in the upper half of the income distribution, especially those at the pinnacle.

The class bias in the Republican stand on tax policy became explicit in August 2011. Democrats sought to extend a "temporary" payroll tax cut as an economic stimulus, a stance seemingly in line with Republican tax policy and a step parallel to the continuing extension of the "temporary" Bush tax cuts of 2001 and 2003. Unlike the Bush cuts, which were heavily tilted in favor of the affluent, the payroll cuts were especially beneficial to low-wage earners for whom the payroll tax is particularly burdensome.

In this case, however, a host of top House and Senate Republicans—including Eric Cantor, Ways and Means Committee chair David Camp (Mich.), and Senator Lamar Alexander (Tenn.)—opposed retention of the payroll tax cut. "[N]ot all tax relief is created equal for the purposes of helping to get the economy moving again," declared House Republican Conference chair Jeb Hensarling (Tex.).[5]

The differing interests of the two parties on tax policy may be seen in data from 2010 exit polls (see Figure 6.5, page 147). A plurality of voters who cast Democratic ballots, 44 percent, come from households making less than fifty thousand dollars a year, many of them below the poverty threshold. Although this group pays little or no federal income tax, it does pay a hefty share of its income in payroll taxes that fund Social Security and Medicare and in excise taxes on gasoline/fuel, alcohol, and cigarettes. Many also pay state or local taxes on sales, income, and property (property taxes often paid in the form of rent). Such taxes consume a greater *proportion* of the income needed for basic necessities of those in the bottom half of the income distribution than do taxes paid by those at the top.

Jonathan Chait of the *New Republic* has noted that

> Americans pay different kinds of taxes to different entities. State
> and local taxes tend to be regressive. Payroll taxes, which fund Social
> Security and Medicare, are also regressive. To balance this out, we have
> a pretty progressive income tax. If you focus only on the income tax,
> it makes it look like the rich are getting screwed. But of course the

| | | | Incomes and Federal, State, and Local Taxes in 2008 Taxes as a Percentage of Income | | | |
|---|---|---|---|---|---|---|
| | Average Cash Income | Total Income | Shares of Total Taxes | Federal Taxes | State & Local Taxes | Total Taxes |
| Lowest 20% | $12,000 | 3.2% | 2.0% | 6.8% | 11.9% | 18.7% |
| Second 20% | 24,500 | 6.7% | 5.0% | 11.0% | 11.2% | 22.3% |
| Middle 20% | 40,000 | 11.1% | 10.1% | 15.9% | 11.1% | 27.0% |
| Fourth 20% | 66,100 | 18.4% | 18.5% | 18.9% | 11.1% | 30.0% |
| Next 10% | 101,000 | 14.0% | 14.8% | 20.3% | 11.1% | 31.5% |
| Next 5% | 144,000 | 10.1% | 10.9% | 21.4% | 10.8% | 32.2% |
| Next 4% | 253,000 | 14.3% | 15.5% | 22.0% | 10.1% | 32.1% |
| Top 1% | 1,445,000 | 22.2% | 23.0% | 22.7% | 8.2% | 30.9% |
| ALL | $70,400 | 100.0% | 100.0% | 19.4% | 10.3% | 29.8% |

*Figure 6.2*

income tax is just one element. And conservatives are working hard to make the tax code more regressive at every level of government.[6]

While the federal income tax is progressive and places a heavier burden on those with high incomes, state and local taxes, as noted, are often regressive. As a result, the total tax burden is relatively flat for those in the middle- to top-income strata, as shown in Figure 6.2[7] from Citizens for Tax Justice.

Just 37.1 percent of Democrats make more than one hundred thousand dollars. Among Republican voters, 47.9 percent make over one hundred thousand dollars, while just 30.8 percent make less than fifty thousand dollars.[8] Clearly, benefit cuts hurt many more Democrats than Republicans, while income tax hikes fall far more heavily on Republicans than Democrats.

### Falsehoods to Some Factions Are Truths to Others

On September 19, 2009, when Obama made his case for health care reform in a televised address to Congress, the nation was momentarily stunned by an unprecedented outburst from the House floor. The president was arguing:

I have no doubt that these reforms would greatly benefit Americans from all walks of life, as well as the economy as a whole. Still, given all the misinformation that's been spread over the past few months,

I realize that many Americans have grown nervous about reform. So tonight I want to address some of the key controversies that are still out there.

Some of people's concerns have grown out of bogus claims spread by those whose only agenda is to kill reform at any cost. The best example is the claim made not just by radio and cable talk show hosts, but by prominent politicians, that we plan to set up panels of bureaucrats with the power to kill off senior citizens. Now, such a charge would be laughable if it weren't so cynical and irresponsible. It is a lie, plain and simple.

There are also those who claim that our reform efforts would insure illegal immigrants. This, too, is false. The reforms—the reforms I'm proposing would not apply to those who are here illegally.[9]

At that point, South Carolina Republican congressman Joe Wilson famously burst out, "You lie!" Even FOX News described the occurrence as "an extraordinary breach of congressional decorum."[10]

But consider for a moment what may have been the thinking underlying Wilson's angry shout. Wilson clearly was not alone in his outburst, given that his constituents reelected him by a 53 to 44 percent margin and that money poured into his campaign immediately afterward, ultimately reaching $4.73 million—all in donations of less than $2,500, more than half from outside his district.[11]

To Wilson and his supporters, Obama was in fact lying: health care reform would do just the opposite of what the president claimed. It would, in Wilson's view, gravely damage Americans from all walks of life, as well as the economy as a whole. To Wilson, Obama's speech was not only a lie of enormous proportion but a patent falsehood designed to cloak a direct assault on the American ethos of self-reliance, responsibility, and independence. Though this was never directly acknowledged, it would also take money from Wilson's white constituents and give it to disproportionately minority beneficiaries.

In his October 31, 2009, critique of ObamaCare, House Speaker-to-be John Boehner declared:

This 1,990 pages of bureaucracy will centralize health care decision making in Washington, DC. It'll require thousands of new federal employees. It'll put unelected boards, bureaus, and commissions in charge of who gets access to what drug and what potentially life-saving treatment. And it won't come cheap. Speaker Pelosi's health care bill will raise the cost of Americans' health insurance premiums; it will kill jobs with tax hikes and new mandates; and it will cut seniors' Medicare benefits.[12]

The Democrats' and Republicans' framing of the health care debate revealed a larger truth: the United States is now split ideologically to the extent that falsehoods to one faction are truths to the other.

### Scarcity and Discord

Incivility is just one of many consequences of polarization—polarization based on disagreements that are unlikely to be settled by conciliation. Contemporary divisions have bred an eat-or-be-eaten mind-set, and the Great Recession and its aftermath have raised the stakes. The hostility underlying contemporary political discourse has a history extending back into the 1960s, when today's racial, ethnic, and sociocultural battles began, but the transition from prosperity to scarcity and the prospect of American decline have ratcheted up the discord.

In legislative terms, issues emanating from the social-moral rights revolutions of the 1960s and 1970s—abortion, gay marriage, stem cell research, euthanasia, affirmative action, civil rights, women's rights, the rights of immigrants, and so forth—have a zero-sum aspect. When the votes in Congress are counted, one side loses and the other side wins.

Once laws are enacted, the consequences are stark: an in utero fetus either lives to term or is aborted. Two men are married with the formal approval and benefits of the state, or they are denied the privilege. Doctors either keep brain-dead Terri Schiavo on life support, or they pull the plug. The strapped state can deny coverage for medication to the impoverished mentally ill, or it can raise taxes, or it can make cuts in another program. Someone takes a loss.

Zero-sum legislative action forces government, individuals, and the private sector to make thousands of similar zero-sum decisions. With jobs, food security, and health care in play, outcomes can determine not only living standards but survival itself.

The scarcity-driven fiscal conflicts now dominating policy agendas across the country often go beyond zero-sum choices to negative-sum disputes in which there are many losers, but few, if any, winners. Take, for example, dirt-poor, crime-ridden, revenue-strapped East St. Louis, Illinois. On December 30, 2010, the city council voted to balance the budget by laying off the sixteen least senior patrolmen—one-quarter of the entire force. The next day the sixteen patrolmen who had been notified that they would lose their jobs—virtually the entire 11:00 P.M. to 7:00 A.M. shift—called in sick.

City officials offered the union, the Fraternal Order of Police Lodge 126, a choice. If members accepted an across-the-board pay cut, the city would not lay off the targeted sixteen. On January 6, 2011, the fraternal order took a vote, and it was decisively unbrotherly. By a five to one margin, the lodge voted to keep full pay and let their junior colleagues walk.[13]

Seven months later, on August 12, 2011, Illinois Democratic senator Richard Durbin obtained special federal law enforcement assistance for East St. Louis, where crime had become endemic and officials had lost control over much of the city.

"Residents of East St. Louis suffer from one of the highest violent crime and homicide rates in the country," Durbin said. "[T]he club scene in the East St. Louis area is better described as a crime scene. I urge the Mayor and other local leaders to take action to rein in these clubs, which are open all night and are the centers of violent, criminal activity according to state and federal law enforcement."[14]

The senator noted that the city of 29,000 had 3,642 serious crimes reported in 2009, the equivalent of 1.3 crimes for every 10 residents.

In Minnesota, a state with a long tradition of taking care of its own, state budget cuts have been brutal to some of the weakest: disabled adults, children, and their caretakers. For Lance Hegland, thirty-eight, who has muscular dystrophy, getting up in the morning requires the help of a personal care assistant who rolls him back and forth in bed to ease a sling under him. Once Hegland is firmly attached, the aide uses a hydraulic Hoyer Lift to swing him from the bed into an electric wheelchair that allows him some mobility in his apartment. With no use of his arms or legs and only some control over his fingers, Hegland had qualified for twenty-two hours a day of help under a state-funded program, Personal Care Assistance (PCA). Hegland's help was reduced in 2010 to eighteen hours, and further cuts are expected. "If my hand falls off my controller, I'm stuck for hours in my wheelchair in the middle of my apartment. What am I supposed to do, sit around and urinate on myself?" he told the *Minneapolis Star Tribune*.[15]

In Tower, Minnesota, Becky Gawboy and her husband adopted twelve children, many of whom suffer from fetal alcohol syndrome. Mrs. Gawboy said the promise of support was crucial to their decision to take on so many troubled children. "These adoptions are predicated on the assumption that you would get these services," she said. "We used to have someone here at night because one of the effects of fetal alcohol syndrome is that they don't sleep. Now, we sleep with a baby monitor to listen to the kids, which means we don't sleep."[16]

In southern Minnesota, the adoptive mother of four disabled children said, "I have a 16-year-old son with Down Syndrome, fetal alcohol syndrome, and autism, who is severely mentally delayed. . . . He had 10 hours a day of personal care. They cut that down to five hours and 15 minutes. It's the new assessment." The state cut back the hours because the boy "can get his own food in his mouth. He can't cut food or know how much to put in his mouth. But as long as he can get food in his mouth, he doesn't get any points." This mother, who did not want her name revealed in order to protect the identities of her children, also has an adopted thirteen-year-old daughter with "fetal alcohol spectrum disorder" who goes into periodic rages during which "[s]he'll kick and bite and pull hair on others. She has pulled her braces off of her teeth. It can go on for a couple of hours." She used to get 10 hours a day of state-paid care; in early 2011 it had been cut to 3.7 hours.[17]

Without prospective adoptive parents, the likelihood is that many of these severely disabled children would be institutionalized at great expense to the state and at an incalculable cost to the children themselves; in the future, it will be harder, if not impossible, to find men and women willing to take on this caregiving burden.

**A**s for the larger national issue of disability, resistance to government spending is again focused on a disproportionately minority beneficiary population: the U.S. Census Bureau reported in 2008 that in every age category from sixteen to sixty-four (the working age population), the percentage of disabled blacks is far higher than the percentage of disabled whites: for sixteen- to twenty-four-year-olds, 3.7 percent of whites are disabled, and 6.8 percent of blacks; for twenty-five- to thirty-four-year-olds, it is 4.9 to 10.3

percent; for thirty-five- to forty-four-year-olds, it is 7.9 to 13.4 percent; for forty-five- to fifty-four-year-olds, it is 12.0 to 21.3 percent; and for fifty-five- to sixty-four-year-olds, it is 20.5 to 30.4 percent.[18]

What stands out in all these examples is that under conditions of austerity, in which there is a limited pot of money in toto for social welfare expenditures, retrenchment is borne by those least equipped to cope and/or to mount a politically effective campaign to have cuts shifted to other competitors for federal dollars.[19]

## No Agreement on the Facts

While the Republican Party has taken a hard right turn on issues of government spending, the ascendant forces in the Democratic Party are pushing, albeit with only intermittent success, from the left. In Congress, the moderate/center-right wing of the Democratic Party has been taking a beating in almost every election, culminating, most recently, in 2010. That year twenty-eight of fifty-four, or more than half the members of the House Blue Dog coalition, the party's center-right faction, lost (twenty-two), retired (four), or ran for higher office and lost (two).[20] In Washington State, centrist Democrats have dubbed themselves the Roadkill Caucus, referring to the adage "Nothing in the Middle of the Road but Yellow Stripes and Dead Armadillos."

With the defeat and retirement of centrist Democrats in Congress and the rise of more explicitly liberal voting constituencies in the Democratic electorate—Hispanics, single women, blacks, and "creatives"—the party has been moving left at both elite and grassroots levels. Responses to key economic questions asked every election year by American National Election Studies reveal that both Democrats and self-identified liberals have shifted toward a more European social democratic view of the role of government.

Take the ANES question that was referred to in Chapter Five (pp. 127–28): "Some people feel that the government in Washington should see to it that every person has a job and a good standard of living. Others think the government should just let each person get ahead on his own. Where would you place yourself on this scale?" In the 1970s, Democrats, by a slight 32.2 to 30.25 percent margin, favored the conservative "let each person get ahead on his own" answer. In the 1980s Democrats shifted slightly, favoring the liberal answer by a modest 33.8 to 32 percent margin. By 2004–2008, however, Democratic voters, convinced that the federal government should see to it that everyone has a job and good standard of living, had shifted decidedly to the left by a 40.5 to 26.5 percent margin.[21]

The same pattern emerges on another ANES test question: "Some people think the government should provide fewer services, even in areas such as health and education, in order to reduce spending. Other people feel that it is important for the government to provide many more services even if it means an increase in spending."[22] In the seventies and eighties Democrats took the liberal side by roughly a two to one margin, 40–18 percent. In 2004–2008, however, this leapfrogged to an overwhelmingly liberal stance, 55–8.5 percent, or more than six to one.[23]

As we have seen, Republicans, who had begun their march to the right earlier, maintained a consistently firm conservative stance on these two questions, declaring that people should get ahead on their own as opposed to the government's having an obligation to help by a 64 to 15 percent margin in 2004–2008 and backing spending cuts over more government spending by a 41 to 26.5 percent margin.[24]

Partisan disagreements are now so wide, and the ideological outlooks of activists and elected officials so antithetical, that there is no agreement on the facts, on what is true and what is false. Increasingly, Democrats and Republicans live in two separate universes with competing realities, assumptions, and moral convictions. Republicans accuse Obama of promoting a "socialist" agenda, arguing that he is responsible for engineering an unprecedented government takeover of two major private corporations, General Motors and Chrysler; a major expansion of the federal role in financing and overseeing the provision of health care; a massive infusion of tax dollars into the financial sector; the federal acquisition of the world's largest insurance company, American International Group (AIG); and the continued unchecked growth of the national debt from $8.95 trillion, or 64.4 percent of the nation's annual economic output (GDP) at the end of fiscal year 2007, to $13.53 trillion, or 93.2 percent of GDP, by the end of FY 2010.[25]

Conversely, liberal Web sites, the progressive netroots, and Democratic officeholders have accused Republicans of "anti-abortion terrorism,"[26] of "leaving lush tax breaks in place for big oil,"[27] etc. Senator Charles Schumer (D-NY), in a direct attack on the motives underlying Republican legislative initiatives, charged that "[r]ight now a very small, very intense ideological tail is wagging the dog over in the [Republican] House of Representatives. . . . Their fervor for spending cuts is not grounded in deficit reduction at all. Instead the far right wing has deliberately confused two separate issues. They've conflated reducing the deficit—which is not their true priority—with cutting government—which is."[28]

On a more idiosyncratic level, the liberal blogger Enufisenuf wrote on February 23, 2011: "Oh, How I Hate You, Republican Party. Yes, you, Republican Party. I. Hate. You. I hate with you with an unrelenting loathing that is sure to send me to straight to Hell, and somehow, I just can't bring myself to care about that."[29]

Not only do right and left see budget cuts, health care reform, and other policy decisions from diametrically opposed points of view, using contrasting value systems, but substantial numbers on each side disagree on empirically verifiable facts.

Pew, for example, found that from October 2008 to August 2010 the percentage of people convinced that Obama is a Muslim grew from 12 to 18 percent, with most of the jump among Republicans, among whom belief in Obama's Muslim convictions doubled from 17 to 34 percent.[30] An August 2010 CNN poll found that 41 percent of Republicans believe that Obama was "definitely" or "probably" born in a foreign country.[31] By February 2011 the percentage of Republican primary voters convinced Obama was born in a foreign country reached 51 percent.[32]

The controversy over Obama's birthplace reached such intensity that he was forced to take "the extraordinary step" of releasing a long-form copy of his Hawaiian birth certificate on April 27, 2011. The certificate showed that he was born August 4, 1961, at the Kapiolani Maternity & Gynecological Hospital in Honolulu.[33]

The arguably paranoid perspective is not restricted to Republicans; Democrats practice it as well.

Brendan Nyhan, a University of Michigan political scientist, examined two surveys, the 2009 Pew study on Obama's birthplace and a 2006 Scripps Howard/Ohio University survey that stated: "There are also accusations being made following the 9/11 terrorist attack. One of these is: People in the federal government either assisted in the 9/11 attacks or took no action to stop the attacks because they wanted the United States to go to war in the Middle East." Nyhan produced the following Figure 6.3[34] showing how partisans split on these two issues. In order to make sure of the findings, Nyhan used only those who said it was "very likely" that there was a 9/11 conspiracy or that Obama is not a citizen.

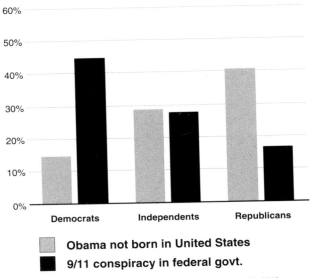

**Obama not born in United States**

**9/11 conspiracy in federal govt.**

*Source: Scripps-Howard poll July 6–24, 2006; CNN poll July 16–21, 2010*

*Figure 6.3*

Clearly, in these and a number of areas, Democrats and Republicans hold irreconcilable views.

MIT political scientist Adam J. Berinsky pursued the same line of inquiry in 2010. His findings—seen in Figure 6.4—show that nearly half of all Republicans at that time believed that Obama was not a U.S. citizen, compared to less than 10 percent of Democrats, and that more than 25 percent of all Democrats believe that government officials in the Bush administration had advance knowledge of 9/11, while only 8 percent of Republicans hold this view.[35]

## The New Imperviousness

A notable consequence of polarization is the increasing unwillingness of either side to acknowledge, much less respond to, criticism. In a zero- or negative-sum conflict, the ability to tune out criticism is a powerful tool. It eliminates what, in other circumstances, would be shame or embarrassment at harm inflicted on the impoverished and deprived. This imperviousness is new in the post–World War II era.

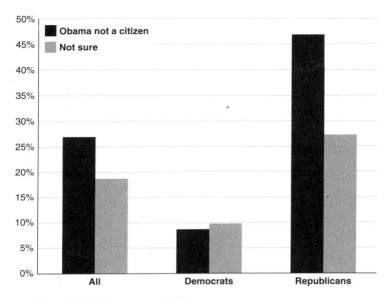

Source: *Polimetrix / Yougov survey, July 2010*

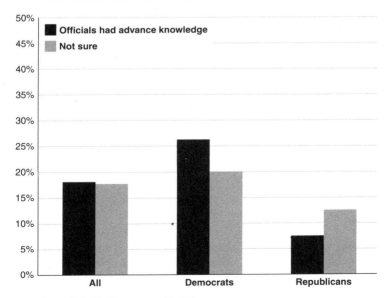

Source: *Polimetrix / Yougov survey, July 2010*

*Figure 6.4*

Thirty years ago, for example, the Reagan White House did a quick about-face when confronted with a palpable untruth. On September 8, 1981, the *Washington Post* reported that the administration, "in major new changes for the nation's school-lunch program, wants to call ketchup and pickle relish vegetables." The idea was to save one billion dollars annually in the program serving twenty-seven million children, many of them poor.

The story created a firestorm. *New York Times* columnist Russell Baker described President Reagan in Dickensian terms as a man who would endorse "an idea by one of Oliver Twist's workhouse bullies."[36] Republican senator John Heinz, heir to the ketchup fortune, denounced the proposal as "ludicrous" on the Senate floor, declaring "ketchup is a condiment."[37]

Two weeks later, on September 25, 1981, the administration backed off and acknowledged a serious mistake. Budget Director David A. Stockman said the Department of Agriculture not only "has egg on its face, but ketchup, too."[38]

By 2001, in contrast, the Republican Party had learned to stonewall in the face of criticism. The George W. Bush administration's two major tax bills provided disproportionate benefits to the wealthy.[39] The administration refused to acknowledge this fact. Instead, officials took delight in passing a "temporary" tax cut that "we knew . . . politically, once you get it into law it becomes almost impossible to remove it. That's not a bad legacy. The fact that we were able to lay the trap does feel pretty good, to tell you the truth," said former Bush spokesman Dan Bartlett in December 2010.[40]

Similarly, George W. Bush and his top political strategist, Karl Rove, in their memoirs disregard the brinksmanship with which they ran the economy aground and with which they launched and conducted the war in Iraq. Their strategy was to write out of the record all adverse information. This approach may be bad for democracy but has been politically advantageous for the GOP.

The aggressive rejection of unfavorable or contrary information has been a crucial factor in the erosion of the once-solid moral boundaries constraining both left and right. Policies and postures untenable in times of greater prosperity have been adopted.

Politicians throughout the government are now displaying a willingness to sacrifice the handicapped, the indigent, the mentally ill, and the disadvantaged, while fighting tooth and nail against tax increases. Scarcity of government resources has coincided with heightened needs among the poor, the out of work, and families facing foreclosure. A commonplace reaction in the political sphere has not, however, been empathy but rather a determination to protect the interests and assets of the haves.

The Texas governor and legislature, facing a two-year budget shortfall of $23 billion in 2012–2013, took this callousness a giant step further. Not only did they rule out a tax increase, but they tapped just $3 billion, or one-third of a $9.4 billion "rainy day" fund set aside for emergencies.[41] This is in a state ranked last, fiftieth, in per capita government spending and forty-fourth in taxes raised per capita, according to the Tax Foundation.[42] In 2011, Governor Rick Perry and Republican leaders of the legislature pushed for slashed spending in two areas to make up the deficit: health and human services programs, especially Medicaid, which was cut from $65.5 billion to $49.4 billion, a $16.1 billion, or 24.6 percent, reduction; and public education for grades K through 12, which dropped from $53.7 billion to $47.7 billion, a seven-billion, or 13.1 percent, reduction.[43]

Without qualm, Texas House Republicans decided to impose the burden of deficit reduction on those least able to defend themselves. The Tea Party's credo "We must live within our means" provides a moral logic in support of the stand taken by Texas Republicans. "America cannot continue to live on borrowed money because the creditors will eventually stop lending and must be paid. Just as any reasonable person or family is forced to make budget cuts when times are lean, so too should the federal and state governments. We're taxed enough already," wrote George H. Rodriguez, president of the San Antonio Tea Party, in support of the Texas cuts. "There is no doubt that a leaner budget is going to cause hardships and distress. But we must face the facts; austere budget shortfalls demand tough decisions by our elected officials in Austin and Washington. . . . The option supported by the Tea Party is to cut spending and live within our means."[44]

Perry's hard-line stance calling for spending cuts, no taxes, and minimal use of the state's "rainy day" fund paid off in spades, helping to push him to the top of all the candidates running for the GOP presidential nomination in the immediate aftermath of his August 13, 2011, announcement. On August 24, Gallup announced that Perry had shot ahead of the previous front-runner, Mitt Romney, leading the former Massachusetts governor 29 to 17, followed by Representatives Ron Paul at 13 and Michele Bachmann at 10.[45]

It should be noted that the Tea Party does not advocate a reduction in consumption in any area other than government spending, leaving private consumer spending and luxury consumption uncriticized. With the unemployment rate above 9 percent at this writing, spending by the rich began to return with a vengeance in 2010–2011. *USA Today* reported on February 21, 2011:

> Retail analysts sensed a coming shopping spree by the affluent as stock prices began climbing last fall. By the holidays, tony retailers such as Neiman Marcus, Saks, Nordstrom and Tiffany were posting December same-store sales gains of up to 10 percent over the previous holiday season. Earlier this month, upscale retailer Ralph Lauren reported a 24 percent gain in quarterly revenue, while high-end grocery chain Whole Foods Market posted a 12.6 percent gain. "Personal embracement of luxury is now back to (pre-recession) 2007 levels," [Jim] Taylor [author of *Selling to the New Elite*] says. "We're seeing that in cars, private jet usage and, finally, in high-end real estate. There's a real change in the way people feel about money. They're making purchases they put off during the recession. Porsche's U.S. sales in 2010 were up 29 percent over 2009; Cadillac's climbed 36 percent. Rolls-Royce sales rocketed 171 percent."[46]

Not only does the right disregard the consumption habits of the rich, but its commentators see inequality as a natural, morally appropriate state of affairs and do not address the dichotomy between the economic conditions at the top and the bottom.

### The Demands of "Others"

Just as a pledge not to raise income taxes appeals to the coalition of the haves, so too does targeting Medicaid for cuts at a time of austerity.

Medicaid serves an overwhelmingly Democratic and disproportionately minority population. For members of the GOP, not only are there few political costs to cutting Medicaid, but such cuts also weaken the vitality of the Democratic opposition.

| Family Income | House Vote Democrat | House Vote Republican |
|---|---|---|
| Under $30,000 (17%) | 57% | 40% |
| $30,000–$49,999 (19%) | 51% | 46% |
| $50,000–$74,999 (21%) | 45% | 51% |
| $75,000–$99,999 (15%) | 42% | 56% |
| $100,000–$199,999 (19%) | 43% | 56% |
| $200,000 or more (8%) | 34% | 64% |

Figure 6.5

The data in from 2010 exit polls in Figure 6.5[47] tell the political story: virtually all Medicaid recipients fall into the category of families making less than thirty thousand dollars, people who in turn voted Democratic by a 57 to 40 percent margin.

The Centers for Medicare & Medicaid Services found that of the 58.24 million enrollees in 2004, blacks and Hispanics, who together make up 27 percent of the total U.S. population, made up 43.8 percent of Medicaid recipients. Whites, who make up 65.1 percent of the total U.S. population, make up 42.8 percent of Medicaid recipients. The remainder of Medicaid recipients are classified as Asian American, Native American, or other.[48]

Here, again, the exit polls, as shown in Figure 6.6,[49] provide the basis for the politicized decision on who should carry the burden of austerity.

Republican opposition to taxes raises a larger question about governance and legitimacy, a question posed succinctly by Francis Fukuyama of Stanford University: "Scandalous as it may sound to the ears of Republicans schooled in Reaganomics, one critical measure of the health of a modern democracy is its ability to legitimately extract taxes from its own elites. The most dysfunctional societies in the developing world are those whose elites succeed either in legally exempting themselves from taxation, or in taking

| Race/Ethnicity | House Vote Democrat | House Vote Republican |
|---|---|---|
| Non-Hispanic White (77%) | 37% | 60% |
| Black (11%) | 89% | 9% |
| Hispanic/Latino (8%) | 60% | 38% |

Figure 6.6

advantage of lax enforcement to evade them, thereby shifting the burden of public expenditure onto the rest of society."[50]

The conservative insurgents of today argue that their antitax, cost-cutting agenda is designed to revive the economy, boost the job market, and get America on the move again. There is, however, another, equally probable motivation. That is, that the cashiering of moral restraint on the right reflects its belief, conscious or unconscious, that we have reached the end of the American Century. In this context, the adamant antitax posture of the right is an implicit abandonment of the state and of the larger American experiment, a decision that the enterprise is failing and that it is time to jump ship.

In 1899, at the start of the twentieth century, Theodore Roosevelt declared that

> [O]ur whole national history has been one of expansion. Under Washington and Adams we expanded westward to the Mississippi; under Jefferson we expanded across the continent to the mouth of the Columbia; under Monroe we expanded into Florida; and then into Texas and California; and finally, largely through the instrumentality of Seward, into Alaska; while under every administration the process of expansion in the great plains and the Rockies has continued with growing rapidity.[51]

By the beginning of the twentieth century, however, Roosevelt's optimistic vision had been gravely compromised. Historian Andrew Bacevich published *Limits of Power: The End of American Exceptionalism*, on August 5, 2008, one month before the catastrophic September 2008 implosion of the U.S. economy.[52] Bacevich describes why the current circumstances of scarcity and austerity are so troubling:

> Expansion made the United States the "land of opportunity." From expansion came abundance. Out of abundance came substantive freedom. Documents drafted in Philadelphia promised liberty. Making good on those promises required a political economy that facilitated the creation of wealth on an enormous scale.
>
> Writing over a century ago, the historian Frederick Jackson Turner made the essential point. "Not the Constitution, but free land and an abundance of natural resources open to a people," he

wrote, made American democracy possible. A half century later the historian David Potter discovered a similar symbiosis between affluence and liberty. "A politics of abundance," he claimed, had created the American way of life, "a politics which smiled both on those who valued abundance as a means to safeguard freedom and those who valued freedom as an aid in securing abundance." William Appleman Williams, another historian, found an even tighter correlation. For Americans, he observed, "abundance was freedom and freedom was abundance."

In short, expansion fostered prosperity, which in turn created the environment within which Americans pursued their dreams of freedom even as they argued with one another about just who deserved to share in that dream. The promise—and reality—of ever-increasing material abundance kept that argument within bounds. As the Industrial Revolution took hold, Americans came to count on an ever-larger economic pie to anesthetize the unruly and ameliorate tensions related to class, race, religion, and ethnicity. Money became the preferred lubricant for keeping social and political friction within tolerable limits. Americans, Reinhold Niebuhr once observed, "seek a solution for practically every problem of life in quantitative terms," certain that more is better.[53]

It is premature to predict with confidence an American future of inevitable decline, but the American conservative movement is taking preemptive action appropriate to a slow but steady collapse. If more than two hundred years of expansion and growth are over, and if the United States is looking toward a future of less, a logical strategy for the haves may be to preserve and protect property, income, and assets from the demands of others. The final chapter will explore that proposition.

# Chapter Seven

## The Big One

In May 1998 ABC correspondent John Miller conducted an hour-long interview with Osama bin Laden at his mountaintop camp in southern Afghanistan. In the interview—a transcript and video of which are maintained by PBS—the Al Qaeda leader declared that the United States had already revealed a fatal weakness five years earlier, in 1993, when U.S. Special Forces were defeated in Mogadishu, Somalia:[1]

> [Muslims] realized that the American soldier was just a paper tiger. He was unable to endure the strikes that were dealt to his army, so he fled, and America had to stop all its bragging and all that noise it was making in the press after the [1990–1991 Gulf War] in which it destroyed the infrastructure and the milk and dairy industry that was vital for the infants and the children and the civilians, and blew up dams which were necessary for the crops people grew to feed their families. Proud of this destruction, America assumed the titles of world leader and master of the new world order. After a few blows, it forgot all about those titles and rushed out of Somalia in shame and disgrace, dragging the bodies of its soldiers.[2]

In the ABC interview, bin Laden claimed:

> Allah has granted the Muslim people and the Afghani mujahedeen, and those with them, the opportunity to fight the Russians and the

Soviet Union. . . . They were defeated by Allah and were wiped out. There is a lesson here. The Soviet Union entered Afghanistan late in December of '79. The flag of the Soviet Union was folded once and for all on the 25th of December just 10 years later. It was thrown in the waste basket. Gone was the Soviet Union forever . . . (today) our battle against the Americans is far greater than our battle was against the Russians. Americans have committed unprecedented stupidity. They have attacked Islam and its most significant sacrosanct symbols. . . . We anticipate a black future for America. Instead of remaining United States, it shall end up separated states and shall have to carry the bodies of its sons back to America.[3]

In a subsequent interview published in the Karachi-based Pakistani daily newspaper *Ummat* on September 28, 2001, seventeen days after 9/11, bin Laden added the following remarks: "Al-Qaida comprises of (*sic*) such modern educated youths who are aware of the cracks inside the Western financial system as they are aware of the lines in their hands. These are the very flaws of the Western fiscal system, which are becoming a noose for it and this system could not recuperate in spite of the passage of so many days."[4]

Bin Laden may well have been overestimating the knowledge that he and his loyalists had of the "cracks" in Western finance, but subsequent developments appeared to provide strong support for his basic premise.

### The Making of a Fiscal Quagmire

In the aftermath of the 9/11 attacks, America launched two wars, one in Afghanistan and one in Iraq. By 2010 these two wars had cost the United States $1.12 trillion, according to the Congressional Research Service.[5] Nobel laureate Joseph Stiglitz of Columbia and Linda Bilmes of Harvard, as noted earlier, estimate the overall costs of the wars in Iraq and Afghanistan at $3 trillion.[6] In 2011 the United States became enmeshed in a third war in Libya. Defense Department officials estimated that the foray in Libya cost $608 million during the first seventeen days of the operation and that continuing costs were running just over $8 million a day.[7]

The degree to which these national security expenditures precipitated the current economic crisis remains a matter of dispute. Explanations of the current conditions of scarcity in the United States run from the conspiratorial—the Huffington Post claimed: "It only took bin Laden 20 men and three hijacked airplanes to hasten the end of the American free market system as we know it"[8]—to the measured. David Leonhardt of the *New York Times*, who sees America's current fiscal quagmire as originating in four domains, "the business cycle, President George W. Bush's policies, policies from the Bush years . . . that Mr. Obama has chosen to extend, and new policies proposed by Mr. Obama."[9] Above and beyond these factors, the deregulation of financial markets—a global development that began in the United States and was supported domestically by both Democrats and Republicans—is often blamed.

Whatever the etiology, the United States currently faces a deficit of staggering proportions. Tax cuts enacted in 2001 and 2003 helped convert a surplus of $236 billion at the end of 2000 (the last year of the Clinton administration) into a decade of annual deficits ranging from $158 billion in 2002 to $1.4 trillion in 2009 to $1.3 trillion in 2010 to an estimated $1.6 trillion at the end of 2011.[10] The two Bush tax cuts resulted in the loss, over ten years, of $1.8 trillion in federal tax revenues, helping swell the national debt[11] to an estimated $15.5 trillion at the end of FY 2011.[12]

The subprime mortgage implosion in turn was fueled by five years of exceptionally low interest rates. The Federal Reserve, under the direction of Alan Greenspan—in the wake of the dot-com bubble and the 9/11 attacks—cut target interest rates eleven times, from 6.5 percent in January 2001 to 1.25 percent in December 2002. These cuts—an effort to keep the U.S. economy from falling into a recession—brought the overnight bank lending rates to their lowest level in nearly forty years. Interest rates did not reach 2.75 percent until May 2005 and rose back to 5 percent only on July 1, 2006.[13] Low rates fueled the housing bubble that was the proximate cause of the mortgage crisis of 2007.[14]

Deregulation opened the door to the engineering of complex and opaque financial instruments—mortgage-backed securities, collateralized debt obligations (CDOs), credit default swaps, and so forth, bought and sold under the umbrella of a shadow banking system consisting of financial intermediaries not subject to regulatory oversight—financial intermediaries that conduct maturity, credit, and liquidity transformation without access to central bank liquidity or public sector credit guarantees.[15]

The U.S. Financial Crisis Inquiry Commission cited among the causes of the financial meltdown of 2008:

the Federal Reserve's failure to stem the tide of toxic mortgages; dramatic breakdowns in corporate governance, including too many financial firms acting recklessly and taking on too much risk; an explosive mix of excessive borrowing and risk by households and Wall Street that put the financial system on a collision course with crisis; key policy makers ill prepared for the crisis, lacking a full understanding of the financial system they oversaw; and systemic breaches in accountability and ethics at all levels.[16]

More succinctly, Nobel laureate A. Michael Spence wrote in November 2008: "Financial innovation, intended to redistribute and reduce risk, appears mainly to have hidden it from view."[17]

### A Sea of Indebtedness

The 2008 financial meltdown devastated the American economy, taking a huge bite out of tax receipts. On the domestic front, federal revenues, which had reached $2.57 trillion in 2007, dropped by more than $500 billion, to $2.10 trillion, in 2009. Total expenditures for the U.S. bailout—including the $787 billion American Recovery and Reinvestment Act of 2009 (the stimulus bill) and the $700 billion Troubled Assets Relief Program (TARP) exceeded $1.4 trillion. This figure does not include a surge in demand for unemployment compensation, food stamps, Medicaid, and other federal benefits, which shot up by more than $500 billion—from $2.73 trillion in 2007 to $3.25 trillion in 2009 to $3.45 trillion in 2010.[18]

The resulting sea of indebtedness and its sources are shown in Figure 7.1, from the Center on Budget and Policy Priorities (CBPP), based on data from the Congressional Budget Office (CBO).[19]

By the end of 2010, the national debt had reached 93 percent of GDP, the highest level since World War II.[20] Without drastic action, the continuing flood tide of red ink presented the danger that sometime in the near future the bond market would either cut off credit or demand exorbitant rates of return. For a country built on debt, such a turn of events signaled disaster.

The accumulation of federal debt—driven by military outlays, tax cuts, expenditures to alleviate the consequences of the financial collapse, and lost tax revenues resulting from the Great Recession—together with widespread

## Deficit, in trillions

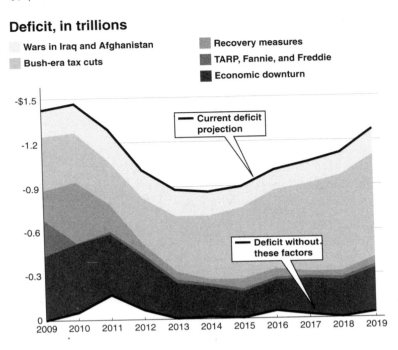

**Source:** Center on Budget and Policy Priorities Analysis,
based on Congressional Budget Office estimates

*Figure 7.1*

reductions in income and job security, have generated a revival of "right populism," pitting American against American.

In 2009 right populism found expression in the emergence of the Tea Party, which became the single most powerful force in the GOP. The Tea Party used its power to control primary and caucus selection of nominees, fundamentally redirecting Republican political strategy for the 2010 and 2012 elections. In many respects, the Tea Party forced the GOP to abandon "compassionate conservatism" and converted the conservative movement from the progrowth optimism of Ronald Reagan, Jack Kemp, Newt Gingrich, and George W. Bush back to the party's deficit-obsessed, "root canal," "eat-your-peas" origins.

This shift in the thrust of the Republican agenda reflected the priorities of the Tea Party. An April 2010 New York Times/CBS poll asked respondents to choose between: (1) "the federal government should spend money to create jobs, even if it means increasing the deficit" and (2) "the federal government should not spend money to create jobs and instead should focus on reducing the budget deficit." All respondents favored government spending to create jobs, 50–42, but Tea Party supporters adamantly preferred cutting the deficit by a 76–16 margin.[21]

This concern over deficits reflected the demographic composition and economic interests of the Tea Party movement. Tea Party members, according to the New York Times/CBS poll, are substantially older than the general public: fully 75 percent are over forty-five, and 29 percent are over sixty-four, compared to 50 percent and 16 percent, respectively, among those surveyed. A third, 32 percent, of polled Tea Party activists were retired, compared to just 18 percent of all adults. Some 88 percent of Tea Party activists were white, compared to 77 percent of all respondents.[22]

Perhaps most important, according to the NYT/CBS poll, 49 percent of Tea Party members and/or their spouses received Social Security benefits in 2010, compared to 32 percent of the general public. Forty-four percent of Tea Party activists or members of their immediate family were covered by Medicare, compared to 34 percent of the general public.[23]

Even though more Tea Party members were retired and no longer worked full-time, compared to the public as a whole, Tea Party members had substantially higher incomes. Only 35 percent of the Tea Party had household incomes of less than fifty thousand dollars a year, compared to 48 percent of all respondents. Some 56 percent of Tea Party activists had incomes of more than fifty thousand dollars a year, compared to 44 percent of all those surveyed, and 20 percent had incomes in excess of one hundred thousand dollars, compared to 14 percent of all those polled.[24]

In sum, poll data showed that Tea Party members were older, richer, whiter, and more commonly beneficiaries of the nation's two biggest entitlement programs, Social Security and Medicare, than the public at large.

Thus, while jobs and income security are important to Tea Party members, federal budget deficits and new government spending (on health care for those currently uninsured or unemployment compensation, for example) are particularly threatening, not only because they promise higher taxes and the diversion of money to programs for the poor but also because they endanger the ability of the federal government to continue Tea Partiers' generous Medicare and Social Security payments.

The Tea Party in effect represents a new faction within the coalition of haves. What its members *have* is their income from savings, which they do not want more heavily taxed, and their Medicare coverage and Social Security benefits, which they do not want diverted to "ObamaCare" or any venture transferring tax dollars to those with lower incomes. When the Obama administration claimed that half of the decade-long cost of expanded health care, five hundred billion dollars, would be achieved through "savings" in Medicare, these conservative voters interpreted that to mean cuts in their own current Medicare benefits—i.e., rationing—and in their current Social Security benefits (a not-unreasonable expectation) as opposed to reductions in the benefits going to future generations, reductions which they are not, in fact, against.

The allegiance of the Tea Party to the coalition of the haves is reflected in the ways in which its views diverge from those of the general public: nearly two-thirds (62 percent) of adult Americans polled by the Public Research Religion Institute (PRRI/RNS Religion News Survey) believe that "one of the biggest problems in this country is that more and more wealth is held by just a few people." Among white evangelical Protestants, more than half, 55 percent, agree, and a plurality, 47 percent, of Republicans agree. Tea Party supporters, however, are split, 40 percent in agreement that wealth concentration is one of the biggest problems, while 41 percent say it "is not that big a problem."[25]

Similarly, 66 percent of all those surveyed agreed that "it is fair for wealthier Americans to pay more taxes than the middle class or those less well off," with even 58 percent of Republicans agreeing. Among Tea Party backers, however, 50 percent disagreed and 49 percent agreed.[26]

Figure 7.2[27] shows the views of the general public, Democrats, Republicans, Independents, and Tea Party supporters on the compatibility of Christian values and capitalism.

Figure 7.2 helps explain another phenomenon, the correlation between rising inequality and partisan polarization in congressional voting. Republicans (and Tea Party members) see rising levels of inequality as a natural outcome of capitalism, in full accord with religious and ethical teachings. Conversely, Democrats by a two to one margin, 53–26, see moral values and capitalism as in opposition. When inequality grows, the inclination of Democrats is to ameliorate income disparities, while Republicans see little or no need for action. And as we've seen on pages 86–87, there is a strong correlation between the political polarization in the House of Representatives and the Gini Index of income inequality.

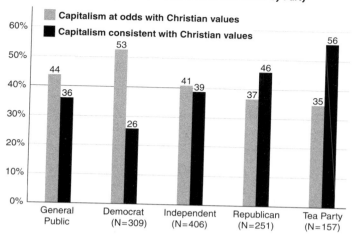

**Compatibility of Capitalism & Christian Values by Party**

Source: PRRI/RNS Religion News Survey, April 2011 (N=1,010)

*Figure 7.2*

While Tea Party members are determined to protect their own Medicare and Social Security benefits, they are largely unaware of two crucial factors underpinning their status as beneficiaries of government largess.

The first factor is that increased longevity now ensures that Medicare and Social Security recipients get far more, on average, from the government than they have contributed for these benefits during their working years. A sixty-five-year-old in 2010 will, on average, have paid a total of $345,000 in Medicare and Social Security taxes, according to the Urban Institute, but can expect to receive Social Security payments and medical coverage under Medicare worth, on average, $417,000. In other words, today's average beneficiary will get $72,000 more in such payments from the federal government than he or she paid in and much more in the case of those who need expensive medical treatment.[28]

Secondly, the decidedly white—78 percent—population of today's Social Security and Medicare beneficiaries[29] will receive these entitlement payments over the next several decades from the payroll taxes of an increasingly black, Hispanic, and Asian workforce.[30] The population aged twenty to forty-five in 2010—the men and women whose payroll taxes will cover the lion's share of benefits for those sixty-five and over—are 39.2 percent minority, and that percentage will grow steadily in coming years.[31]

With minorities increasingly carrying the social insurance costs for aging whites, the issue of who is financially responsible, in the form of payroll taxes, for the welfare of the elderly takes on a novel cast. Even as a large proportion of today's white electorate has come to resist the obligation to care for the "least among us"—and has given birth to the current wave of right populism—it is this very cohort that will be in need of taxpayer-financed care carried by tomorrow's Hispanic, African American, and Asian working majority.

The Tea Party not only seeks to maintain benefits flowing from payroll taxes contributed by minority employees but disputes any parallel obligation on the part of its members to underwrite government benefits for predominantly minority low-income Americans, explicitly rejecting Obama's "North Star"—the belief that "I am my brother's keeper, I am my sister's keeper."[32]

The embattled and self-protective character of the Tea Party movement was reflected at a key moment in its development. The initial mobilization of the Tea Party was not a populist outcry over the bailout of the banks or of General Motors, Chrysler, and AIG. Instead, it was a yowl of anger over government assistance to homeowners facing foreclosure, an impromptu rant on CNBC, the network beloved by older viewers (median age: fifty-two) keeping an eye on their stock portfolios and mutual funds.[33]

On February 19, 2009, CNBC commentator Rick Santelli declared in a broadcast from the floor of the Chicago Merchant Exchange:

> How about this, Mr. President and new administration. Why don't you put up a website to have people vote on the Internet as a referendum to see if we really want to subsidize the losers' mortgages? Or would they like to at least buy cars, buy a house that is in foreclosure, give it to people who might have a chance to actually prosper down the road and reward people that can carry the water·instead of drink the water? This is America! How many people want to pay for your neighbor's mortgages that has an extra bathroom and can't pay their bills. . . . It's time for another tea party. What we are doing in this country will make Thomas Jefferson and Benjamin Franklin roll over in their graves.[34]

The Santelli message caught fire with millions of Americans, even as it turned a blind eye to the subprime lending industry, to the creators of exotic financial products, reckless risk management practices, and Wall Street firms that made billions in fees, commissions, and trading revenue from packaging and selling subprime mortgages as bonds.

In terms of the previously cited work of Haidt, Carney, and Jost (see Chapters Two and Three), the significance of Santelli's comments lies in their striking lack of empathy, one of the first emotions to go when the going gets tough and a hallmark of contemporary conservatism.

### The Moral Peril of Debt

House Speaker John Boehner is in many respects ideally suited to reflect the views of the Tea Party. He believes that cutting spending is less an economic issue than a profoundly ideological one. "We have a moral responsibility to address the problems we face. That means working together to cut spending and rein in government," Boehner told the National Religious Broadcasters on February 27, 2011. "We have a moral responsibility to deal with this threat to freedom and liberate our economy from the shackles of debt and unrestrained government."[35]

Boehner's views of the moral peril posed by deficit spending are widely shared. Indiana governor Mitch Daniels declared in a February 11, 2011, speech at the Conservative Political Action Conference (CPAC) Ronald Reagan Centennial Dinner:

[T]he American project is menaced by a survival-level threat. We face an enemy, lethal to liberty, and even more implacable than those America has defeated before. We cannot deter it; there is no countervailing danger we can pose. We cannot negotiate with it, any more than with an iceberg or a Great White [shark]. I refer, of course, to the debts our nation has amassed for itself over decades of indulgence. It is the new Red Menace, this time consisting of ink. . . . If a foreign power advanced an army to the border of our land, everyone in this room would drop everything and look for a way to help. We would set aside all other agendas and disputes as secondary, and go to the ramparts until the threat was repelled.[36]

Mitch Daniels served as director of the Office of Management and Budget under George W. Bush, and during Daniels's twenty-nine-month tenure, a $236 billion federal budget surplus was turned into a $400 billion deficit.[37] At the time Daniels made no reference to the "new Red Menace," which first reared its head on his watch. When Bush's economic adviser Lawrence Lindsey estimated that cost of the Iraq invasion could range from $100 to $200 billion (a fraction of the real cost), Daniels quickly stepped in to discredit Lindsey, describing the estimate as "very, very high" and stating that a more correct figure was likely to be in the $60 to $70 billion range.[38] As noted above, data from the Congressional Research Service and from Stiglitz and Bilmes peg the costs of the Iraq and Afghanistan wars at between $1.12 trillion and $3 trillion.[39]

For decades conservatives have sought to chip away at the infrastructure of contemporary liberal democracy. The right—between Presidents Reagan and Bush—successfully halved the top income tax rate from 70 percent in 1980 to 35 percent in 2010.[40] Regulation of the financial sector, designed to protect consumers and the general public from excessive risk, was weakened by the 1999 Gramm-Leach-Bliley Act (GLBA), which repealed the Glass-Steagall Act of 1933 and removed the separation that previously existed between Wall Street investment banks and depository banks.

The 1999 GLBA legislation allowed investment banks, securities firms, and insurance companies to merge with commercial banks and eliminated conflict-of-interest prohibitions "against simultaneous service by any officer, director, or employee of a securities firm as an officer, director, or employee of any member bank." Gramm-Leach-Bliley was followed by passage in 2000 of the Commodity Futures Modernization Act (CFMA), which deregulates the trading of financial derivatives in general and, more narrowly, the trading in energy markets. Both measures were shepherded through Congress by Republican senator Phil Gramm of Texas.

In 2004, under the aegis of the Bush administration, the Securities and Exchange Commission (SEC) lowered capital requirements to allow securities firms to make highly leveraged investments.[41] The result in 2007, according to Ray Kurzweil—winner of the Lemelson-MIT Prize and founder of Financial Accelerating Transactions, which specializes in the application of algorithms to stock market decisions—was:

excessive leverage just like in 1929 and the 1930's. We put bank regulations in place that limited leverage and that worked for many decades, but recently a shadow banking system arose that was not covered by the banking regulations. Wall Street firms were leveraged 30:1. It was not just an American problem; European banks were leveraged 60:1. That's extremely unstable. It only worked when the real estate assets that were used to collateralize the loans kept going up in value. When that bubble burst, the excessive leverage caused the meltdown.[42]

The Republican assault on the regulation of financial markets was accompanied by an attack on other pillars of the regulatory state, particularly an offensive mounted against environmental restrictions, an attack reaching a crescendo as George W. Bush prepared to depart from the White House in 2008. Bush left behind new rules that exempted major farming operations from Clean Air Act regulation, weakened the Endangered Species Act, loosened rules governing mining discharges into nearby waterways, and lowered standards allowing power plants to emit higher levels of pollutants.[43]

These were among the many substantial conservative triumphs over three decades. Such victories, however, were unable to crack the edifice built by Democrats during the two great liberal moments of the twentieth century, the New Deal, from roughly 1933 to 1938, and the Great Society, from 1964 to 1966, still largely intact, much to conservative frustration.

### The Left Opens the Window of Opportunity for the Right

On Tuesday, April 5, 2011, the economic and ideological confrontation that had been building for nearly half a century reached a critical point. On that day, House Budget Committee chairman Paul Ryan, Republican of Wisconsin, proposed the actual dismantling of much of the modern welfare state. Ryan proposed to end Medicare and Medicaid as programs guaranteeing medical coverage to those meeting eligibility criteria. Instead, Medicaid would be converted into fixed-sum block grants allowing the federal government to cap funding and allowing states to cut off services when the money runs out.

In the case of Medicare, the Ryan Committee budget would end the system in which the federal government serves as insurer, directly paying hospitals and doctors. Instead, those covered under Medicare would get government subsidies—a "premium" or voucher—to buy coverage from private insurers. Such vouchers would be inadequate to cover the level of medical services now provided and would leave many patients unable to pay for care. The rationing of medical services here is implicit rather than explicit, but it is nonetheless rationing.

In addition, such present guaranteed programs as food stamps and unemployment compensation would be converted to block grants to the states, with the size to be determined annually by Congress. In times of added need, both programs would simply run out of cash, forcing either a cutoff of benefits or a sharp reduction.

The House proceeded to pass the 2011 Republican budget on April 15, 2011, 235–193, with no Democratic support, and Republicans almost unanimous, casting only four no votes. The overwhelming support for the GOP House Budget Committee plan, despite its highly controversial proposal to convert Medicare into a voucher program, reflected the GOP's recognition that 2011 was a crucial year for the right. Not only did the conservative movement have the momentum of the 2010 elections and the Tea Party behind it, but liberal policy intellectuals joined their conservative counterparts in warning of the need to cut spending.

"We have to do something about health care costs, which means that we have to find a way to start saying no. In particular, given continuing medical innovation, we can't maintain a system in which Medicare essentially pays for anything a doctor recommends. And that's especially true when that blank-check approach is combined with a system that gives doctors and hospitals—who aren't saints—a strong financial incentive to engage in excessive care," wrote leading liberal *New York Times* columnist Paul Krugman on April 21, 2011. "Before you start yelling about 'rationing' and 'death panels,' bear in mind that we're not talking about limits on what health care you're allowed to buy with your own (or your insurance company's) money. We're talking only about what will be paid for with taxpayers' money."[44]

Similarly, Democratic centrists like Alice Rivlin and Erskine Bowles cochaired commissions—Rivlin, the Bipartisan Policy Center's Debt Reduction Task Force, and Bowles, the National Commission on Fiscal Responsibility and Reform—calling for major fiscal retrenchment. In addition, the

## Focus Shifts to the Deficit

Number of articles in the *Los Angeles Times, New York Times, USA Today, Wall Street Journal,* and *Washington Post* whose headline or lead mentioned unemployment or the deficit.

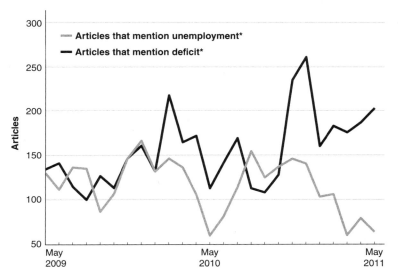

\* *Excludes articles with the words* Greek, Greece, Europe, *and* European

*Source: The papers*

*Figure 7.3*

Obama administration and a substantial bloc of Democratic senators were on the defensive, acknowledging the dangers posed by growing entitlement obligations. With much of the left conceding basic points to conservatives, the window of opportunity was open for the right.

The effectiveness of conservative efforts to shift the debate to the deficit and to the need to cut spending was perhaps best reflected in the changing focus of media coverage. A *National Journal* trend analysis tracking the number of articles referring to the deficit compared to those mentioning unemployment shows the deficit beginning to sharply eclipse unemployment as the focus of news articles by the end of 2010 (see Figure 7.3[45]).

Despite their success in focusing the national debate on the deficit, conservative strategists knew that they faced a daunting future with not only growing numbers in progovernment constituencies—African Americans, single women, and Hispanics—but, equally important, with the whites who were mobilized to turn out in force for the GOP in 2010, who were unlikely to stay energized indefinitely. The left coalition demonstrated in 2006 and 2008 that it was no longer moribund and not only could elect a Democratic Congress and a Democratic president but could provide the momentum to enact just what the right most detested, a major new entitlement—in this case, health care reform.

In that light, conservative elites had to move fast to exploit a possibly unique opportunity to demolish key structures of the liberal state. The Ryan budget set the stage to turn the election of 2012 into a referendum on the scope and obligations of government. Concern was bipartisan that mounting debt would constrict future policy options and ensure American decline. In this political climate, the Ryan proposal represented a high-risk gamble: that the Republican Party could run on an agenda of radical retrenchment and that despite the liabilities of a Spartan platform, the GOP could sweep to victory in 2012, winning both branches of Congress and the White House. Armed with such a mandate, the GOP in 2013 would actually be positioned to enact a version of the Ryan budget, in what could well prove to be a climactic victory for the conservative movement.

With his April 5 budget resolution, Ryan, in his role as committee chairman, laid down the gauntlet. The challenge of the right to the left had escalated into an all-out crusade. Ryan and his allies portrayed the resolution—"The Path to Prosperity: Restoring America's Promise: Fiscal Year 2012"—not only in economic but once again in moral terms:

> Above all, this "Path to Prosperity" calls for a government faithful to its limited but noble mission: securing every American's right to pursue a destiny of his or her choosing. This budget rejects a culture of complacency, offers reforms that promote initiative by rewarding effort, and aims to restore the dynamism that has defined America over the generations. . . . Decline is antithetical to the American Idea. America is a nation conceived in liberty, dedicated to equality, and defined by limitless opportunity. In all the chapters of human history, there has never been anything quite like America. This budget's goal is to keep it exceptional, and to preserve its promise for the next generation.[46]

The Big One | 165

The *Wall Street Journal*'s opinion pages were jubilant. Columnist Daniel Henninger declared that the underlying rationale of the 2011 Republican House budget "is to reorder the relationship between Washington and the American people—country first, Washington behind. That notion is what November's startling Tea Party and independent vote for the GOP was about, and what the party's Senate and House freshmen appear to understand. Properly understood, this is the first presidential budget message of the new Republican Party."[47]

"House Budget Chairman Paul Ryan did what the president has not. Demonstrating leadership and more than a little courage, Mr. Ryan laid out a thoughtful, ambitious blueprint for the next decade," wrote GOP strategist and *Wall Street Journal* columnist Karl Rove. "The contrast between the GOP's boldness and the president's cowardice is striking. The question is whether the president and his party will pay a political price for their abdication of leadership."[48]

Rove and Henninger were joined on the *Wall Street Journal*'s April 7, 2011, op-ed page by Roger Pilon of the Cato Institute, whose column was provocatively titled "Is It Immoral to Cut the Budget?" He wrote:

> [A] nation, unlike a family, is not bound by tendrils of intimacy and affection. America, especially, is not one big family. "We the People" constituted ourselves for the several reasons set forth in our Constitution's Preamble, but chief among those—the reason we fought for our independence—was to "secure the Blessings of Liberty to ourselves and our Posterity." Yet nowhere today is that liberty more in jeopardy than in a federal budget that reduces us all, in so many ways, to government dependents. . . . The budget battle is thus replete with moral implications far more basic than Sojourners[49] and Catholics for Choice seem to imagine. They ask, implicitly, how "we" should spend "our" money, as though we were one big family quarreling over our collective assets. We're not. We're a constitutional republic, populated by discrete individuals, each with our own interests. Their question socializes us and our wherewithal. The Framers' Constitution freed us to make our own individual choices.

Pilon stated his belief that the morality of the Ryan House budget coincided with long-established religious teachings:

The irony is that Jesus, properly understood, saw this clearly—both when he asked us to render unto Caesar what is Caesar's and unto God what is God's, and when he spoke of the Good Samaritan. [Liberal groups] imagine that the Good Samaritan parable instructs us to attend to the afflicted through the coercive government programs of the modern welfare state. It does not. The Good Samaritan is virtuous not because he helps the fallen through the force of law but because he does so voluntarily, which he can do only if he has the right to freely choose the good, or not.[50]

Clearly articulating the distance between their own moral values and those of their supporters, on the one hand, and those of their opponents on the center-left, on the other, Ryan and the *Wall Street Journal* editorial pages ignore the following issues, which are of grave moral concern to political progressives:

- The 2011 House budget plan rescinds Obama's 2010 health care legislation and, in doing so, eliminates medical coverage for thirty-two million people currently uninsured.[51]
- The plan will double the out-of-pocket medical costs for seniors once the Medicare premium support plan goes into effect in 2022. The annual cost to individuals will rise, doubling from an average of $6,150 to $12,500 according to the Center on Budget and Policy Priorities, using data from the CBO.[52]
- The Ryan Committee budget would radically alter long-standing entitlement programs. The CBO wrote: "the large projected reduction in payments [in the Ryan proposal] would . . . require states to decrease payments to Medicaid providers, reduce eligibility for Medicaid, provide less extensive coverage to beneficiaries, or pay more themselves than would be the case under current law."[53]
- Under the Ryan plan, total spending for housing, transportation, social services, foreign aid, food stamps, unemployment, the FBI and Department of Justice, etc. would fall from the 2010 level of 12 percent of gross domestic product to 3.5 percent in 2050, according to the Congressional Budget Office.[54] The Center on Budget and Policy Priorities estimated that at least two-thirds of these budget cuts would come out of benefits currently flowing to the poor (see

Figure 7.4[55]). The Ryan budget would in effect achieve the goal of the Americans for Tax Reform president Grover Norquist: "I don't want to abolish government. I simply want to reduce it to the size where I can drag it into the bathroom and drown it in the bathtub."[56]

· The tax provisions in the Ryan Committee plan penalize those at the bottom of the income distribution, while granting major new breaks to the affluent. An analysis by the Urban Institute and Brookings Institution Tax Policy Center of an earlier, very similar Ryan plan, "Roadmap for America's Future," found that those making $75,000 a year or less—the majority of Americans—would pay higher taxes. Those with incomes between $30,000 and $40,000, for example, would pay $398 more in federal taxes. Those making more than $75,000 would pay less. Those with incomes exceeding $1 million a year would pay an average of $628,190 less.[57]

Even some conservative economists were taken aback. "Distributionally, the Ryan plan is a monstrosity," wrote Bruce Bartlett, former Republican Joint Economic Committee executive director, senior fellow at the Heritage

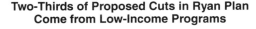

**Two-Thirds of Proposed Cuts in Ryan Plan
Come from Low-Income Programs**

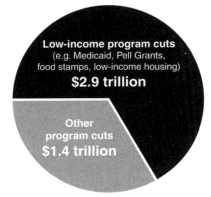

Source: "The Path to Prosperity," FY2012 Budget Resolution

*Figure 7.4*

Foundation, senior policy analyst in the White House for Ronald Reagan, and deputy assistant treasury secretary for economic policy under George H. W. Bush: "The rich would receive huge tax cuts while the social safety net would be shredded to pay for them."[58]

## The Scent of Decline

Over time there are significant costs to a sustained climate of scarcity and austerity. There are few things that more quickly sap national initiative and enterprise than joblessness and the fear of diminishing resources. Here in the United States "the scent of decline is in the air. Imperial overreach, political polarization, and a costly financial crisis are weighing on the economy," writes Berkeley economics and political science professor Barry Eichengreen in an essay titled "Is America Catching the 'British Disease'?":

> Doomed to slow growth, the U.S. of today, like the exhausted Britain that emerged from World War II, will be forced to curtail its international commitments. This will create space for rising powers like China, but it will also expose the world to a period of heightened geopolitical uncertainty. . . . Herein lies the most convincing explanation for British decline. The country failed to develop a coherent policy response to the financial crisis of the 1930's. Its political parties, rather than working together to address pressing economic problems, remained at each other's throats. The country turned inward. Its politics grew fractious, its policies erratic, and its finances increasingly unstable. In short, Britain's was a political, not an economic, failure. And that history, unfortunately, is all too pertinent to America's fate.[59]

A related concept is cited by Jonathan Haidt of the University of Virginia: "Wage leveling has a destructive impact not only on the economy, but on people's morality, and their entire way of thinking and acting. It diminishes the prestige of conscientious, creative labor, weakens discipline, destroys interest in improving skills, and is detrimental to the competitive spirit in work."[60]

Pessimism arising from economic stagnation has been reinforced by the decreasing comparative stature of the United States. More and more frequently questions are asked on whether the door is closing on America and Western Europe. Gideon Rachman writes in *Zero-Sum Future*:

> Over the past thirty years the world's major powers have all embraced "globalization"—an economic system that promised rising living standards across the world and that created common interests between the world's most powerful nations. In the aftermath of the cold war, America was obviously the dominant global power, which added to the stability of the international system by discouraging challenges from other nations.
>
> But the economic crisis that struck the world in 2008 has changed the logic of international relations. It is no longer obvious that globalization benefits all the world's major powers. It is no longer clear that the United States faces no serious international rivals. And it is increasingly apparent that the world is facing an array of truly global problems—such as climate change and nuclear proliferation—that are causing rivalry and division between nations. After a long period of international cooperation, competition and rivalry are returning to the international system. A win-win world is giving way to a zero-sum world.
>
> Both as individuals and as a nation, Americans have begun to question whether the "new world order" that emerged after the cold war still favors the United States. The rise of Asia is increasingly associated with job losses for ordinary Americans and with a challenge to American power from an increasingly confident China. The crash has heightened awareness of American economic vulnerability and the country's reliance on continued Chinese and Middle Eastern lending. Of course, even after the crash, the United States remains the most powerful country in the world—with its largest economy, its most powerful military, and its leading universities. But the United States will never recover the unchallenged superiority of the "unipolar moment" that began with the collapse of the Soviet Union in 1991.[61]

This pessimism is evident in the growing convergence of both public and elite opinion. A July 2010 FOX News poll found that 62 percent of voters believe the United States is in decline, more than double the 26 percent who believe it is on the rise.[62] More recently, a January 2011 *Washington Post* survey found that only 36 percent believe the ability of the United States to compete globally is "excellent" or "good." Nearly two-thirds, 63 percent, described the country's ability to meet challenges from abroad as either "just fair," 35 percent, or "not so good" or "poor," 28 percent.[63]

At gatherings of the G-20 countries and in negotiations with such rising powers as South Korea and China, the United States no longer receives the deference to which it has been accustomed. As early as 2025, China's economy is predicted to overtake America's—and perhaps earlier.[64] According to the consulting firm PriceWaterhouse Coopers, a plurality of Americans believe that China has already surpassed the United States.[65]

This pessimism on the global front is reinforced by the employment situation at home. In June 2011 the overwhelming majority of the four million people who had been unemployed for a year or more and seeking work were older workers: 83 percent were fifty-five or older.[66] As noted, the combination of being old and out of work for a year or more makes it increasingly difficult to find a job. In fiscal year 2011, overall unemployment benefits were expected to cost $129 billion.[67]

Corporate profits surged in 2010 but failed to translate into a burst of new hiring, and economists cite three factors, each suggesting lasting damage to the job market. Even in early 2011, as some markers of recovery became more apparent, hiring remained sluggish.

"Why have corporate profits (and that market thermometer, the Dow) spiked even as 15 million Americans remain mired in unemployment, a number without precedent since the Great Depression?" asked journalist Michael Powell in the *New York Times*. "More so than in the past, many American-based corporations earn a great portion of their profits overseas. And thanks to porous tax laws, these companies return fewer of those profits to American shores than in the past."[68]

At the same time, U.S.-based multinational firms are steadily cutting employment in America while they hire more and more overseas. U.S. multinational corporations cut domestic employment by 2.9 million during the 2000s while adding 2.4 million workers overseas, according to the Department of Commerce. Figure 7.5[69] shows the overall pattern and specific changes in domestic and foreign employment by Oracle, General Electric, and Caterpillar.

In addition, corporations found that recession-forced layoffs resulted

## What's Happening to American Jobs?

**During the last decade, American multinational companies increased jobs abroad but eliminated them in the U.S.**

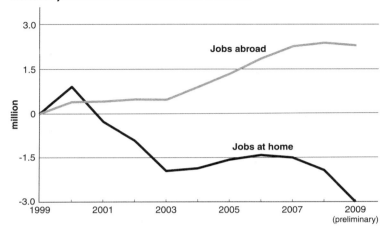

## Sample Data

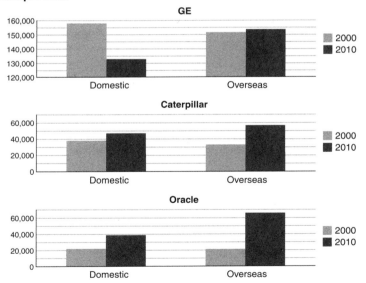

*Source: Commerce Department, the companies*

*Figure 7.5*

in increased productivity, which in turn translated into higher profits with fewer workers. "The nation's workers may be struggling, but American companies just had their best quarter ever. . . . This breakneck pace can be partly attributed to strong productivity growth—which means companies have been able to make more with less—as well as the fact that some of the profits of American companies come from abroad," wrote Catherine Rampell on the *New York Times* Economix blog.[70]

It would be difficult to overestimate the detrimental consequences of these developments for American confidence. Over a decade, from 2001 to 2011, Americans have become increasingly apprehensive about globalization. In 2001, 60 percent believed the trend toward a global economy was a good thing, and only 24 percent said it was detrimental. By 2003 the favorable view was held by only a slim plurality, 42–38. By January 2011 the public had turned negative by a 42–36 margin.[71]

The recession that began in late 2007 was exceptionally brutal. Figure 7.6[72] compares the job losses of past recessions to the 2008–2009 downturn. For the eleven recessions since World War II, the figure illustrates how long it took for employment rates to return to the level at the start of each recession. The bottom line in the figure represents the recession of 2008–2009; even after thirty-eight months, the employment rate remains far below the level of late 2007. This most recent recession stands in stark contrast to the ten preceding it.

As the chart makes clear, even as the recovery was gaining steam in March 2011, the job market had a long way to go before returning to anything like the employment levels of 2007.

As the rate of unemployment began to fall, there was a disturbing development: the proportion of people out of work for a very long time was growing. In March 2011 the average length of unemployment reached record levels, thirty-nine weeks. Why? "Layoffs during the Great Recession were unusually concentrated," wrote Catherine Rampell in the *New York Times*. Whereas in previous recessions a large swatch of American workers churned in and out of unemployment, "this time around the ax fell on relatively few Americans. And as the economy has marched onward, this smaller group of workers has been left further and further behind." This bleak situation is compounded, Rampell continued, by the fact that "unemployment begets unemployment. The longer a person is out of work, the less likely he is to find new work in the coming few weeks, whether because of

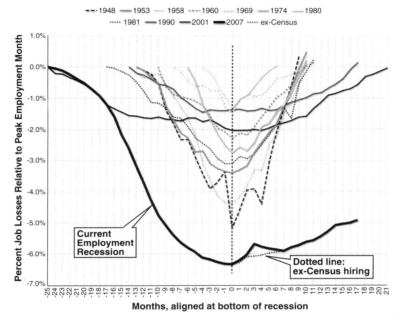

**Percent Job Losses in Post-WWII Recessions, aligned at maximum job losses**

Source: Bureau of Labor Statistics

*Figure 7.6*

stigma, less intensive searching, skill deterioration, or other factors."[73] Her point is illustrated in Figure 7.7.[74]

University of Michigan economist Mark Parry agrees that corporations have sharply curtailed hiring despite a surge in economic activity, because businesses have dramatically increased the productivity of their workforces or profits per worker. "[R]eal corporate profits per private sector job reached an all-time record historical high of $11,552 in the fourth quarter of 2010 (measured in inflation-adjusted 2010 dollars). That's 65 percent higher than the recession-low of about $7,000 per worker in the fourth quarter of 2008 and 7.5 percent above the pre-recession high of $10,740 in 2006."[75]

The results of the high productivity and low hiring rates can be seen in Figure 7.8.[76] As the nation pulls sharply out of the recession—as measured by the growth in the gross domestic product, which, by the end of 2010, was

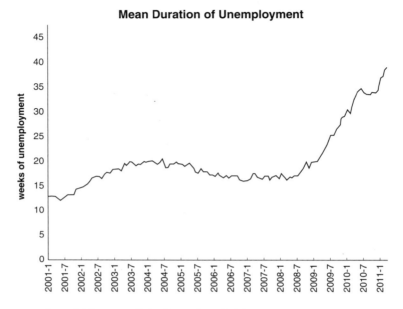

**Mean Duration of Unemployment**

*Source: U.S. Department of Labor, Bureau of Labor Statistics*

*Figure 7.7*

slightly above 2007 highs—private sector jobs had barely begun to pick up, down 7.3 million, or 6.32 percent, below 2007 highs.

In many respects, the economic pressures at the start of the second decade of the twenty-first century call to mind predictions made by Yale historian Paul Kennedy in his 1987 book *The Rise and Fall of the Great Powers*:

> [W]ealth is usually needed to underpin military power, and military power is usually needed to acquire and protect wealth. If, however, too large a proportion of the state's resources is diverted from wealth creation and allocated instead to military purposes, then that is likely to lead to a weakening of national power over the longer term. . . . The United States now runs the risk, so familiar to historians, of the rise and fall of previous great powers, of what might roughly be called "imperial overstretch"; that is to say, decision makers in Washington must face the awkward and enduring fact that

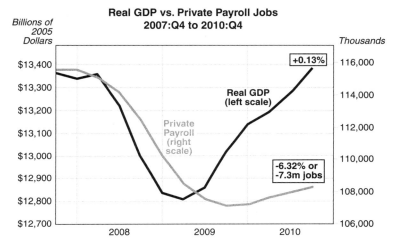

Source: Bureau of Economic Analysis and Bureau of Labor Statistics

*Figure 7.8*

the sum total of the United States' global interests and obligations is nowadays far larger than the country's power to defend them all simultaneously.[77]

Kennedy posed a question far more pertinent in 2012 than in 1987: Is the United States digging itself into a hole by devoting the highest percentage of revenues among all nations to its military?

Along the same lines, Stiglitz and Bilmes in *The Three Trillion Dollar War* (2008) wrote that U.S. commitments in Iraq and Afghanistan were at that time projected to cost almost ten times the price of the first Gulf War, a third more than the Vietnam War, and twice the price of America's participation in the First World War.[78]

Furthermore, American expenses for national defense are by no means limited to threats from radical Islamic movements. The Congressional Research Service reports:

> China is modernizing and expanding its missile force. North Korea, Iran, Israel, India, and Pakistan are building short- and medium-range missiles and are developing longer-range missiles.

Dozens of countries have or are developing short-range ballistic missiles and more are likely to buy them. Over 80 countries have cruise missiles; about 40 manufacture or have the ability to manufacture them. And terrorists continue their efforts to acquire nuclear, biological, and chemical [NBC] capabilities. . . . Elements in North Korea, Russia, China, India, Pakistan, and other countries continue to export weapons technology. The potential for secondary proliferation markets has grown. . . . [79]

All these developments require attention from and, in some cases, military responses by the United States.

The fragility of America's status in the world was more recently noted by neoconservative Harvard economic historian Niall Ferguson:

[I]f empires are complex systems that sooner or later succumb to sudden and catastrophic malfunctions, rather than cycling sedately from arcadia to apogee to Armageddon, what are the implications for the United States today? First, debating the stages of decline may be a waste of time—it is a precipitous and unexpected fall that should most concern policymakers and citizens. Second, most imperial falls are associated with fiscal crises. All the above cases [of imperial decline and fall] were marked by sharp imbalances between revenues and expenditures, as well as difficulties with financing public debt. Alarm bells should therefore be ringing very loudly, indeed, as the United States contemplates a deficit for 2009 of more than $1.4 trillion—about 11.2 percent of GDP, the biggest deficit in 60 years—and another for 2010 that will not be much smaller. [80]

As if to reinforce Ferguson's warnings, in early 2011, two major credit agencies, Standard & Poor's and Moody's Investors Service, were openly discussing the possibility of downgrading the ratings of bonds issued by the U.S. government. "[T]here are questions about the willingness of the U.S. to take the necessary steps" to reduce its deficit, the January 13, 2011, Moody's report said. "[T]he medium-term trajectory for the deficit and debt ratios continues to present a worsening picture." [81]

Then, in early April 2011, the International Monetary Fund (IMF) publicly rebuked the United States, its biggest shareholder, declaring that America lacks a "credible strategy" to limit mounting public debt. The level of debt, in excess of fourteen trillion dollars, created a small but dangerous risk of a global economic crisis.[82]

Later that month, on April 18, 2011, Standard & Poor's sent a shock wave through financial markets by adding a "negative outlook" to its highly favorable AAA ratings of U.S. securities: "Our negative outlook on our rating on the U.S. sovereign signals that we believe there is a likelihood of at least one-in-three of a downward rating adjustment within two years. We currently expect that if we do lower the rating, it would be by no more than one notch to 'AA+,' reflecting only a small degree of deterioration in our opinion of the U.S.'s creditworthiness."[83]

### Worse than the Great Depression?

According to the Congressional Budget Office, these trends translate into a bleak future without radical intervention and adjustment, as demonstrated in its report "The Budget and Economic Outlook: Fiscal Years 2011 to 2021":

> The United States faces daunting economic and budgetary challenges. The economy has struggled to recover from the recent recession, which was triggered by a large decline in housing prices and a financial crisis—events unlike anything this country has seen since the Great Depression. During the recovery, the pace of growth in the nation's output has been anemic compared with that during most other recoveries since World War II, and the unemployment rate has remained quite high.[84]

There are a variety of factors that make the current situation more serious than past periods of high deficits, including the Great Depression and the Second World War. First and foremost, during prior periods of stress, the general expectation—and expectations are a powerful force in economics—was that the downturns were temporary, that the economy would recover, that the war would end, and that the nation would get back on an even keel. In the current situation, there is an expectation only of a short-term return to economic growth and declining deficits. For the mid and long term, there is widespread agreement on the left and right that relentless structural forces, among them, the cost of increasingly technologically sophisticated health care and longer life spans, are pushing federal spending up at a higher rate than anticipated revenues, leading to levels of accumulated debt which threaten the credibility of the country in the bond market.

As two economists, Alan J. Auerbach and William G. Gale, of the relatively liberal Urban Institute in Washington, described in 2011, the growing national debt poses a major threat:

> The unsustainability of federal fiscal policy has been discussed at least since the 1980s. But the problem has increased in importance and urgency in recent years for several reasons. First, the medium-term projections have deteriorated significantly. Second, the issues driving the long-term projections—in particular, the retirement of the baby boomers and the aging of the population and the resulting pressure on Medicare and to some extent Social Security—which were several decades away in the 1980s—are now imminent. Third, there are increasing questions about the rest of the world's appetite for U.S. debt, as the United States has changed from a net creditor country in 1980 to a vast net debtor currently. Fourth, many countries around the world and many of the U.S. states also face daunting fiscal prospects currently. . . .
>
> The real concerns lie in the . . . long-term outlook. The medium-term and long-term budget shortfalls will create growing burdens on the economy. These burdens can happen gradually or suddenly. In the gradual scenario, budget shortfalls will reduce national saving. In the absence of increased capital inflows, the reduction in national saving will raise interest rates, reduce investment and reduce future national output. Increased capital inflows from abroad can mitigate or eliminate the increase in interest rates and/or the decline in investment. This in turn will offset some of the decline in future national income, but of course the inflows create increasing claims on the domestic capital stock and hence still reduce future national income. In either case, under the gradual scenario, sustained large deficits will reduce future national income and living standards. In the sudden scenario, long-term budget shortfalls could trigger a political or market reaction that leads to a sudden change in interest rates, exchange rates, capital

outflows, etc. Avoiding these outcomes will require significant and sustained changes to spending and revenue policies, much larger changes than have received serious consideration in the policy process to date.[85]

The phrase "significant and sustained changes to spending and revenue policies" is a euphemism for substantial cuts in programs with widespread popular support and for the bête noire of American politics, tax hikes.

Ever since 1984, when Democratic presidential nominee Walter F. Mondale famously proposed raising taxes, only to lose every state to Ronald Reagan with the exception of his native Minnesota ("Let's tell the truth. It must be done, it must be done. Mr. Reagan will raise taxes, and so will I. He won't tell you. I just did"), proposals to raise revenues have been shunned by both parties.[86] For Republicans, this stance is now the most deeply ingrained element of conservative orthodoxy; for Democrats, it is a matter of survival on election day.

The stark reality, however, is that if long-range deficit reduction is the goal, a failure to raise taxes means disproportionately penalizing Democratic constituencies. There are a host of alternative forms in which tax hikes can be presented, including creation of a value-added tax (a type of national sales tax), increased income tax rates, extended coverage of the payroll tax, and the elimination or modification of such tax expenditures as the mortgage interest deduction or the tax exemption for employer-paid health insurance.

For Democrats seeking to represent the interests of core constituencies, a substantial tax hike would seem to be an essential policy tool. Given the fact that the deficit and the debt will rank high in the 2012 election debate, Democrats will face major hurdles evading the subject of raising federal revenues.

For the GOP, however, the focus of attention on the debt is a win-win situation.

The party experienced striking success in early skirmishes over the FY 2011 budget, giving additional momentum to the austerity movement. The GOP triumphed in pressing Obama and Senate Democrats to agree on April 8, 2011, to a record-setting thirty-eight billion dollars in spending cuts, some seven billion dollars more than House Speaker John Boehner had originally called for.

At the same time, House passage of the Ryan budget forced the Obama administration to radically alter its FY 2012 budget proposal and to produce a plan calling for major surgery on federal spending, including reductions in basic entitlement programs.[87]

The preliminary battle lines over competing plans to achieve massive reductions in federal expenditures were drawn when Obama presented his new budget plan on April 13, 2011, drawing strong contrasts with the Ryan budget. Obama charged:

> [The Republican proposal] paints a vision of our future that is deeply pessimistic. It's a vision that says if our roads crumble and our bridges collapse, we can't afford to fix them. If there are bright young Americans who have the drive and the will but not the money to go to college, we can't afford to send them. . . . It says that 10 years from now, if you're a 65-year-old who's eligible for Medicare, you should have to pay nearly $6,400 more than you would today. It says instead of guaranteed health care, you will get a voucher. . . . And worst of all, this is a vision that says even though Americans can't afford to invest in education at current levels, or clean energy, even though we can't afford to maintain our commitment on Medicare and Medicaid, we can somehow afford more than $1 trillion in new tax breaks for the wealthy. . . . They want to give people like me a $200,000 tax cut that's paid for by asking 33 seniors each to pay $6,000 more in health costs. That's not right. And it's not going to happen as long as I'm President.[88]

Just hours after Obama spoke, Ryan shot back:

> I'm very disappointed in the president. I was excited when we got invited to attend his speech today. . . . Instead, what we got was a speech that was excessively partisan, dramatically inaccurate and hopelessly inadequate to addressing our country's pressing fiscal challenges. . . . This is very sad and very unfortunate. Rather than building bridges, he's poisoning wells. By failing seriously to confront the most predictable economic crisis in our nation's history, the president's policies are committing us and our children to a diminished future.[89]

Early polling showed widespread opposition to some of the Ryan Committee proposals, especially the conversion of Medicare from an entitlement into a voucher program that would not cover the full cost of medical treatment. Newt Gingrich, recognizing the political liabilities of cutting Medicare benefits, described the plan as "right-wing social engineering."[90]

Despite these concerns, the public, according to an April 27, 2011, Gallup poll, was evenly split when asked to choose between the Ryan Committee budget, 43 percent, and the Obama budget, 44 percent. In a warning shot to Democrats, when voters were asked which party in Congress was better able to deal with the federal budget, Republicans came out ahead, 48–36, including independents, 47–30, a seventeen-point advantage among the key swing segment of the electorate.[91]

The very fact that the Republican House and the Democratic Obama administration were fighting over competing plans to perform major surgery on federal spending was in itself a huge victory for conservatism. The movement's "starve the beast" strategy had finally worked to force Democrats and Republicans to compete over austerity measures.

Given the complexity of the deliberations over the deficit and the wide variation in fiscal policies advocated by economists and budget specialists, the success of the GOP and the Tea Party in defining the terms of the debate in 2011 is an extraordinary feat.

### Economists Dissent

Many, if not most, economists argue that contrary to Republican orthodoxy, substantial revenue increases are a needed part of a long-term deficit reduction program and that new levies should be more substantial than Obama's proposal to impose a tax hike on the rich.

In addition, while there is a general consensus that the trajectory of growing debt as a percentage of GDP is unsustainable, there are credible economists who dissent from this view. James K. Galbraith of the University of Texas, for example, contends:

> Everything depends on the interest rate assumptions. And the interest rate assumptions that everyone makes, which are nearly hidden, are completely implausible [and] the effect is to create an exploding debt/GDP projection, almost entirely out of whole cloth. . . . When

you make a realistic interest rate assumption—that is, assume interest rates will stay close to where they are, then the current primary
deficits are not unsustainable and all the attacks on Social Security
and Medicare and Medicaid are revealed for what they are: the same
old crowd going after their habitual target.[92]

Nobelist Michael Spence argues that the intense, almost obsessive, concern with deficits and debt oversimplifies, and perhaps masks, a much more
complex and difficult-to-manage issue: the increasingly powerful role of
emerging market economies in shaping the United States, especially its job
market: "The American economy does not exist in a vacuum; some of its
most striking evolving characteristics are tied to long-term trends in the
developing world and especially the large emerging economies."[93]

Globalization, in this view, has put America in an uncomfortably passive
position, subject to external forces that it cannot control—that it can at best
moderate or fine-tune. Employment exported from the United States started
with low-skilled jobs and, over time, moved up the employment ladder to
higher-quality, better-paying work. "A growing emerging economy shifts to
higher value-added components of international supply chains as physical,
human, and institutional capital deepen and emerging economies begin to
compete directly with rich ones," Spence writes.[94]

Spence and his co-author Sandile Hlatshwayo, a researcher at the Stern
School of Business, New York University, use the shifting pattern of exports
from China to illustrate their point. In 1992, the dark bars in Figure 7.9[95]
show, exports from China were dominated by textiles, apparel, and footwear.
By 2005, the light bars in the figure show, export production in China had
shifted "up the value-added chain" to telecom, office machines, and electronic
machinery. In other words, China was taking many more higher-skilled and
better-paying jobs away from developed countries in 2005 than it had done
thirteen years earlier.

Until the start of the Great Recession in 2008, the United States was able
to absorb the loss of jobs in the tradable sector because of strong employment growth in the nontradable sectors, especially jobs in government and
in health care. From 1990 to 2008 the United States gained a total of 27.3 million jobs, enough to absorb population growth, almost all of them, 26.7 million, in nontradable sectors. Together, health care and government produced
10.4 million jobs, or nearly 40 percent of total new employment.[96]

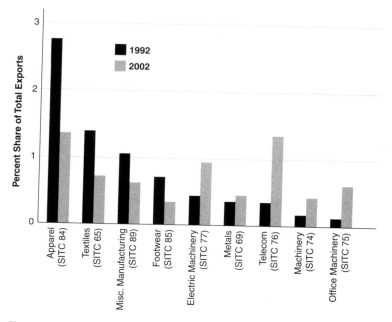

*Figure 7.9*

Now, however, governments at every level in the United States are shedding jobs, while simultaneously searching for ways to reduce health care costs. The United States is caught in a tightening free-market vise. Multinationals, businesses that operate in the global economy, and those that have a role in creating and managing global supply chains, are good at what they do and are getting better all the time. They are knowledgeable about doing business in multiple national environments; they identify and respond to market and supply chain opportunities.

The global economy has an abundance of human resources, and these resources are becoming more accessible. The supply of human capital and skill increases as emerging economies develop. The sectors of the supply chain in which these economies have the potential to be competitive are enlarging. Multinational companies, operating in such a way as to gain access to these assets and to growing markets, are doing exactly as expected. The resulting efficiency of the global system is rising. The result is that first low-skill, then mid-skill, and increasingly high-skill workers in the United States "are seeing employment options narrow and incomes stagnate."[97]

The dilemma facing the United States is not the result of liberal policies, market failure, or a calculated effort on the part of foreign powers to undermine the United States. Instead, it is a natural outcome of market competition. Spence notes:

> The transaction costs of complex and geographically dispersed supply chains are coming down because of a combination of management expertise and information technology that allows efficient coordination of complex, geographically dispersed systems. The costs of remoteness are declining. . . . [O]peratives in the system adapt to the shifting sands of comparative advantage and market size, and move economic activity (think of parts of the value-added or global supply chains) to the places where it can be performed at high efficiency and low cost.[98]

The undermining of decent-paying jobs for workers at all skill levels is exacerbating inequality: "[T]he distributional effects may be negative. Within countries, inequality may rise. Between countries, the success of the emerging economies may impose costs on richer ones, straining public support for globalization."[99]

In a damning op-ed published August 10, 2011, in the *Washington Post*, Bill Gross, founder and co–chief investment officer of the investment management firm Pimco, wrote about the debt ceiling/debt legislation:

> To Republicans, and even many co-opted Democrats, the debate starts with spending cuts and how much must be done to appease voters and the markets. . . . But while our debt crisis is real and promises to grow to Frankenstein proportions in future years, debt is not the disease—it is a symptom. Lack of aggregate demand or, to put it simply, insufficient consumption and investment is the disease. . . . [A]n anti-Keynesian, budget-balancing immediacy imparts a constrictive noose around whatever demand remains alive and kicking. Washington hassles over debt ceilings instead of job creation in the mistaken belief that a balanced budget will produce a balanced economy. It will not.[100]

## The Political Reality

Policy makers and economists differ over what strategies are most effective given the nation's dilemma. Many have suggested a call for more spending on higher education, fundamental research, and infrastructure.

The political reality, however, is that the GOP and Tea Party have, for the present at least, effectively vetoed any approach involving increased government expenditures in what could prove to be a dangerous constraint on American policy, worsening prospects for global competitiveness and thus recovery.

Conflicting left and right austerity strategies will shape the 2012 election. And if the past is precedent, it is unlikely that the election will resolve the debate. Incentives to sustain partisan warfare far outweigh the potential rewards of constructive bipartisan cooperation:

- Both parties have found that fear and anger are the best motivators to boost voter turnout. The advantage on election day lies with keeping a dangerous and threatening enemy (the other party) front and center in the minds of supporters. The payoff for cooperation across party lines and diffusion of conflict is, in political terms, negligible.
- Conservative priorities have gained more traction from fiscal collapse than has liberalism. The contemporary economic climate has dealt a blow to the instinct of generosity essential to the left and has strengthened the instincts of greed, callousness, and self-preservation.
- The threat of a debt crisis is most likely to emerge as an immediate danger toward the end of the decade, in 2018–2020, when health care and other social insurance costs begin to once more balloon. For a politician, an event six or eight years way is so far into the future that it does not warrant attention.
- As documented earlier, centrists of both parties—those most likely to press for consensual, bipartisan agreement on long-range fiscal policy—have been decimated, their numbers declining each year.
- The willingness of Democrats to compromise in the face of Republican challenges has had the unanticipated consequence of making

collaboration between the parties less and less likely. The Republican Party has no reason to negotiate a broad peace if it keeps winning incremental victories on tax policy, spending cuts, and deregulation, as it has repeatedly over the past three decades.

- Insofar as America's global stature declines and its economy is eclipsed, voters will be forced inexorably to accommodate a lower standard of living and may become more extreme in their political views.

### An Underdog Mentality?

America has thrived on growth. It is a commercial republic of creative, but also predatory, risk-taking entrepreneurs. The American economy, at least until recently, has been—for such purposes—an ideal environment. In 1913 the S&P was at 8.51. By April 2011 the S&P 500 was at 1,363, an inflation-adjusted increase of 710 percent.[101] The gross domestic product has grown from $997 billion in 1929 to $13 trillion in 2009, in inflation-adjusted 2005 dollars, a 1,304 percent increase.[102] Per capita disposable income has grown fivefold from $6,498 in 1929 to $32,518 in 2009 in inflation-adjusted 2005 dollars.[103]

These growth trends have flattened in recent years and in some cases declined. Per capita income rose from $13,835 in 1967 to $27,833 in 2000 in inflation-adjusted 2009 dollars but then failed to move during the next decade, falling during the current downturn to $26,530 in 2009.[104] The same pattern is true of median household income, which peaked at just over $52,000 in 1999 and 2000, only to drop even before the Great Recession began.[105]

In this bleak climate, there is always an outside chance of positive change. Theoretically, a major new technological advance on the level of the Internet could revive the economy, pulling the nation out of debt. There are strong believers on the left and right in the power of American ingenuity, initiative, and innovation. Some optimists believe that when America falls into second place relative to China, subordination will serve as an incentive, a challenge to the nation's self-regard, even to its honor.

"We need an underdog mentality. America is like the rich, dysfunctional family that lives in the ramshackle mansion at the top of the hill. We're living off of our past and have lost the habit of working hard to earn our liveli-hood," wrote Rick Newman, chief business correspondent for *U.S. News &*

*World Report.* "If falling to No. 2 would generate a common sense of purpose and give Americans something to rally around, it might help generate the kind of determination to solve problems that no blue-ribbon commission or bipartisan study group can generate."[106]

A less palatable path out of economic stagnation was suggested by liberal Princeton Nobelist Paul Krugman and Harvard economist Martin Feldstein, a major player on the right, appearing together in October 2010 at the forum "America's Fiscal Choices." The two economists suggested the possibility of "an exogenous shock"—an economic, terrorist, climate-induced, military, or other calamity that would force a major alteration in the political system. The *National Journal* reported the exchange:

> Krugman and Feldstein, though often on opposite sides of the political fence on fiscal and tax policy, both appeared to share the view that political paralysis in Washington has rendered the necessary fiscal and monetary stimulus out of the question. Only a high-impact "exogenous" shock like a major war—something similar to what Krugman called the "coordinated fiscal expansion known as World War II"—would be enough to break the cycle. . . ."I don't think we're about to launch a war against anybody," Feldstein said. "But Paul is right. That was the fiscal move that got us out of the last downturn comparable to this one, the Great Depression."[107]

The dangers of chemical or biological or nuclear war today are self-evidently not suited to serve the purposes of "coordinated fiscal expansion," but catastrophic wars are not always planned.

There is the more likely probability that the institutions, countries, and individuals that buy U.S. debt will balk sooner than expected. As already noted, such a development would force policy makers to adopt harsh tax and spending policies—similar to those imposed on Ireland, Portugal, and Greece—to restore U.S. credibility in the bond market. If the nation's politics and fiscal policies remain in stasis, the odds will increasingly favor a debt crisis.

When, and if, that happens, the current environment of hostile competition over scarce resources will be looked back upon as a benign, indeed halcyon, moment.

# Coda

The United States considered Osama bin Laden so great a threat that the country devoted ten years of warfare, espionage, surveillance, and high-tech pursuit to his capture and assassination. The effort succeeded on May 1, 2011, when bin Laden was shot by an elite squad of Navy SEALS in a firefight within his walled compound outside Islamabad. To avoid making his tomb a martyr's shrine, the U.S. government announced that on May 2, 2011, bin Laden had been buried at sea.

In the immediate aftermath of bin Laden's death, there was American celebration, followed quickly by a deeper concern over his legacy for the United States. Apprehension was widespread over the possibility of retribution, retaliation, and revenge, with Interpol warning on May 2 of heightened risk from Al Qaeda–affiliated or Al Qaeda–inspired terrorists.

Warnings of fundamental threats are unlikely to subside. Richard C. Clarke, counterterrorism coordinator at the National Security Council from 1993 to 2001, wrote, "The government that was overthrown in Egypt was corrupt and feckless, as are the regimes now under siege in Libya, Syria, and Yemen, but the groups poised to take advantage of the upheaval in those countries include many who share bin Laden's vision for repressive religious rule." Clarke noted that similar situations exist in Afghanistan and Pakistan. "In many Muslim societies there remains a radical stratum born of a sense of victimization by the West, fueled by inefficient and corrupt governments, and carried forward by an enormous youth population."[1]

Looking inward, Peter Goodman of the Huffington Post argued that the victory over bin Laden celebrated on May 2 failed to acknowledge the immense costs to the country: "A decade ago we watched people we knew or might have known hurtle to their deaths from a landmark building. Someone had to pay."

Goodman continued:

> The trouble is that we ourselves paid as a nation. And we have kept paying even as the price has climbed to impossible heights, via disastrous choices made in anger and vengeance more than reason and enlightened self-interest. We rushed into Afghanistan without the will to remake it. We embarked on an unnecessary war in Iraq, chasing the phantom of our national fears. We squandered our treasure on ill-conceived military misadventures just as we needed it most here at home, to rebuild our schools and invest in productive industries that might put people back to work.[2]

Barry Ritzholtz, founder of the influential Big Picture blog, wrote on the morning after the announcement of bin Laden's death:

> Today's news of Osama bin Laden being brought to justice was long overdue. It brought up bittersweet feelings of closure regarding that fateful day a decade ago. . . . I have always wondered how much Osama bin Laden had to do with the 2008–09 collapse. In a weird way, Greenspan's overreaction on rates post 9/11 was a key element in the run up to the collapse. Indirectly, the 9/11 attacks were a factor in the 2008–09 crisis. The Butterfly Effect is why great nations should not be over-extended militarily except for emergencies; why they should not take on too much collective debt; why their peoples should not be over-leveraged. In short, intelligent nations should have a margin of safety that allows them to absorb unanticipated externalities and random events, tragedies and even attacks easily.
>
> We may not know where the next Black Swan is coming from, but we do know it's coming. I don't want to rehash the prior arguments I have made; rather, I am compelled to point out the horrific cost of our incompetency; from those ultra-low rates to the wrongheaded response of the United States pulling troops away from Afghanistan

to invade a country that had nothing to do with 9/11 served to postpone Osama bin Laden's day of reckoning. That this fucker did not meet the Devil 10 years ago is yet another part of this tragedy.[3]

The next Black Swan—a wildly unexpected event or process[4]—may stem from the current role of the United States, a country with just under 5 percent of the world population, but one that consumes 20 percent of all energy—a level, as illustrated in Figure C.1,[5] that the rest of the world is unlikely to continue to tolerate or accept.

The same will inevitably prove true of the disproportionate share of virtually every major commodity consumed by the United States, as shown in Figure C.2.[6]

Global challenges to continued American security and prosperity shed additional light on the strategy of the Tea Party and its allied Republican forces. Just as the goal of the conservative movement on the domestic front is to protect the income, assets, and wealth of its supporters from the demands of ascendant, Democratic constituencies, conservatives also recognize the threat to their standard of living from developing economies, emerging mar-

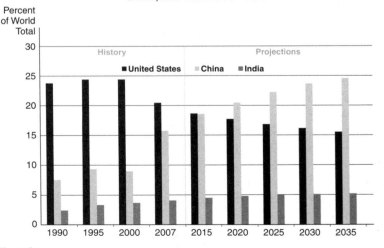

Figure C.1

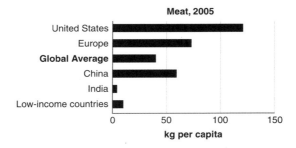

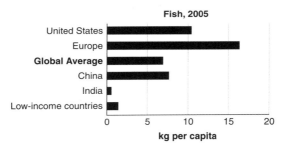

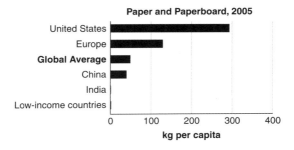

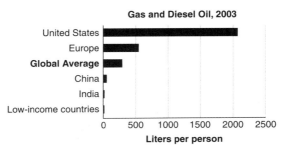

*Figure C.2*

kets, and migrants fleeing the world's most impoverished regions—the "bottom billion," as Oxford economist Paul Collier put it.[7] External threats to America's command of a disproportionate share of the world's resources add further urgency to the Republican agenda of a major political victory in 2012.

"2012 is the big one," Republican South Carolina senator Jim DeMint, a leader of the Tea Party movement, told conservatives gathered at a presidential forum on April 29, 2011. "Frankly, I think it could be our last chance."[8]

## Acknowledgments

This book could not have been written without help from a broad array of people and institutions. I am grateful to Columbia University and the Graduate School of Journalism for providing an ideal environment in which to think and write. Thanks to Nick Lemann and to the Columbia community, including Todd Gitlin and Laurel Cook, Sam Freedman, Michael Shapiro and Susan Chira, Victor and Annie Navasky, Sandro Stille, and David Klatell. Particular thanks to David and Katherine Moore.

I am grateful to my editor at Doubleday, Gerald Howard, and his uncanny skill. It has been my exceptional good fortune to work with him.

To my agent, the former CEO of W. W. Norton, Donald Lamm, my deepest thanks.

A special tribute to *The New Republic*—Frank Foer, Richard Just, and John Judis.

My thanks to those who opened doors for me along the way: Ben Bradlee, David Broder, Irving Howe, Arianna Huffington, Haynes Johnson, Seymour Martin Lipset, Robert Merry, John O'Sullivan, Charles Peters, Carla Anne Robbins, Andrew Rosenthal, Andre Schiffrin, and Robert Silvers.

I am fortunate to have had a home at the *Washington Post,* where I covered national politics for twenty-five years. My thanks to Dan Balz, Peter Behr, Ceci Connolly, E. J. Dionne, Juliet Eilperin, Mike Getler, Jim Grimaldi, Bill Hamilton, John Harris, Al Kamen, Kevin Klose, Ruth Marcus, Kevin Merida, Larry Meyer, Dana Milbank, Ellen Nakashima, Steve Pearlstein,

Hanna Rosin, Keith Richburg, Maralee Schwartz, Pete Silberman, Frank Swoboda, and Jim VandeHei.

I have benefitted from working with and reading the following journalists: Mike Barone, Jack Beatty, Chris Bowers, John Breshnahan, Ron Brownstein, Jon Chait, Richard Ben Cramer, Nina Easton, Howard Fineman, Jack Germond, Bob Healy, Jacob Heilbrunn, Jim Mann, Jane Mayer, Harold Meyerson, David Plotz, Dave Rogers, Jeff and Christine Rosen, Noam Scheiber, William F. Schmick III, Sam Stein, Scott Stossel, Mike Tomasky, Roger Wilkins, Frank Wilkinson, and Jules Witcover.

Among those whose professional and personal friendship I treasure are Sidney Blumenthal, Eric Alterman, Pietro Nivola, Guy Gugliotta, Peter Reuter, and Mark Kleiman. In addition, I have been blessed with a circle of stimulating friends: Jonathan Kempner and Lise Van Susteren, Jim Jaffe and Leslie Sewell, Abigail Trafford, Kay Moseley, Becky Lescaze and Mark Borthwick, Bill Fritzmeier, Geoff Lamb and Caroline Atkinson, Jeffrey Owen Jones, Judith Milliken, Mark London, Robert Dowling, Trip and Heddy Reid, and Wendy Lynn Gray.

Thanks to David Brady at Stanford, to the Hoover Institution, and to the Woodrow Wilson Center for Scholars. Bob Barnett at Williams and Connolly has provided me with invaluable help.

To Joe Foote and Eric Pfeufer, my enduring appreciation, and to my cousins David and Nicholas Edsall.

I am grateful for guidance from Harold Ickes, Bill Galston, Bill McInturff, Fred Wertheimer, Andy Kohut, Alex Castellanos, Steve Rosenthal, Stan Greenberg, Alex Gage, Geoff Garin, Mark Gersh, Bob Greenstein, Alice Rivlin, Isabel Sawhill, Ralph Reed, Celinda Lake, Rob Shapiro, Simon Rosenberg, Steve Murphy, Tom King, Wendell Primus, John Lawrence, Karl Rove, Rahm Emmanuel, Paul Begala, Bill Carrick, Larry O'Brien, Jim Wetzler, Richard Kogan, Whit Ayres, Tom Doherty, Bob Shrum, Craig Shirley, Bob Bauer, Andy Stern, Heather and Paul Booth, Howard Berman, Ron Kaufman, Jim Manley, Mike Meehan, Will Feltus, Tony Fabrizio, Tom Matzzie, Donna Brazile, David Lyles, Jim Duffy, Howard Wolfson, Kent Cooper, Jonathan Prince, Bob Borosage, Mike Whouley, Tamara Luzzatto, Steve Elmendorf, Jim Jordan, Charles Baker III, Mark McKinnon, Marcia Hale, Bob McIntyre, Hal Malchow, Doug Sosnik, Ben Ginsberg, Joel Benenson, David Axelrod, Joe Trippi, Don Fowler, William Drayton, and Howard Gleckman.

I want to recognize those who have shared their insights and data with me: Hank Aaron, Alan Abramowitz, Elijah Anderson, Steve Ansolabehere, Larry Bartels, Peter Berkowitz, Richard Betts, Earl Black, Merle Black, Robert Blendon, Philip Bobbitt, Gary Burtless, Bruce Cain, Ted Carmines, Bob Erickson, Mo Fiorina, Robert H. Frank, Charles Franklin, William Frey, Benjamin Friedman, Jamie Galbraith, Curtis Gans, Andy Gelman, John Green, James Guth, Jonathan Haidt, Fredrick Harris, Doug Hibbs, Ray Horton, Ravi Iyer, Gary Jacobson, Don Kinder, Richard Kogan, Sandy Maisel, Michael Malbin, Tom Mann, David Mayhew, Nolan McCarty, Sara McLanahan, Massimo Morelli, Norm Ornstein, Carl Pinkele, Sam Popkin, Robert Putnam, Larry Sabato, Byron Schafer, David O. Sears, Robert Y. Shapiro, Derek Shearer, Theda Skocpol, Paul Sniderman, Gene Steurle, Charles Stewart III, James Stimson, Ruy Teixeira, Michael Tesler, Philip Tetlock, Michael Ting, Dorian Warren, Greg Wawro, Drew Westen, and John White.

Thanks to Hannah Wood of Doubleday, a miracle worker. Thanks, as well, to Melissa Chincillo at the literary agency Fletcher & Company.

I am in debt to Sally Regal and to Judy Ng for their loyal assistance.

Finally, I want to honor the memory of my uncle John Tileston Edsall, and my father-in-law, Karl W. Deutsch.

# Notes

PROLOGUE: THE NOOSE

1. Bill Heniff Jr., "The Sequestration Process," Congressional Research Service, available at http://democrats.rules.house.gov/archives/RS20007.pdf.

2. Richard Kogan, "How the Potential Across-the-Board Cuts in the Debt Limit Deal Would Occur," Center on Budget and Policy Priorities, August 8, 2011, available at http://www.cbpp.org/cms/index.cfm?fa=view&id=3557.

3. E-mail from Henry Aaron to author, August 28, 2011.

4. E-mail from John Feehery to author, August 28, 2011.

5. E-mail from Gregory Wawro to author, August 31, 2011.

6. Susan Hockfield, "Manufacturing a Recovery," New York Times, August 29, 2011, available at http://www.nytimes.com/2011/08/30/opinion/manufacturing-a-recovery.html.

7. Frank Newport, "Americans Blame Wasteful Government Spending for Deficit; Prefer Cutting Spending over Raising Taxes as Way for Congress to Reduce Deficit," Gallup, April 29, 2011, available at http://www.gallup.com/poll/147338/Americans-Blame-Wasteful-Government-Spending-Deficit.aspx.

8. CNN, "New CNN Poll: Majority Want Tax increase for Wealthy and Deep Spending Cuts," by CNN Political Unit, August 10, 2011, available at http://politicalticker.blogs.cnn.com/2011/08/10/new-cnn-poll-majority-want-tax-increase-for-wealthy-and-deep-spending-cuts/.

9. Kate Zernike and Megan Thee-Brenan, "Poll Finds Tea Party Backers Wealthier and More Educated," New York Times, April 14, 2010, available at http://www.nytimes.com/2010/04/15/us/politics/15poll.html and http://documents.nytimes.com/new-york-timescbs-news-poll-national-survey-of-tea-party-supporters?ref=politics.

10. Center on Budget and Policy Priorities, "Policy Basics: Introduction to the Federal Budget Process," January 3, 2011, available at http://www.cbpp.org/cms/?fa=view&id=155.

11. Kenneth Rogoff, "The Second Great Contraction," August 2, 2011, available at http://www.project-syndicate.org/commentary/rogoff83/English.

12. Jon Carson, "Myths and Facts About the Debt-Ceiling Compromise," The White

House Blog, August 4, 2011, available at http://www.whitehouse.gov/blog/2011/08/04/myths-and-facts-about-debt-ceiling-compromise.

13. "S&P Downgrades U.S. Debt Rating," *Wall Street Journal*, August 5, 2011, available at http://blogs.wsj.com/marketbeat/2011/08/05/sp-downgrades-u-s-debt-rating-press-release/?mod=WSJ_markets_article_liveupdate.

14. Obama, Barack, "Remarks at the Opening of the White House Fiscal Responsibility Summit." Transcript, *Federal News Service*, February 23, 2009, available at http://www.nytimes.com/2009/02/23/us/politics/23text-summit.html?pagewanted=print.

15. Sue Kirchhoff, "How Will the $787 Billion Stimulus Package Affect You?," *USA Today*, February 17, 2009, available at http://www.usatoday.com/money/economy/2009–02–12-stimulus-package-effects_N.htm.

16. Douglas W. Elmendorf, "Analysis of the Major Health Care Legislation Enacted in March 2010." Statement before the Subcommittee on Health Committee on Energy and Commerce, U.S. House of Representatives, March 30, 2011, available at http://www.cbo.gov/ftpdocs/121xx/doc12119/03–30-HealthCareLegislation.pdf.

17. Jake Tapper, "How Much Did the Auto Bailout Cost Taxpayers?" ABC News, June 3, 2011, available at http://blogs.abcnews.com/politicalpunch/2011/06/how-much-did-the-auto-bailout-cost-taxpayers-.html.

18. Congressional Budget Office, "The Budget and Economic Outlook: Fiscal Years 2010 to 2020," January 2010, available at http://www.cbo.gov/ftpdocs/108xx/doc10871/frontmatter.shtml. See Chapter Three, "The Spending Outlook."

19. Barack Obama interview by Steve Kroft, "Transcript: President Barack Obama, Part 1," *60 Minutes*, CBS, November 4, 2010, available at http://www.cbsnews.com/stories/2010/11/07/60minutes/main7032276.shtml.

20. "Remarks by President Barack Obama; Secretary of Education Arne Duncan; and Jacob Lew, Director, Office of Management and Budget," transcript, Federal News Service, February 14, 2011, available at http://m.whitehouse.gov/the-press-office/2011/02/14/remarks-president-unveiling-budget-baltimore-maryland.

21. Sahadi, Jeanne, "America's Debt Crisis: Painful Cuts in $3.7 Trillion Budget," CNN, February 14, 2011, available at http://money.cnn.com/2011/02/14/news/economy/obama_budget/index.htm.

22. Ibid.

23. "Rep. Paul D. Ryan Holds a Hearing on the President's Fiscal Year 2012 Budget Proposal." Transcript, CQ Transcriptions, LLC, Financial Markets Regulatory Wire, February 15, 2011.

24. Congressional Budget Office, "Preliminary Analysis of the President's Budget for 2012," March 2011, available at http://www.cbo.gov/doc.cfm?index=12103.

25. Congressional Budget Office, "Economic Impacts of Waiting to Resolve the Long-Term Budget Imbalance," December 2010, available at http://www.cbo.gov/ftpdocs/119xx/doc11998/12–10-CostWaitingBrief.pdf.

26. CBS News, "Boehner: I Got 98 Percent of What I Wanted," August 1, 2011, available at http://www.cbsnews.com/stories/2011/08/01/eveningnews/main20086598.shtml.

27. The Conference Board, "The Conference Board Consumer Confidence Index® Declines," August 20, 2011, available at http://www.conference-board.org/data/consumerconfidence.cfm.

28. Bill McInturff, "Consequences of the Debt Ceiling Negotiations," Public Opinion Strategies, August 31, 2011, http://pos.org/2011/08/mcinturff-consequences-of-the-debt-ceiling-negotiations.

29. John Gray, review of "That Used to Be Us," *Financial Times*, September 2, 2011, http://www.ft.com/intl/cms/s/2/059dda68-d30f-11e0–9aae-00144feab49a .html#axzz1WlT5qh35.

30. Timothy Snyder, *Bloodlands: Europe Between Hitler and Stalin* (New York: Basic Books, 2010), passim; Anne Applebaum, "The Worst of the Madness," *New York Review of Books*, November 11, 2010, http://www.nybooks.com/articles/archives/2010/ nov/11/worst-madness/?pagination=false.

31. World War II, http://www.u-s-history.com/pages/h1661.html.

32. "Source List and Detailed Death Tolls," Second World War (1939–45), http:// necrometrics.com/20c5m.htm#Second; "World War 2 Death Count," http://www .hitler.org/ww2-deaths.html; "Second World War," http://secondworldwar.co.uk/ index.php/fatalities; "World War II Casualties," http://en.wikipedia.org/wiki/ World_War_II_casualties.

## CHAPTER ONE: AUSTERITY

1. Bureau of Labor Statistics, "Employment Situation Summary," Washington, D.C., U.S. Department of Labor, August 5, 2011, accessed August 23, 2011, available at http://www.bls.gov/news.release/empsit.nr0.htm.

2. Phil Izzo, "Nearly 1 in 3 Unemployed Out of Work More Than a Year," *Wall Street Journal*, June 3, 2011, http://blogs.wsj.com/economics/2011/06/03/nearly-1-in-3 -unemployed-out-of-work-more-than-a-year/.

3. Bureau of Labor Statistics, "Job Openings and Labor Turnover Survey Highlights—June 2011," http://www.bls.gov/web/jolts/jlt_labstatgraphs.pdf.

4. U.S. Census Bureau, "Median and Average Sales Prices of New Homes Sold in United States," Washington, D.C.: U.S. Department of Commerce, accessed March 21, 2011, available at http://www.census.gov/const/uspricemon.pdf.

5. CoreLogic, "U.S. Housing and Mortgage Trends," July, 2011, http://www.corelogic .com/about-us/researchtrends/asset_upload_file530_8290.pdf.

6. E. S. Browning, "Retiring Boomers Find 401(k) Plans Fall Short," *Wall Street Journal*, February 19, 2011, available at http://online.wsj.com/article/SB10001424052748703959 604576152792748707356.html.

7. Steven Greenhouse, "Making the Most out of Less," *New York Times*, March 2, 2011, available at http://www.nytimes.com/2011/03/03/business/RETIREmentspecial/ 03SOCIAL.html?ref=pensionsandRETIREmentplans&pagewanted=all.

8. McKinsey & Company, Financial Services Practice, *Restoring Americans' Retire- ment Security: A Shared Responsibility*, 2009, available at http://www.mckinsey.com/ clientservice/Financial_Services/Knowledge_Highlights/Recent_Reports/~/media/ Reports/Financial_Services/RETIREment_Security.ashx.

9. Carole Fleck, "Boomers Report No Savings at All; with Fewer Pensions and More Debt, They Face Retirement Challenges Their Parents Didn't," *AARP Bulletin*, February 3, 2011, available at http://www.aarp.org/work/retirement-planning/ info-02–2011/many_boomers_report_no_savings_at_all.html.    ·

10. Gary Burtless and Joseph F. Quinn, "Retirement Trends and Policies to Encour- age Work Among Older Americans," presented at the Annual Conference of the National Academy of Social Insurance, Washington, D.C., January 26–27, 2000, available at http://fmwww.bc.edu/ec-p/wp436.pdf.

11. U.S. Census Bureau, "Aging Boomers Will Increase Dependency Ratio, Census Bureau Projects Older American Population to Become More Diverse," Washington,

D.C.: U.S. Department of Commerce, accessed May 20, 2010, available at http://www.census.gov/newsroom/releases/archives/aging_population/cb10–72.html.

12. Department of Health and Human Services, Administration for Children and Families, "TANF: Total Number of Recipients Fiscal and Calendar Year 2011," May 26, 2011, available at http://www.acf.hhs.gov/programs/ofa/data-reports/caseload/2011/2011_recipient_tan.htm.

13. Food and Nutrition Service, "Supplemental Nutrition Assistance Program: Number of Persons Participating," Washington, D.C.: U.S. Department of Agriculture, accessed March 21, 2011, available at http://www.fns.usda.gov/pd/29snapcurrpp.htm.

14. Food and Nutrition Service, "Supplemental Nutrition Assistance Program: Average Monthly Benefit per Person," Washington, D.C.: U.S. Department of Agriculture, accessed March 21, 2011, available at http://www.fns.usda.gov/pd/18SNAPavg$PP.htm.

15. Matt Kennard, "Hardship on Rise for Middle Class," *Financial Times*, March 7, 2011, available at http://www.ft.com/cms/s/0/328aaab2–48ed–11e0-af8c-00144feab49a.html#axzz1G2xQqzjy.

16. Kaiser Commission on Medicaid and the Uninsured, John Holahan and Irene Headen, *Medicaid Coverage and Spending in Health Reform: National and State-by-State Results for Adults at or Below 133% FPL* (Washington, D.C.: Henry J. Kaiser Family Foundation, May 2010), available at http://www.kff.org/healthreform/upload/Medicaid-Coverage-and-Spending-in-Health-Reform-National-and-State-By-State-Results-for-Adults-at-or-Below-133-FPL.pdf.

17. Roberton Williams, "Who Pays No Income Tax?," *Tax Notes*, Tax Policy Center, June 29, 2009, available at http://www.taxpolicycenter.org/UploadedPDF/1001289_who_pays.pdf.

18. Memorandum, "U.S. Congress Joint Committee on Taxation, Information on Tax Liability for Tax Year 2009," accessed April 29, 2011, available at http://dontmesswithtaxes.typepad.com/JCT_Analysis_2009_Income_Tax.pdf.

19. Stephen Ohlemacher, "Nearly Half of U.S. Households Escape Fed Income Tax: Recession, New Tax Credits Have Nearly Half of US Households Paying No Federal Income Tax," Associated Press, April 7, 2010, available at http://finance.yahoo.com/news/Nearly-half-of-US-households-apf-1105567323.html.

20. Media Matters for America, "Hannity Falsely Claimed '50 Percent of American Households No Longer Pay Taxes,' " April 9, 2010, available at http://mediamatters.org/research/201004090085.

21. Dennis Cauchon, "Private Pay Shrinks to Historic Lows as Gov't Payouts Rise," *USA Today*, May 26, 2010, available at http://www.usatoday.com/money/economy/income/2010–05–24-income-shifts-from-private-sector_N.htm.

22. Congressional Budget Office, "Monthly Budget Review," Washington, D.C., November 2010, available at http://www.cbo.gov/doc.cfm?index=11873.

23. Douglas Elmendorf, "Federal Budget Deficit in First Four Months of Fiscal Year 2011 $424 Billion," Congressional Budget Office Director's Blog, February 7, 2011, accessed June 4, 2011, available at http://cboblog.cbo.gov/?p=1819.

24. Congressional Budget Office, "Federal Debt and Interest Costs," and "Debt Held by the Public Consists Mostly of Securities that the Treasury Issues to Raise Cash to Fund the Activities of the Government, Including the Securities Sold to Pay Off Maturing Securities," December 14, 2007, available at http://cboblog.cbo.gov/?p=1726.

25. Congressional Budget Office, "CBO's 2011 Long-Term Budget Outlook," July

2011, accessed August 23, 2011, available at http://www.cbo.gov/ftpdocs/122xx/
doc12212/06–21-Long-Term_Budget_Outlook.pdfhttp://www.cbo.gov/ftpdocs/120xx/
doc12039/01-26_FY2011Outlook.pdf.

26. Ibid.

27. Leslie Eaton, "Strapped City Cuts and Cuts and Cuts," *Wall Street Journal*, April 13,
2010, available at http://online.wsj.com/article/SB1000142405270230341160457516803
0083419748.html.; Michael Booth, "Colorado Springs Cuts into Services Considered
Basic by Many," *Denver Post*, January 31, 2010, available at http://www.denverpost
.com/news/ci_14303473; Michael Cooper and Mary Williams Walsh, "Alabama
Town's Failed Pension Is a Warning," *New York Times*, December 22, 2010, available
at http://www.nytimes.com/2010/12/23/business/23prichard.html.

28. Chris Christie, Address to the Legislature, February 22, 2011, available at http://www
.state.nj.us/governor/news/news/552011/approved/20110223c.html.

29. Lee Bergquist and Jason Stein, "Walker Looks at Showdown with State Employee
Unions: Governor-elect May Try to Gut Bargaining Power," *Milwaukee Journal
Sentinel*, December 7, 2010, available at http://www.jsonline.com/news/
statepolitics/111463779.

30. Neil King, Jr., and Scott Greenberg, "Poll Shows Budget-Cuts Dilemma," *Wall Street
Journal*, March 3, 2011, available at http://online.wsj.com/article/SB1000142405274870
4728004576176741120691736.html.

31. John R. Parkinson and Matthew Most, "House Cuts F-35 Engine from Spending Bill: Bipartisan Vote to Amend the GOP's Spending Package and Cut the F-35
Extra-Engine Program," ABC News, February 16, 2011, available at http://abcnews
.go.com/Politics/budget-cut-house-kills-35-joint-strike-fighter/story?id=12933195.

32. Jim DeMint, "DeMint Statement on Rising Unemployment," September 3, 2010,
available at http://demint.senate.gov/public/index.cfm?p=PressReleases&Content
Record_id=bf03390b-5570–421e-a6c9–84285f349bdd.

33. John Boehner, "Weekly Address Highlights: Rep. Jaime Herrera Beutler on Ending
Uncertainty & Helping Small Businesses Hire Again," March 19, 2011, available at
http://www.speaker.gov/blog/?p=3123.

34. "Statement on Using the Chained CPI for Social Security Cost of Living Adjustments: Switch to Chained CPI Would Lead to Benefit Cuts for Current and Future
Retirees," Center for Economic and Policy Research (CEPR), http://www.cepr.net/
index.php/press-releases/press-releases/statement-on-using-the-chained-cpi
-for-social-security-cost-of-living-adjustments.   .

35. U.S. Office of Personnel Management, "Federal Civilian Workforce Statistics, The
Fact Book," Washington, D.C., 2007, accessed March 21, 2011, available at http://www
.opm.gov/feddata/factbook/2007/2007FACTBOOK.pdf.

36. U.S. Equal Employment Opportunity Commission, "EEOC FY 2009 Annual Report
on the Federal Work Force, Part II, Profiles for Selected Federal Agencies," Washington, D.C., accessed March 21, 2011, available at http://www.eeoc.gov/federal/reports/
fsp2009/profiles.cfm.

37. U.S. Equal Employment Opportunity Commission, "Equal Employment Opportunity Commission, State and Local Government Information (EEO-4), 2007
Employment Summary by Job Category," Washington, D.C., accessed March 21, 2011,
available at http://www.eeoc.gov/eeoc/statistics/employment/jobpat-eeo4/2007/
us.html; U.S. Bureau of Labor Statistics, "Employment Status of the Civilian
Non-institutional Population by Age, Sex, and Race," Washington, D.C., accessed

June 3, 2011, available at ftp://ftp.bls.gov/pub/special.requests/lf/aat3.txt; U.S. Census Bureau, "Census 2000 Brief: The Black Population: 2000," Washington, D.C.: U.S. Department of Commerce, accessed June 12, 2011, available at http://www.census .gov/prod/2001pubs/c2kbr01–5.pdf.

38. David Rogers, "One-Two Punch Hits Food Stamps," Politico, August 6, 2010, available at http://www.politico.com/news/stories/0810/40739.html.

39. Ibid.

40. Jane E. Allen, "Two Dead Since Arizona Medicaid Program Slashed Transplant Coverage," ABC News Medical Unit, January 6, 2011, available at http://abcnews.go.com/ Health/News/arizona-transplant-deaths/story?id=12559369.

41. Tim Gaynor, "A Pacemaker and Defibrillator Fitted to Carpenter Douglas Gravagna's Failing Heart Makes Even Rising from the Couch of His Phoenix-Valley Home a Battle," Reuters, March 5, 2011, available at http://www.reuters.com/ article/2011/03/06/us-arizona-transplants-idUSTRE7242GN20110306.

42. Steve Nuñez, "Tucson Woman Denied Transplant Speaks Out," KGUN9 (ABC affiliate), March 5, 2011, available at http://www.kgun9.com/story/14194759/tucson -transplant-pa.

43. Michelle Ye Hee Lee, "Budget Stops Phoenix Man from Getting New Liver," *USA Today,* November 17, 2010, available at http://www.usatoday.com/news/nation/2010 –11–17-arizona-cuts-liver-transplant_N.htm.

44. Steven Greenhouse, "Labor's New Critics: Old Allies in Elected Office," *New York Times*, June 27, 2010, available at http://www.nytimes.com/2010/06/28/ business/28union.html?ref=us.

45. Mike Sunnucks, "Phoenix Extends Sales Tax to Food Items," *Phoenix Business Journal*, February 3, 2010, available at http://phoenix.bizjournals.com/phoenix/ stories/2010/02/01/daily25.html.

46. Craig Schneider and Tammy Joyner, "Housing Crisis Reaches Full Boil in East Point; 62 Injured," *Atlanta Journal-Constitution*, August 11, 2010, available at http://www .ajc.com/news/atlanta/housing-crisis-reaches-full-589653.html.

47. White House, "The Federal Budget, Fiscal Year 2012," accessed March 21, 2011, available at http://www.whitehouse.gov/omb/factsheet_department_housing/.

48. Brian Reed, "Months Later, Cuts to Newark Police Have Residents on Edge," WNYC News, May 10, 2011, http://www.wnyc.org/articles/wnyc-news/2011/may/10/months -later-cuts-newark-police-have-residents-edge/.

49. Christopher Beam, "Officers Down: What Happens to Camden, N.J., Now that It's Lost Half Its Police Force?," Slate, January 19, 2011, available at http://www.slate.com/ id/2281694/.

50. Mike Newall, James Osborne, and Darran Simon, "Camden Lays Off Nearly Half of Its Police Force," *Philadelphia Inquirer*, January 17, 2011, available at http://www .philly.com/philly/news/breaking/20110117_Camden_lays_off_nearly_half_of_its _police_force.html?page=1&c=y.

51. Barbara Boyer and Darran Simon, "Violent Crime Spikes 19% in Camden," *Philadelphia Inquirer*, May 2, 2011, available at http://www.philly.com/philly/news/ breaking/20110302_Crime_up_in_Camden_so_far_in_2011.html?c=r.

52. Frank Newport, "Americans on Healthcare Reform: Top 10 Takeaways," Gallup, July 31, 2009, available at http://www.gallup.com/poll/121997/Americans-Healthcare -Reform-Top-Takeaways.aspx.

53. White House, "Table 3.2—Outlays by Function and Subfunction: 1962–2015, Line

84, Historical Tables, Office of Management and Budget," accessed August 23, 2011, available at http://www.whitehouse.gov/sites/default/files/omb/budget/fy2012/assets/histo3z2.xls.

54. Ronald Brownstein, "The Grey and the Brown: The Generational Mismatch," *National Journal* (July 24, 2010), available at http://www.nationaljournal.com/njmagazine/cs_20100724_3946.php?mrefid=site_search.

55. David Leonhardt, "After the Great Recession," *New York Times*, April 28, 2009, available at http://www.nytimes.com/2009/05/03/magazine/03Obama-t.html?_r=3&partner=rss&emc=rss&pagewanted=all.

56. Pew Research Center for the People and the Press, "Distrust, Discontent, Anger and Partisan Rancor," April 18, 2010, available at http://people-press.org/report/?pageid=1700.

57. Democracy Corps, 1994–2010: Report on the Democracy Corps and Resurgent Republic Bipartisan Post Election Poll," November 9, 2010, available at http://www.democracycorps.com/wp-content/files/DCorps-Resurgent-Republic-Post-Election-Memo.FINAL_.pdf.

58. GOP, "A Pledge to America," accessed March 21, 2011, available at http://pledge.gop.gov/resources/library/documents/pledge/a-pledge-to-america.pdf.

59. http://www.nunneleeforcongress.com/Blog/BlogRead.aspx?guid=2bcd67cc-6d42-425f-9efc-f21d17b788a8.

60. Jeremy P. Jacobs, "Starting Lineup: 60 Plus Steps into the Election," *National Journal* (September 9, 2010), available at http://hotlineoncall.nationaljournal.com/archives/2010/09/starting_lineup_9.php.

61. The Lonely Conservative, "Video: Paul Ryan Explains Plan to Save Medicare," May 25, 2011, http://lonelyconservative.com/2011/05/video-paul-ryan-explains-plan-to-save-medicare/.

62. The Heritage Foundation, "Heritage Myth Buster: Ryan Budget saves Medicare for those 55 and over," May 26, 2011, http://www.hawaiifreepress.com/ArticlesMain/tabid/56/articleType/ArticleView/articleId/4356/Heritage-Myth-Buster-Ryan-Budget-saves-Medicare-for-those-55-and-over.aspx.

63. Peter Hart and Bill McInturff, "Survey: Study 10651," NBC News/Wall Street Journal, August 5–9, 2010, available at http://msnbcmedia.msn.com/i/MSNBC/Sections/NEWS/A_Politics/___Politics_Today_Stories_Teases/Aug%20NBC-WSJ%20Filled-in%20_for%208–11–10%20release_.pdf.

64. Strengthen Social Security, "Highlights of 2010 Election Voters' Opinions on Social Security Based on Lake Research Partners Survey," October 31–November 2, 2010, available at http://socialsecurity-works.org/wp-content/uploads/2010/11/SSSCHighlightsofElectionPollonSocialSecurity.pdf.

65. Pew Research Center, "A Balance Sheet at 30 Months: How the Great Recession Has Changed Life in America," June 30, 2010, available at http://pewsocialtrends.org/assets/pdf/759-recession.pdf.

66. Rakesh Kochhar, Richard Fry, and Paul Taylor, "Wealth Gaps Rise to Record Highs Between Whites, Blacks, Hispanics Twenty-to-One," Pew Research Center, July 26, 2011, available at http://pewsocialtrends.org/2011/07/26/wealth-gaps-rise-to-record-highs-between-whites-blacks-hispanics/.

67. Jack Farchy and Javier Blas, "IMF Warns Food Prices to Stay High," *Financial Times*, March 3, 2011, available at http://www.ft.com/cms/s/0/4c46da8c-45ca-11e0-acd8-00144feab49a.html#ixzz1FrERpsJ3.

68. Ed Crooks, "A Guide for Business in Turbulent Times," *Financial Times*, February 2, 2011, available at http://www.ft.com/cms/s/0/620cdf32-2f19-11e0-88ec-00144feabdc0 .html#axzz1FrDvWbKZ.

CHAPTER TWO: THE MORAL UNDERPINNINGS OF PARTISAN CONFLICT, PART I

1. "Election 2010 House Exit Polls," *New York Times*, accessed March 21, 2011, available at http://elections.nytimes.com/2010/results/house/exit-polls.

2. Pew Research Center, "GOP Makes Big Gains Among White Voters Especially Among the Young and Poor," July 22, 2011, available at http://people-press .org/2011/07/22/gop-makes-big-gains-among-white-voters/.

3. Alan Abramowitz, "The Incredible Shrinking Republican Base," *Rasmussen Reports*, May 2, 2008, available at http://www.rasmussenreports.com/public_content/ political_commentary/commentary_by_alan_i_abramowitz/the_incredible _shrinking_republican_base.

4. Alan Abramowitz, "Diverging Coalitions: The Transformation of the American Elec- torate," University of Virginia Center for Politics, April 9, 2009, available at http:// www.centerforpolitics.org/crystalball/articles/aia2009040901/.

5. John B. Judis and Ruy Teixeira, *The Emerging Democratic Majority* (New York: Scrib- ner, 2002); John B. Judis and Ruy Teixeira, "Back to the Future: The Re-emergence of the Emerging Democratic Majority," *American Prospect* (June 19, 2007).

6. Alan Abramowitz, "Diverging Coalitions: The Transformation of the American Elec- torate," University of Virginia Center for Politics, April 9, 2009, accessed June 4, 2011, available at http://www.centerforpolitics.org/crystalball/articles/aia2009040901/.

7. Thomas B. Edsall and James V. Grimaldi, "On Nov. 2, GOP Got More Bang for Its Billion, Analysis Shows," *Washington Post*, December 30, 2004, available at http:// www.washingtonpost.com/ac2/wp-dyn/A35062-2004Dec29?language=printer.

8. Jim Rutenberg and Jeff Zeleny, "Democrats Outrun by a 2-Year G.O.P. Comeback Plan," *New York Times*, November 3, 2010, available at http://www.nytimes .com/2010/11/04/us/politics/04campaign.html.

9. Faiz Shakir, "Mitch McConnell: I Want to Be Senate Majority Leader in Order to Make Obama a One-Term President," October 25, 2010, available at http:// thinkprogress.org/politics/2010/10/25/126242/mcconnell-obama-one-term/.

10. Robert Pear, "G.O.P. to Fight Health Law with Purse Strings," *New York Times*, November 6, 2010, available at http://www.nytimes.com/2010/11/07/health/ policy/07health.html?_r=1&hp.

11. Women's Voices. Women's Vote, "Understanding the 2009 Elections: Implications for 2010," November 2009, available at http://wvwv.org/assets/2009/11/6/nj-va-post -election-presentation.pdf.

12. Greenberg Quinlan Rosner Research, "Agenda and Advocacy Survey: Keeping Obama Surge Voters Engaged," February 11, 2009, available at http://www.gqrr.com/ articles/2316/5129_wvwv%20_Rising%20American%20Electorate%20agenda %20Survey_%20m1.%20doc.pdf.

13. Stan Greenberg, e-mail message to author, September 2010.

14. Lydia Saad, "More Americans Say U.S. a Nation of Haves and Have-Nots," Gallup, July 11, 2008, available at http://www.gallup.com/poll/108769/More-Americans-Say -US-Nation-Haves-HaveNots.aspx.

15. Frank Newport, "Socialism Viewed Positively by 36% of Americans," Gallup, Febru-

ary 4, 2010, available at http://www.gallup.com/poll/125645/Socialism-Viewed
-Positively-Americans.aspx.

16. Lydia Saad, "Likely Voters Demographically Typical, but Skew Conservative," Gallup,
October 8, 2010, available at http://www.gallup.com/poll/143468/Likely-Voters
-Demographically-Typical-Skew-Conservative.aspx.

17. Ibid.

18. Ibid.

19. Linda J. Skitka and Philip E. Tetlock, "Providing Public Assistance: Cognitive
and Motivational Processes Underlying Liberal and Conservative Policy
Preferences," *Journal of Personality and Social Psychology* 65 (1993): 1205–23,
available at http://faculty.haas.berkeley.edu/tetlock/Vita/Philip%20Tetlock/
Phil%20Tetlock/1992–1993/1993%20Providing%20Public%20Assistance. . . . pdf.

20. Pew Research Center for the People and the Press, "Independents Oppose Party in
Power . . . Again: More Conservative, More Critical of National Conditions," September 23, 2010, available at http://people-press.org/report/658/.

21. Ibid.

22. Ibid.

23. Ibid.

24. Ibid.

25. YourMorals.org, accessed March 21, 2011, available at http://www.yourmorals.org/
aboutus.php.

26. Thomas B. Edsall, *Building Red America* (New York: Basic Books, 2006). "The
Democratic Party, conversely, is the party of the so-called 'subdominant' and of
those who identify with the subdominant, including those upper-income voters who
have taken the side of the insurgents in the sexual, women's rights, and civil rights
revolutions. Roughly two-thirds of the Democratic Party's adherents are Americans
who struggle to survive in an increasingly brutal competitive environment. The
party is also the representative of organized labor and of the leadership of old-line
religious denominations—institutions in decline," p.1.

27. Polipsych.com, accessed March 21, 2011, available at http://www.polipsych.com/.

28. Polipsych.com, "Differences Between White Male Liberals and White Male Conservatives," October 27, 2010, available at http://www.polipsych.com/2010/10/27/
differences-between-white-male-liberals-and-white-male-conservatives/. The site
has a link to the same data for white female liberals and conservatives.

29. Ibid. Data on the www.Polipsych.com Web site confirms that divisions between
conservative and liberal white women are very similar to those between conservative
and liberal white men.

30. Polipsych.com, "Differences Between White Male Liberals and White Male Conservatives," October 27, 2010, available at http://www.polipsych.com/2010/10/27/
differences-between-white-male-liberals-and-white-male-conservatives/. The site
has a link to the same data for white female liberals and conservatives.

31. Ibid.

32. Thomas B. Edsall, "Women's Political Muscle Shapes 2000 Race," *Washington Post*,
March 11, 1999.

33. James C. Dobson, *Dare to Discipline* (Wheaton, Ill.: Tyndale House, 1977). "[P]ain is
a marvelous purifier. . . . It is not necessary to beat the child into submission; a little
bit of pain goes a long way for a young child. However, the spanking should be of
sufficient magnitude to cause the child to cry genuinely," pp. 16 and 23.

34. George Lakoff, *Moral Politics* (Chicago: University of Chicago Press, 2002). "The conservative/liberal division is ultimately a division between strictness and nurturance as ideals at all levels—from the family to morality to religion and, ultimately, to politics. It is a division at the center of our democracy and our public lives, and yet there is no overt discussion of it in public discourse. The reason is that the details are largely unconscious, part of what cognitive scientists call the Cognitive Unconscious—a deep level of mind that we have no direct access to. Yet it is vitally important that we do so if Americans are to understand, and come to grips with, the deepest fundamental division in our country, one that transcends and lies behind all the individual issues: the role of government, social programs, taxation, education, the environment, energy, gun control, abortion, the death penalty, and so on. These are ultimately not different issues, but manifestations of a single issue: strictness versus nurturance," p. x.

35. Nicholas Winter, "Masculine Republicans and Feminine Democrats: Gender and Americans' Explicit and Implicit Images of the Political Parties." Paper presented at the American Political Science Association Toronto Meeting, 2009, available at http://papers.ssrn.com/sol3/papers.cfm?abstract_id=1451343.

36. Ibid.

37. Ibid.

38. Ibid.

39. Jim Sidanius and Felicia Pratto, *Social Dominance: An Intergroup Theory of Social Hierarchy and Oppression* (New York: Cambridge University Press, 2001), passim, and Markus Kemmelmeier, "Social Dominance Theory," in Ritzer, George (ed.), *Blackwell Encyclopedia of Sociology* (Blackwell Publishing, 2007), Blackwell Reference Online, September 5, 2011, http://www.sociologyencyclopedia.com/public/tocnode?id=g9781405124331_yr2010_chunk_g978140512433125_ss1–321.

40. James Sidanius, e-mail message to author, December 19, 2010.

41. Bear ad, accessed March 21, 2011, available at http://www.youtube.com/watch?v=NpwdcmjBgNA.

42. Fred Barnes, "Kerry Nation?," *Weekly Standard* (February 23, 2004), accessed June 6, 2011, available at http://www.weeklystandard.com/Content/Public/Articles/000/000/003/740mrvbh.asp.

43. Wolves ad, accessed March 21, 2011, available at http://www.youtube.com/watch?v=MU4t9O_yFsY.

44. Ibid.

CHAPTER THREE: THE MORAL UNDERPINNINGS OF PARTISAN CONFLICT, PART II

1. Cliff Montgomery, "Yankee Republicans May Be on Last Legs," *American Spark*, available at http://www.americanspark.com/bytes_11–15–06.html.

2. U.S. House of Representatives, "Clerk of the House, Final Vote Results for Roll Call 71," accessed June 12, 2011, available at http://clerk.house.gov/evs/2011/roll071.xml.

3. Ibid.

4. Norman Ornstein, e-mail message to author, March 12, 2011.

5. Stephen Ansolabehere, e-mail message to author, March 12, 2011.

6. David Mayhew, e-mail message to author, March 12, 2011.

7. Robert Erikson, e-mail message to author, March 13, 2011.

8. Urban Institute and Brookings Institution, "Options to Limit the Extension of the

2001–2006 Tax Cuts, February 11, 2008, available at http://www.taxpolicycenter.org/numbers/displayatab.cfm?DocID=1782&topic2ID=40&topic3ID=58&DocTypeID=5.

9. "Rules for Smaller Government: The House GOP Is Making It Harder to Tax and Spend," *Wall Street Journal*, January 5, 2011, available at http://online.wsj.com/article/SB10001424052748704111504576060222252953518.html.

10. Jonathan Haidt, "What Makes People Vote Republican?," *Edge* (September 9, 2008), available at http://www.edge.org/3rd_culture/haidt08/haidt08_index.html.

11. Susan Page, "Poll: Dems, GOP Divided on How to Move Forward," *USA Today*, November 8, 2010, available at http://www.usatoday.com/news/politics/2010-11-08-post-election-poll_N.htm.

12. Jonathan Weisman and Danny Yadron, "Poll Supports Shift to Center," *Wall Street Journal*, December 14, 2010, available at http://online.wsj.com/article/SB10001424052748704828104576021900230935000.html?mod=WSJ_WSJ_US_News_5.

13. Lester Thurow, *The Zero-Sum Society: Distribution and the Possibilities for Economic Change* (New York: Basic Books, 1980).

14. Alan I. Abramowitz, *The Disappearing Center: Engaged Citizens, Polarization, and American Democracy* (New Haven: Yale University Press, 2010).

15. Dana R. Carney, John T. Jost, Samuel D. Gosling, and Jeff Potter, "The Secret Lives of Liberals and Conservatives: Personality Profiles, Interaction Styles, and the Things They Leave Behind," *Political Psychology* 29 (2008): 807–40, available at http://www.psych.nyu.edu/jost/Carney,%20Jost,%20&%20Gosling%20(2008)%20The%20secret%20olives%20of%20liberals%20.pdf.

16. Ibid.

17. Ibid.

18. Ibid.

19. Felicia Pratto, James Sidanius, and Shana Levin, "Social Dominance Theory and the Dynamics of Intergroup Relations: Taking Stock and Looking Forward," *European Review of Social Psychology* 17 (2006): 271–320. The appendix lists the questions used to determine SDO.

20. Ibid.

21. Felicia Pratto, James Sidanius, Lisa M. Stallworth, and Bertram F. Malle, "Social Dominance Orientation: A Personality Variable Predicting Social and Political Attitudes," *Journal of Personality and Social Psychology* 67 (1994): 741–63, available at http://dash.harvard.edu/bitstream/handle/1/3207711/Sidanius_SocialDominance Orientation.pdf?sequence=1.

22. Jesse Graham, Jonathan Haidt, and Brian A. Nosek, "Liberals and Conservatives Rely on Different Sets of Moral Foundations," American Psychological Association, *Journal of Personality and Social Psychology* 96 (2009): 1029–46, available at http://people.virginia.edu/~jdh6n/.

23. Jesse Graham, Jonathan Haidt, and Brian A. Nosek, "Liberals and Conservatives Rely on Different Sets of Moral Foundations," *Journal of Personality and Social Psychology* 96 (2009): 1029–46, available at http://www4.gsb.columbia.edu/rt/null?&exclusive=filemgr.download&file_id=7214828&rtcontentdisposition=filename%3DGraham_Jesse_paper.pdf.

24. Jonathan Haidt and Jesse Graham, "When Morality Opposes Justice: Conservatives Have Moral Intuitions that Liberals May Not Recognize," *Social Justice Research* (2007), available at http://papers.ssrn.com/sol3/papers.cfm?abstract_id=872251.

25. P. E. Tetlock and P. G. Mitchell, "Liberal and Conservative Approaches to Jus-

tice: Conflicting Psychological Portraits," in *Psychological Perspectives on Justice*, B. Mellers and J. Baron, eds. (Cambridge: Cambridge University Press, 1993), available at http://faculty.haas.berkeley.edu/tetlock/Vita/Philip%20Tetlock/Phil %20Tetlock/1992–1993/1993%20Liberal%20and%20Conservative%20Approaches %20to%20Justice.pdf.

26. Ibid.

27. American National Election Studies, "Military Spending, 7 Point Scale (1980–2008)," accessed July 12, 2011, available at http://www.electionstudies.org/nesguide/toptable/ tab4d_3b.htm.

28. Suzanne Goldenberg and Elana Schor, "Obama Supports Supreme Court Reversal of Gun Ban: Candidate's Stance at Odds with Former Position: Democrat Backs Death Penalty for Child Rapist," *GuardianUK*, June 27, 2008, available at http://www .guardian.co.uk/world/2008/jun/27/barackobama.usa.

29. Paul Kane, "Obama Supports FISA Legislation, Angering Left," *Washington Post*, June 20, 2008, available at http://voices.washingtonpost.com/44/2008/06/20/obama _supports_fisa_legislatio.html.

30. Barack Obama, "We Need Fathers to Step Up," *Parade* (June 21, 2009), available at http://www.parade.com/news/2009/06/barack-obama-we-we-need-fathers-to-step-up .html.

31. Mark Gersh, "Swing Voters," Democratic Leadership Council, accessed June 12, 2011, available at http://www.dlc.org/print.cfm?contentid=252802.

32. Michiko Kakutani, "The Republican Collapse May Not Be So Imminent," *New York Times*, September 12, 2006, available at http://www.nytimes.com/2006/09/12/ books/12kaku.html?pagewanted=all.

33. Alan I. Abramowitz and Bill Bishop, "Myth of the Middle," *Washington Post*, March 1, 2007, available at http://www.washingtonpost.com/wp-dyn/content/ article/2007/02/28/AR2007022801817.html.

34. Lester Thurow, *The Zero-Sum Society* (New York: Basic Books, 1980, 2001 rep. ed.), pp. 12–13.

35. Ibid., 10.

36. U.S. Census Bureau, "Statistical Abstract of the United States, 2011, Table No. HS-25: Money Income of Families—Median Income in Current and Constant (2001) Dollars by Race and Type of Family, 1947 to 2001," Washington, D.C.: U.S. Department of Commerce, accessed June 12, 2010, available at http://www.census.gov/statab/hist/ HS-25.pdf.

37. U.S. Bureau of Labor Statistics, "Productivity Change in the Nonfarm Business Sector, 1947–2010," Washington, D.C., accessed June 12, 2010, available at http://www.bls .gov/lpc/prodybar.htm.

38. U.S. Census Bureau, "Statistical Abstract of the United States, 2011, Table No. HS-31: Nonfarm Establishments—Employees, Hours, and Earnings by Industry, 1919 to 2002," Washington, D.C.: U.S. Department of Commerce, accessed June 12, 2010, available at http://www.census.gov/statab/hist/HS-31.pdf.

39. Federal Reserve Archival System for Economic Research, "The 1970s: Inflation, High Interest Rates, and New Competition," accessed June 12, 2010, available at fraser .stlouisfed.org/publications/erp/page/6688/ . . . /6688_ERP.pdf.

40. U.S. Census Bureau, "Statistical Abstract 1995, Table No. 761, Consumer Price Indexes (CPI-U), by Major Groups, 1960 to 1994," Washington, D.C.: U.S. Department of Commerce, accessed June 12, 2010, available at http://www.census.gov/ prod/1/gen/95statab/prices.pdf.

41. Silverstone Investment Group Inc., "Prime Rate from April 1974 to Present," accessed June 12, 2011, available at http://ssiginc.com/uploads/Prime_rate_from_April_1974 _to__Present.pdf.

42. U.S. Bureau of Labor Statistics, "Unemployment Rate 16 Years and Over," Washington, D.C.: U.S. Department of Commerce, accessed June 12, 2010, available at http:// data.bls.gov/pdq/SurveyOutputServlet.

43. U.S. Census Bureau, "Statistical Abstract of the United States 2011, Table No. HS-54, U.S. International Transactions by Type of Transaction, 1960 to 2001," accessed June 12, 2010, available at http://www.census.gov/statab/hist/HS-54.pdf.

44. Thomas and Mary Edsall, *Chain Reaction* (New York: Norton, 1992), ch. 9, "The Reagan Attack on Race Liberalism," pp. 172–97.

45. *Gramm-Latta* is shorthand for the Omnibus Budget Reconciliation Act of 1981, which included steep increases in military spending, steep cuts in nondefense expenditures, and a large tax cut.

46. Helen Dewar and Richard Lyons, "Reagan Triumphs in House Budget Vote," *Washington Post*, June 27, 1981.

47. Social Security Online, "Vote Tallies: 1996 Welfare Amendments," accessed June 12, 2011, available at http://www.ssa.gov/history/tally1996.html.

48. U.S. Department of Health and Human Services, "TANF: Total Number of Families: Fiscal and Calendar Year 2010," accessed June 12, 2011, available at http://www.acf .hhs.gov/programs/ofa/data-reports/caseload/2010/2010_family_tan.htm.

49. U.S. House of Representatives, House Appropriations Committee, "FY 2011 Continuing Resolution Reductions (in Millions of Dollars)," accessed June 12, 2011, available at http://appropriations.house.gov/_files/ProgramCutsFY2011Continuing Resolution.pdf.

50. U.S. House of Representatives, Clerk of the House, "Final Vote Results for Roll Call 179," March 15, 2011, available at http://clerk.house.gov/evs/2011/roll179.xml.

51. Thomas B. Edsall, *Building Red America* (New York: Basic Books, 2006), pp. 1–2.

52. Ronald Brownstein, *The Second Civil War* (New York: Penguin, 2007), p. 139.

53. Juli Weiner, "An Unabridged Guide to All of Newt Gingrich's Wives," *Vanity Fair*, August 10, 2010, available at http://www.vanityfair.com/online/daily/2010/08/an -unabridged-guide-to-all-of-newt-gingrichs-wives.html.

54. Howard Kurtz, "Report of Hyde Affair Stirs Anger," *Washington Post*, September 17, 1978, available at http://www.washingtonpost.com/wp-srv/politics/special/clinton/ stories/hyde091798.htm.

55. Dwight Garner, "The Hypocrite Broke Up My Family," Salon, September 18, 1998, available at http://www.salon.com/news/1998/09/cov_16newsb.html.

56. Congressional Research Service, accessed June 12, 2011, available at http://www.loc .gov/crsinfo/. "The Congressional Research Service (CRS) works exclusively for the United States Congress, providing policy and legal analysis to committees and Members of both the House and Senate, regardless of party affiliation. As a legislative branch agency within the Library of Congress, CRS . . . is well-known for analysis that is authoritative, confidential, objective and nonpartisan. Its highest priority is to ensure that Congress has 24/7 access to the nation's best thinking."

57. Amy Belasco, "The Cost of Iraq, Afghanistan, and Other Global War on Terror Operations Since 9/11," Congressional Research Service, September 2, 2010, available at http://www.fas.org/sgp/crs/natsec/RL33110.pdf.

58. Joseph E. Stiglitz and Linda J. Bilmes, *The Three Trillion Dollar War: The True Cost of the Iraq Conflict* (New York: Norton, 2008).

59.  DEALBOOK, "At Plants, G.M. Bankruptcy Feels Like a Funeral," *New York Times*, June 2, 2009, http://dealbook.nytimes.com/2009/06/02/for-some-gm-bankruptcy -has-the-feel-of-a-funeral/.

CHAPTER FOUR: THE ECONOMICS OF IMMIGRATION

1.   Tim Carpenter, "Dems Accuse O'Brien of Racism," *Topeka Capital-Journal*, February 14, 2011, available at http://cjonline.com/legislature/2011-02-14/dems-accuse-obrien -racism.

2.   Scott Rothschild, "Kansas Legislator Suggests Using Hunters in Helicopters to Con- trol Illegal Immigration, Likens Immigrants to Feral Hogs," *Lawrence Journal-World*, March 14, 2011, available at http://www2.ljworld.com/news/2011/mar/14/legislators -comment-illegal-immigration-criticized/.

3.   CBS News, "New Tancredo Spot Warns of Illegal Immigrants 'Raping Kids,' " December 4, 2007, available at http://www.cbsnews.com/8301-502163_162-3575110 -502163.html.

4.   Associated Press, "Dream Act Passes House, Likely Doomed in Senate," December 8, 2010, available at http://www.cbsnews.com/stories/2010/12/08/politics/main7132292 .shtml.

5.   David Kurtz, "Rock the Casbah," Talking Points Memo, March 8, 2008, available at http://www.talkingpointsmemo.com/archives/182343.php.

6.   Pro-Con.org, "Is the 2006 Kennedy-McCain Comprehensive Immigration Reform Act (CIRA) a Good Piece of Legislation?," accessed March 21, 2011, available at http:// immigration.procon.org/view.answers.php?questionID=000791.

7.   John Heilemann and Mark Halperin, *Game Change: Obama and the Clintons, McCain and Palin, and the Race of a Lifetime* (New York: HarperCollins, 2010), pp. 283–84, available at http://www.ontheissues.org/Archive/Game_Change _Immigration.htm.

8.   Associated Press, "McCain Adjusts Immigration Stance: GOP Hopeful Emphasizes Securing Borders First," November 3, 2007, available at http://www.msnbc.msn.com/ id/21614851/ns/politics-decision_08/.

9.   Randal C. Archibold, "McCain's Tough Stance on Arizona Immigration Bill," *New York Times*, April 20, 2010, available at http://thecaucus.blogs.nytimes .com/2010/04/20/mccains-tough-stance-on-arizona-immigration-bill/.

10.  Kasie Hunt, "John McCain Tacks Right on Immigration," Politico, April 19, 2010, available at http://www.politico.com/news/stories/0410/36022.html.

11.  U.S. Customs and Border Protection, "Total Illegal Alien Apprehensions by Fiscal Year (Oct. 1st Through Sept. 30th)," Washington, D.C.: U.S. Department of Home- land Security, accessed March 21, 2011, available at http://www.cbp.gov/linkhandler/ cgov/border_security/border_patrol/apps.ctt/apps.pdf.

12.  U.S. Immigration and Customs Enforcement, "ACTT Helps Secure Southwest Border," February 11, 2011, available at http://www.ice.gov/about/offices/leadership/corner/.

13.  Pew Hispanic Center, Rakesh Kochhar, C. Soledad Espinoza, and Rebecca Hinze-Pifer, "After the Great Recession: Foreign Born Gain Jobs; Native Born Lose Jobs," October 29, 2010, available at http://pewhispanic.org/reports/report .php?ReportID=129.

14.  Brookings Institution, Matthew Hall, Audrey Singer, Gordon F. De Jong, and Debo- rah Roempke Graefe, "The Geography of Immigrant Skills: Educational Profiles of Metropolitan Areas: Immigration, Jobs and the Economy, Demographics, Ethnicity,"

June 9, 2011, available at http://www.brookings.edu/papers/2011/06_immigrants _singer.aspx.

15. Nolan McCarty, Keith T. Poole, and Howard Rosenthal, *Polarized America: The Dance of Ideology and Unequal Riches* (Cambridge: MIT Press, 2006).

16. BusinessDictionary.com, "Gini Index Definition," accessed March 21, 2011, available at http://www.businessdictionary.com/definition/gini-index.html.

17. Nolan McCarty, Keith T. Poole, and Howard Rosenthal, *Polarized America: The Dance of Ideology and Unequal Riches* (Cambridge, MA: MIT Press, 2006). The charts are in *Polarized America*, but they are best viewed on a Web site maintained by one of the authors, Keith Poole, available at http://voteview.com/Inequality_and _Polarization_Overheads_2.pdf.

18. Ibid.

19. 89th Congress, 1965 Immigration and Nationality Act, H.R. 2580, October 3, 1965, available at http://library.uwb.edu/guides/USimmigration/1965_immigration_and _nationality_act.html.

   "The 1965 Hart-Celler Act abolished the national origins quota system that had structured American immigration policy since the 1920s, replacing it with a preference system that focused on immigrants' skills and family relationships with citizens or residents of the U.S. Numerical restrictions on visas were set at 170,000 per year, not including immediate relatives of U.S. citizens, nor 'special immigrants' (including those born in 'independent' nations in the Western hemisphere; former citizens; ministers; employees of the U.S. government abroad)."

20. Arizona Legislature, "Ballot Proposition # 204: Healthy Arizona," August 17, 2000, available at http://www.azleg.gov/jlbc/ballotprop204.pdf.

21. Diggers Realm, "Arizona Governor Janet Napolitano Faces Backlash for Vetoing Illegal Immigration Bills," June 3, 2005, available at http://www.diggersrealm.com/ mt/archives/001095.html.

22. Arizona Governor's Office, "Inaugural Address, Second Term, Governor Janet Napolitano," January 4, 2007, available at http://www.azgovernor.gov/dms/upload/ Inaugural07_PUBLIC%20VERSION.pdf.

23. Elliott D. Pollack & Company, "Employment Revisions Point to Record Year in 2006," March 2007, available at http://www.edpco.com/files/azbc_07-03.pdf.

24. University of Arizona, Economic and Business Research Center, Marshall J. Vest, "Recession Is Over: Let Recovery Begin!," March 1, 2010, available at http:// azeconomy.eller.arizona.edu/AZE10Q1/Recession_Is_Over.aspx.

25. Jane E. Allen, "Two Dead Since Arizona Medicaid Program Slashed Transplant Coverage; Hospital Confirms Former Patient Died While Awaiting Liver Transplant," ABC News Medical Unit, January 6, 2011, available at http:// abcnews.go.com/Health/News/arizona-transplant-deaths/story?id=12559369. This information was corroborated in a June 6, 2011, e-mail to the author from Rainer Gruessner, M.D., professor of surgery and immunology, chairman, Department of Surgery at the University of Arizona.

26. CNBC, "States with Highest Foreclosure Rates," accessed March 21, 2011, available at http://www.cnbc.com/id/29655038/States_with_the_Highest_Foreclosure_Rates ?slide=10.

27. Google, "Unemployment rate 1990–January 2011," accessed March 21, 2011, available at http://www.google.com/publicdata?ds=usunemployment&met=unemployment _rate&idim=state:ST040000&dl=en&hl=en&q=arizona+unemployment.

28. Mary Jo Pitzl, "Arizona Budget Passes; the Cuts Total $1.1 Billion," *Arizona Republic*,

March 12, 2010, available at http://www.azcentral.com/news/articles/2010/03/12/2010 0312budgetvote0312.html.

29. Janice K. Brewer, "The Executive Budget Summary, Fiscal Year 2011," Arizona Office of Strategic Planning and Budgeting, January 15, 2010, available at http://www.ospb .state.az.us/documents/2010/FY2011_BudgetSummaryFINAL.pdf.

30. U.S. Customs and Border Protection, "Total Illegal Alien Apprehensions by Fiscal Year (Oct. 1st Through Sept. 30th)," Washington, D.C.: U.S. Department of Homeland Security, accessed March 21, 2011, available at http://www.cbp.gov/linkhandler/ cgov/border_security/border_patrol/apps.ctt/apps.pdf.

31. Access Integrity Unit of the Arizona Department of Public Safety, "Crime in Arizona Reports: An Annual Report," accessed March 21, 2011, available at http://www .azdps.gov/about/reports/Crime_In_Arizona/.

32. Arizona State Legislature, Arizona State Senate, "Second Regular Session, 2010, Senate Bill 1070," accessed March 21, 2011, available at http://www.azleg.gov/ legtext/49leg/2r/bills/sb1070s.pdf.

33. Cannon and Gill, Inc., "Proposition 204—Healthy Arizona II, An Arizona Health Futures Report," prepared for St. Luke's Health Initiatives, accessed March 21, 2011, available at http://www.slhi.org/publications/studies_research/pdfs/Step_By_Step .pdf.

34. Henry J. Kaiser Family Foundation, "Arizona: People in Poverty," accessed March 21, 2011, available at http://www.statehealthfacts.org/profileind. jsp?sub=2&rgn=4&cat=1.

35. Mary K. Reinhart, "Arizona Medicaid Cuts OK, Feds Say; Ending Coverage for 250,000 Won't Threaten U.S. Funds," *Arizona Republic*, February 16, 2011, available at http://www.azcentral.com/arizonarepublic/news/articles/2011/02/16/20110216arizona -health-care-cuts.html#ixzz1EMoatJ3w.

36. Economic and Business Research Center, Eller College of Management, University of Arizona, "Current Indicators, Arizona," accessed March 21, 2011, available at http://ebr.eller.arizona.edu/DataEntry/CurrentIndicators.aspx?CurrID=9.

37. Ibid.

38. Ibid.

39. Haya El Nasser, "Hispanic Growth Outpaced Estimates," *USA Today*, March 3, 2011, available at http://www.usatoday.com/news/nation/census/2011–03–15-hispanics15 _ST_N.htm.

40. Tessa Muggeridge, "Experts Call Arizona's Census Results Lower than Expected," Cronkite News, March 10, 2011, available at http://cronkitenewsonline.com/2011/03/ experts-call-arizonas-census-results-lower-than-expected/.

41. Arizona State Legislature, Arizona State Senate, "Immigration Omnibus, Fiftieth Legislature, First Regular Session, 2011, SB 1611," accessed March 21, 2011, available at http://www.azleg.gov/legtext/50leg/1r/bills/sb1611p.pdf.

42. FOX News, "Arizona Senate Hailed for Halting Anti-immigrant Bills," March 18, 2011, available at http://latino.foxnews.com/latino/news/2011/03/18/arizona-senate -hailed-halting-anti-immigrant-bills/.

43. Greater Phoenix Chamber of Commerce, "CEOs on Immigration Letter," March 15, 2011, available at http://www.phoenixchamber.com/news/ceos-immigration-letter.

44. Bureau of Labor Statistics, "Economy at a Glance, Arizona," Washington, D.C.: U.S. Department of Labor, accessed March 21, 2011, available at http://www.bls.gov/eag/ eag.az.htm.

45. University of Arizona, Economic and Business Research Center, Eller College of

Management, "Arizona's Economic Outlook, Current Indicators," accessed March 21, 2011, available at http://ebr.eller.arizona.edu/indicators/.

46. Bureau of Economic Analysis, "Regional Economic Accounts, Personal Income," Washington, D.C.: U.S. Department of Commerce, accessed March 21, 2011, available at http://www.bea.gov/regional/sqpi/drill.cfm.

47. Gallup Poll, Frank Newport, "Americans Oppose Federal Suit Against Ariz. Immigration Law: Republicans Are Highly Opposed; a Majority of Democrats Are in Favor," July 9, 2010, available at http://www.gallup.com/poll/141209/Americans -Oppose-Federal-Suit-Against-Ariz-Immigration-Law.aspx.

48. Conservatives from Rush Limbaugh to FOX News were outraged by a September 2011 report that the federal government had paid $4.2 billion in earned income tax credits to illegal immigrants. Lisa Rein, "Undocumented Workers Got Billions from IRS in Tax Credits, Audit Finds," *Washington Post*, September 2, 2011, http://www .washingtonpost.com/blogs/federal-eye/post/undocumented-workers-got-billions -from-irs-in-tax-credits-audit-finds/2011/03/23/gIQAhtaKvJ_blog.html.

49. CNN Politics, CNN Wire Staff, "Take Back Our Country," March 27, 2011, available at http://articles.cnn.com/2010–03–27/politics/reid.tea.party_1_tea-party-express-reid -campaign-sarah-palin?_s=PM:POLITICS.

50. U.S. Census Bureau, Jennifer Cheeseman Day, "National Population Projections," Washington, D.C.: U.S. Department of Commerce, accessed March 21, 2011, available at http://www.census.gov/population/www/pop-profile/natproj.html.

51. University of Virginia Center for Politics, Alan I. Abramowitz, "Beyond 2010: Demographic Change and the Future of the Republican Party," March 11, 2010, available at http://www.centerforpolitics.org/crystalball/articles/aia2010031101/.

52. Ibid.

53. Stephen Castle, "Swedish Anti-Immigration Party Claims Seats," *New York Times*, September 19, 2010, available at http://www.nytimes.com/2010/09/20/world/ europe/20sweden.html.

54. Refugees United Australia, "Immigration Backlash Spreads in Europe," Reuters, accessed March 21, 2011, available at http://refuniteaustralia.wordpress.com/2010/ 09/19/immigration-backlash-spreads-in-europe/.

55. Number10.gov.uk, "PM's Speech at Munich Security Conference: Prime Minister David Cameron Has Delivered a Speech Setting Out His View on Radicalisation and Islamic Extremism," February 5, 2011, available at http://www.number10.gov .uk/news/speeches-and-transcripts/2011/02/pms-speech-at-munich-security -conference-60293.

56. Harris Interactiv, "Immigration Hostility Widespread in U.S. and 5 Largest European Countries: Many People in All Six Countries See Negative Impact on Economy, Jobs and Public Services," September 10, 2010, available at http://www.harrisinteractive .com/NewsRoom/HarrisPolls/FinancialTimesHarrisPolls/tabid/449/ctl/ReadCustom %20Default/mid/1512/ArticleId/561/Default.aspx.

57. John Price and Michael Sandelson, "Norwegians Claim Immigration Policy Failing," *Foreigner*, July 7, 2011, http://theforeigner.no/pages/news/norwegians-claim -immigration-policy-failing/.

58. Bloomberg, Thomas Penny, "U.S. White Population Will Be Minority by 2042, Government Says," August 14, 2008, available at http://www.bloomberg.com/apps/ news?pid ewsarchive&sid=afLRFXgzpFoY.

59. GOP, "GOP 2008 Platform," accessed March 21, 2011, available at http://www.gop .com/2008Platform/2008platform.pdf.

60. Steve Forbes, "Fact and Comment," *Forbes*, April 24, 2006, available at http://www
.forbes.com/forbes/2006/0424/023.html.
61. Ibid.
62. Richard Freeman, "The Global Expansion of Higher Education," National Bureau
of Economic Research, May 2009, available at http://www.nber.org/digest/oct09/
w14962.html.
63. Vivek Wadhwa, "Why Policy Makers Should Review the Facts Before Marching to
the Drumbeat of the Xenophobes," *Techcrunch*, May 29, 2010, available at http://
techcrunch.com/2010/05/29/why-policy-makers-should-review-the-facts/.

CHAPTER FIVE: RACE

1. T. Keung Hui, "Garner Draws Line on Students; Asks Assurance that Too Many in
New School Won't Be Poor," *Raleigh News & Observer*, April 9, 2008.
2. T. Keung Hui, "Whites No Longer a Majority," *Raleigh News & Observer*,
November 24, 2010, available at http://www.newsobserver.com/2010/11/24/
822737/whites-outnumbered-in-wake-schools.html#storylink=misearch.
3. Ibid.
4. Ibid.
5. U.S. Census Bureau, "2010 State and County QuickFacts: Wake County, North
Carolina," Washington, D.C.: U.S. Department of Commerce, accessed April 7, 2011,
available at http://quickfacts.census.gov/qfd/states/37/37183.html.
6. Wake County Board of Elections, Voter Registration Statistics, March 1, 2011, available at http://msweb03.co.wake.nc.us/bordelec/downloads/7stats/7statslist/Historical
PrecinctStats/20110301stats.pdf.
7. WRAL News, "Unemployment Rate Hits Record in Raleigh-Cary, Durham-Chapel
Hill," July 24, 2009, http://www.wral.com/business/story/5649405/.
8. Mike Baker, "Debate over School Busing in NC County Gets Uglier," Associated
Press, March 5, 2010, available at http://www.deseretnews.com/article/700014293/
Debate-over-school-busing-in-NC-county-gets-uglier.html.
9. T. Keung Hui, "Uncivil Tone in Wake School Debate," *Raleigh News & Observer*,
March 3, 2010, available at http://blogs.newsobserver.com/wakeed/uncivil-tone-in
-wake-school-debate#storylink=misearch#ixzz1HOUC1LJq.
10. Wake County, "Wake County Board of Commissioners, Regular Meeting (Minutes),"
December 6, 2010, available at http://wake.granicus.com/DocumentViewer
.php?file=wake_2d297a9d-97e0-4d06-b36b-383c09a0cc21.pdf.
11. Ibid.
12. Thomas Goldsmith, "Wake Schools Catch Bill Clinton's Critical Eye," *Raleigh News
& Observer*, February 24, 2011, available at http://www.newsobserver
.com/2011/02/24/1009894/wake-schools-catch-clintons-critical.html.
13. Arne Duncan, letter to the editor, "Maintaining Racial Diversity in Schools," *Washington Post*, January 13, 2011, available at http://www.washingtonpost.com/wp-dyn/
content/article/2011/01/13/AR2011011305529.html.
14. Katherine Kersten, "Busing Students for Integration Failed Elsewhere, but Eden
Prairie Wants to Try," *Minneapolis-St. Paul Star Tribune*, November 13, 2010, available
at http://www.startribune.com/opinion/commentary/107585253.html?elr=KArksc8P
:Pc:UockkD:aEyKUiD3aPc:_Yyc:aUoc7Ok:Pia_eyckciU.
15. Ibid.

16. Ibid.

17. Neil Riemann, "Socioeconomic Diversity and 'White Flight,'" Wake Reassignment: Notes on Proposed School Reassignment Plans in Wake County, North Carolina, November 20, 2010, accessed April 7, 2011, available at http://www.wakereassignment .info/home/tag/private-school.

18. Jason Langberg and Cary Brege, "The Racial Achievement Gap in the Wake County Public School System," Legal Aid of North Carolina, March 2010, available at http:// www.legalaidnc.org/public/Learn/Statewide_Projects/ACS/ACS_Publications/ IssueBrief_Mar-10_WCPSSAchievementGap.pdf.

19. Ibid.

20. Ibid.

21. Southern Coalition for Social Justice, "Title VI Complaint Wake County School Board," September 24, 2010, available at http://www.southerncoalition.org/ documents/education/Title-VI-Complaint-WCSB-9–24–2010-FINAL.pdf.

22. November 24, 2010, comments on T. Keung Hui, "Whites No Longer a Majority," *Raleigh News & Observer*, November 24, 2010, available at http://www.newsobserver .com/2010/11/24/822737/whites-outnumbered-in-wake-schools.html#story_tab _comments#disqus_thread.

23. Ibid.

24. Ibid.

25. Public Religion Research Center, "Old Alignments, Emerging Fault Lines: Religion in the 2010 Election and Beyond: Findings from the 2010 Post-election American Values Survey," accessed April 7, 2011, available at http://www.publicreligion.org/ research/published/?id=428.

26. NAACP, "NAACP Delegates Unanimously Pass Tea Party Amendment," July 13, 2010, available at http://www.naacp.org/press/entry/naacp-delegates-unanimously-pass -tea-party-amendment/.

27. St. Louis Tea Party Coalition, Bill Hennessey, "St. Louis Tea Party Condemns NAACP Slur," July 13, 2010, available at http://stlouisteaparty.com/2010/07/13/ st-louis-tea-party-condemns-naacp-slur/.

28. Manny Fernandez and Emily Ramshaw, "As a States' Rights Stalwart, Perry Draws Doubts," *New York Times*, August 28, 2011, http://www.nytimes.com/2011/08/29/us/ politics/29perry.html.

29. Thomas B. Edsall, *Building Red America: The New Conservative Coalition and the Drive for Permanent Power* (New York: Basic Books, 2006), pp. 8–10. "Coded Rhetoric: A candidate affirming his or her support for 'family values' or for the physical display of religious symbols such as the Ten Commandments in public areas, using the noun *Democrat* as an adjective (as in 'Democrat senator praises bin Laden'), or simply describing himself or herself as a conservative is indicating, in the symbolic language of politics, opposition to taxes, to 'big government,' to gay marriage, to affirmative action, and to key court-ordered remedies for racial segregation, while supporting deregulation, religious expression in the public sphere—including in the schools—the overturn of *Roe v. Wade*, lower taxes, and abstinence education. . . ."

30. Tea Party Patriots, "Tea Party Patriots Mission Statement and Core Values," http:// www.teapartypatriots.org/mission.aspx.

31. Devin Burghart and Leonard Zeskind, "Tea Party Nationalism: A Critical Examination of the Tea Party Movement and the Size, Scope, and Focus of Its National

Factions," Institute for Research & Education on Human Rights, Fall 2010, available at http://www.teapartynationalism.com/pdf/TeaPartyNationalism.pdf.

32. Michael Tesler and David Sears, "President Obama and the Growing Polarization of Partisan Attachments by Racial Attitudes and Race." Paper presented at the annual meeting of the American Political Science Association, Washington, D.C., September 2010, available at http://mst.michaeltesler.com/uploads/sample_2.pdf.

33. Joshua L. Rabinowitz, David O. Sears, James Sidanius, and Jon A. Krosnick, "Why Do White Americans Oppose Race-Targeted Policies? Clarifying the Impact of Symbolic Racism," *Political Psychology* 30 (2009): 805, available at http://communication .stanford.edu/faculty/krosnick/Why%20do%20white%20Americans%20oppose %20racial%20policies.pdf.

34. Tea Party Patriots, "Mission Statement and Core Values," accessed April 7, 2011, available at http://www.teapartypatriots.org/Mission.aspx.

35. John Katsillis and J. Michael Armer, "Education and Mobility," in *Encyclopedia of Sociology*, Edgar F. Borgatta and Rhonda J. V. Montgomery, eds. (New York: Macmillan, 2000), available at http://edu.learnsoc.org/Chapters/20%20education/ 4%20education%20and%20mobility.htm: "*Education and Mobility*" regarding "ascriptive": "The class or status positions that individuals occupy in society are usually attributed to both ascriptive and achievement processes. These are generally viewed as opposite or contradictory processes involving either ascribed characteristics based on biological factors and family of origin or achieved characteristics based on individual traits and behaviors. Stratification systems that emphasize ascriptive characteristics for class or status placement are defined as 'closed' and lead to status inheritance or class reproduction. Those stratification systems that emphasize achieved characteristics are defined as 'open' and are expected to lead to social mobility"; Joan Ferrante, *Sociology: A Global Perspective* (Belmont, Calif.: Wadsworth, 2010), available at http://books.google.com/books?isbn=0840032048. "Ascribed characteristics include hair texture and color, eye shape. . . . Findings that announce an ascribed characteristic as a 'cause' can be used to stereotype and stigmatize people "

36. United for a Fair Economy, "State of the Dream 2011: Austerity for Whom?," January 14, 2011, available at http://www.faireconomy.org/files/State_of_the_Dream_2011.pdf.

37. Ibid.

38. Ibid.

39. U.S. Census Bureau, "Alternative Poverty Estimates Based on National Academy of Sciences Recommendations, by Selected Demographic Characteristics and by Region: 2009," Washington, D.C.: U.S. Department of Commerce, accessed April 7, 2011, available at http://www.census.gov/hhes/povmeas/data/nas/tables/2009/ web_tab2_NAS_demogCE_2009.xls.

40. Public Agenda, "Race of TANF Recipients," December 2006, available at http://www .publicagenda.org/charts/race-tanf-recipients.

41. United for a Fair Economy, "State of the Dream 2011: Austerity for Whom?," January 14, 2011, available at http://www.faireconomy.org/files/State_of_the_Dream_2011.pdf.

42. William W. Beach, "Relying on Government Coming to Tipping Point," *Washington Times*, March 11, 2011, available at http://www.washingtontimes.com/news/2010/ mar/11/relying-on-government-coming-to-tipping-point/print/.

43. Kathleen S. Swendiman and Thomas J. Nicola, "Social Security Reform: Legal Analysis of Social Security Benefit Entitlement Issues," Congressional Research Service, August 11, 2010, available at http://aging.senate.gov/crs/ss2.pdf.

44. Mary Meeker, "Analysis of the Financial Condition of the United States," KPCB, February 2011, available at http://images.businessweek.com/mz/11/10/1110_mz_49meekerusainc.pdf. Or Henry Blodget, "Here's the only chart you need to see to understand why the US is screwed," Business Insider, February 28, 2011, available at http://www.businessinsider.com/the-only-chart-you-need-to-see-to-understand-why-the-us-is-screwed-2011-2.

45. Editorial, "Tinker, Tailor, Soldier, ObamaCare," *Wall Street Journal*, March 7, 2010, available at http://online.wsj.com/article/SB100014240527487039152045751034241471 9264.html.

46. Google. Image search, accessed April 7, 2011, available at http://www.google.com/images?hl=en&source=hp&biw=1024&bih=653&q=You+Are+Not+Entitled+To+What+I+Earn&gbv=2&aq=f&aqi=&aql=&oq=.

47. Thomas B. Edsall, *Building Red America: The New Conservative Coalition and the Drive for Permanent Power* (New York: Basic Books, 2006), pp. 9–10; and Maureen Dowd, "Bush Paints Rival as Elitist, with 'Harvard Yard' Views," June 10, 1988, http://www.nytimes.com/1988/06/10/us/bush-paints-rival-as-elitist-with-harvard-yard-views.html; and Michael Prell, "Obama's White House Is a Harvard Frat House," *Human Events*, September 3, 2011, http://www.humanevents.com/article.php?id=45947.

48. Eric Kleefeld, "Bachmann: 'Wean Everybody Off' Social Security and Medicare," Talking Points Memo DC, February 9, 2010, available at http://tpmdc.talkingpointsmemo.com/2010/02/bachmann-wean-everybody-off-social-security-and-medicare.php.

49. "Sarah Palin on Cutting the Budget, Reforming Entitlement Programs," *The O'Reilly Factor*, March 4, 2011, transcript available at http://senatorteaparty.com/sarah-palin-on-cutting-the-budget-reforming-entitlement-programs/.

50. New Boston Tea Party, "Dismantling the Entitlement System," accessed April 7, 2011, available at http://thenewbostonteaparty.com/2011/03/15/dismantling-of-the-entitlement-system.aspx.

51. Elise Foley, "John Boehner on Entitlement Cuts; 'Everything Is on the Table,'" Huffington Post, February 15, 2011, available at http://www.huffingtonpost.com/2011/02/15/john-boehner-budget-cuts-on-the-table_n_823408.html; John Boehner, posts tagged "budget," accessed April 7, 2011, available at http://www.johnboehner.com/?tag=budget.

52. Stephen Hayes, "All In: GOP Embraces Entitlement Reform," *Weekly Standard* (February 15, 2011), available at http://www.weeklystandard.com/blogs/all-gop-embraces-entitlement-reform_550184.html.

53. Rush Limbaugh, "Chris Christie Hits the Entitlement Mentality Right Between the Eyes," March 23, 2011, available at http://www.rushlimbaugh.com/home/daily/site_032311/content/01125109.guest.html.

54. Ohio State University, Kirwan Institute for the Study of Race and Ethnicity, "Unemployment Insurance, the Recession, and Race," July 2010, available at http://4909e99d35cada63e7f757471b7243be73e53e14.gripelements.com/publications/unemployment_insurance_the_recession_and_race_july_2010.pdf.

55. Ibid.

56. Glenn Beck, "Increasing the Minimum Wage Is Like Hugging a Polar Bear," July 24, 2009, available at http://www.foxnews.com/story/0,2933,534771,00.html.

57. Social Security Administration, "Monthly Statistical Snapshot, July 2011," http://www.ssa.gov/policy/docs/quickfacts/stat_snapshot/#table3.

58. R. M. Bottger, "Mental Conditions in Children Applying for SSI Disability Benefits,"

The Disability Expert, http://www.thedisabilityexpert.com/Mental%20Conditions%20in%20Children%20Applying%20for%20SSI%20Disability%20Benefits.html.

59. Arif Mamun, Paul O'Leary, David C. Wittenburg, and Jesse Gregory, "Employment Among Social Security Disability Program Beneficiaries, 1996–2007," *Social Security Bulletin*, Vol. 71, No. 3, Social Security Administration, Office of Retirement and Disability Policy, 2011, http://www.ssa.gov/policy/docs/ssb/v71n3/v71n3p11.html, and Robert Verbruggen, "Containing the Disability Explosion" (a book review of *The Declining Work and Welfare of People with Disabilities* by Cornell economics professor Richard V. Burkhauser and Federal Reserve Bank of San Francisco economist Mary C. Daly), *National Review*, August 31, 2011, http://web2.nationalreview.com/articles/275809/containing-disability-explosion-robert-verbruggen?page=1.

60. American National Election Studies, "ANES Guide to Public Opinion and Electoral Behavior," August 5, 2010, available at http://www.electionstudies.org/nesguide/toptable/tab4a_4b.htm.

61. Pew Center for the People and the Press, "Mixed Views of Economic Policies and Health Care Reform Persist: Support for Health Care Principles, Opposition to Package," October 8, 2009, available at http://people-press.org/2009/10/08/section-2-opinions-of-health-care-proposals/.

62. Public Religion Research Institute, Robert P. Jones and Daniel Cox, "Old Alignments, Emerging Fault Lines: Religion in the 2010 Election and Beyond: Findings from the 2010 Post-election American Values Survey," November 2010, available at http://www.publicreligion.org/objects/uploads/fck/file/AVS%202010%20Post-election%20report%20FINAL.pdf; Public Religion Research Institute, Robert P. Jones and Daniel Cox, "Religion and the Tea Party in the 2010 election," October 2010, available at http://www.publicreligion.org/objects/uploads/fck/file/AVS%202010%20Report%20FINAL.pdf.

63. Beth Fouhy, "Paladino Gives Welfare Plan: Candidate Says Prison Space Could Be Dorms for Employment Training," Associated Press, August 22, 2010, available at http://www.timesunion.com/news/article/Paladino-gives-welfare-plan-625187.php#ixzz1ILKrRwC7.

64. Stephanie McCrummen, "Republican School Board in N.C. Backed by Tea Party Abolishes Integration Policy," *Washington Post*, January 12, 2011, available at http://www.washingtonpost.com/wp-dyn/content/article/2011/01/11/AR2011011107063.html.

CHAPTER SIX: BRUTALITY, COARSENESS, AND THE FRACTURE
OF AMERICAN POLITICS

1. Robert Novak, "No Permanent GOP Minority," Real Clear Politics, July 7, 2008, available at http://www.realclearpolitics.com/articles/2008/07/no_permanent_gop_minority.html.

2. Americans for Tax Reform, "Taxpayer Protection Pledge," accessed April 17, 2011, available at http://www.atr.org/userfiles/Congressional_pledge(1).pdf.

3. Americans for Tax Reform, "About Americans for Tax Reform," accessed April 17, 2011, available at http://www.atr.org/index.php?content=about.

4. Roberton Williams, "Why Nearly Half of Americans Pay No Federal Income Tax," Tax Policy Center, 2010, available at http://www.taxpolicycenter.org/Uploaded PDF/412106_federal_income_tax.pdf.

5. Charles Babington, "GOP May OK Tax Increase that Obama Hopes to Block," Asso-

ciated Press, August 22, 2011, available at http://news.yahoo.com/gop-may-ok-tax
-increase-obama-hopes-block-124016578.html.

6. Jonathan Chait, "No, Half of All Workers Aren't Freeloaders," *New Republic* (April 22, 2011), http://www.tnr.com/blog/jonathan-chait/87204/no-half-all-workers-arent
-freeloaders.

7. "Is 'Tax Day' Too Burdensome for the Rich? The U.S. Tax System Is Not as Progressive as You Think," Citizens for Tax Justice, April 13, 2009, available at http://www
.ctj.org/pdf/taxday2009.pdf.

8. CNN News, "2010 Exit Polls," 2010, available at http://www.cnn.com/ELECTION/
2010/results/polls/#val=USH00p1.

9. Barack Obama, "Remarks by the President to a Joint Session of Congress on Health Care," White House, September 9, 2009, available at http://www.whitehouse.gov/
the-press-office/remarks-president-a-joint-session-congress-health-care.

10. FOX News, "Congressman Yells 'You Lie' at Obama During Speech," September 10, 2009, available at http://www.foxnews.com/politics/2009/09/10/congressman-yells
-lie-obama-speech/.

11. Center for Responsive Politics, "Geography Data: South Carolina District 02, 2010 Race," 2010, available at http://www.opensecrets.org/races/geog.php
?cycle=2010&id=SC02.

12. Byron York, "GOP on Health Care: In 568 Words, What's Wrong with 1,990 Pages," *Washington Examiner*, October 31, 2009, available at http://washingtonexaminer
.com/blogs/beltway-confidential/gop-health-care-568-words-what039s-wrong-1990
-pages#ixzz1JBTCJFl8.

13. Carolyn Smith, "ESL Police Reject Deal that Would Have Brought Back Laid-off Cops," Fraternal Order of Police, July 1, 2011, available at http://www.fop.net/
servlet/display/news_article?id=3074&XSL=xsl_pages/public_news_individual
.xsl&nocache=1764487.

14. E News Park Forest, "Durbin: East St. Louis Mayor's Decision to Enforce 1 A.M. Cut-off for Liquor Sales Is Step in Right Direction—More Needs to Be Done," August 12 2011, available at http://www.enewspf.com/latest-news/police-reports/26055-durbin
-east-st-louis-mayors-decision-to-enforce-1-am-cutoff-for-liquor-sales-is-step-in
-right-direction-more-needs-to-be-done.html.

15. Jim Spencer, "Balancing the Cost of Care: Cuts Mean Many Disabled Minnesotans Get Less Help with at-Home Care," *Minneapolis Star Tribune*, January 13, 2011, available at http://www.startribune.com/local/113428589.html?elr=KArksLckD8EQDUoa
EyqyP4O:DW3ckUiD3aPc:_Yyc:aUeDyic:E7PNDh_oaE3miUsZ.

16. Ibid.

17. Ibid.

18. U.S. Census Bureau, Statistical Abstract of the United States: 2011, "Persons with Work Disability by Selected Characteristics: 2008," Washington, D.C.: U.S. Department of Commerce, accessed June 17, 2011, available at http://www.census.gov/
compendia/statab/cats/social_insurance_human_services/unemployment
_disability_workers_compensation.html.

19. Douglas J. Besharov, "Social welfare's twin dilemmas: Universalism versus Targeting and Support versus Dependency," American Enterprise Institute, January 25, 1998, available at http://www.aei.org/paper/22208.

20. Amanda Terkel, "Blue Dog Coalition Crushed by GOP Wave Election," Huffington Post, March 10, 2011, available at http://www.huffingtonpost.com/2010/11/03/

blue-dog-coalition-gop-wave-elections_n_778087.html; Daily Caller, Jon Ward, "Conservative Democrat Blue Dog Caucus Cut in Half," November 3, 2010, available at http://dailycaller.com/2010/11/03/conservative-democrat-blue-dog-caucus-cut-in-half/.

21. American National Election Studies, "Government Services and Spending 1982–2008," August 5, 2010, available at http://www.electionstudies.org/nesguide/toptable/tab4a_5.htm.

22. Ibid.

23. Ibid.

24. Ibid.

25. Office of Management and Budget, White House, "Table 7.1—Federal Debt at the End of Year: 1940–2016, Historical Tables," accessed June 17, 2011, available at http://www.whitehouse.gov/sites/default/files/omb/budget/fy2012/assets/hist07z1.xls.

26. Avenging Angel, comment on "Republicans Push to Legalize Anti-abortion Terrorism," Daily Kos, February 25, 2011, available at http://www.dailykos.com/story/2011/02/25/949771/-Republicans-Push-to-Legalize-Anti-Abortion-Terrorism.

27. UPI, "Big Oil Protected by GOP, Democrats Say," April 6, 2011, available at http://www.upi.com/Science_News/Resource-Wars/2011/04/06/Big-oil-protected-by-GOP-Democrats-say/UPI-47451302094252/.

28. Brian Beutler, "Schumer Calls GOP Bluff on Spending and Deficits," Talking Points Memo, March 9, 2011, available at http://tpmdc.talkingpointsmemo.com/2011/03/schumer-calls-gop-bluff-on-spending-and-deficits.php.

29. Enufisenuf, comment on "Oh, How I Hate You, Republican Party," Daily Kos, February 23, 2011, available at http://www.dailykos.com/story/2011/02/23/948821/-Oh,-How-I-Hate-You,-Republican-Party.

30. Pew Research Center, "Growing Number of Americans Say Obama Is a Muslim: Religion, Politics and the President," August 19, 2010, available at http://pewresearch.org/pubs/1701/poll-obama-muslim-christian-church-out-of-politics-political-leaders-religious.

31. Ibid. Pew report on CNN survey.

32. Public Policy Polling, "Huckabee Tops GOP Field, 51% Are Birthers and Love Palin," February 15, 2011, available at http://www.publicpolicypolling.com/pdf/PPP_Release_US_0215.pdf.

33. Michael A. Memoli, "White House releases long-form Obama birth certificate," *Los Angeles Times*, April 27, 2011, available at http://articles.latimes.com/2011/apr/27/news/la-pn-obama-birth-certificate-20110427.

34. Brendan Nyhan, "9/11 and Birther Misperceptions Compared," August 10, 2009, available at http://www.brendan-nyhan.com/blog/2009/08/911-and-birther-misperceptions-compared.html.

35. Adam J. Berinsky, "Rumors, Truths, and Reality: A Study of Political Misinformation," working paper presented at the 2011 Midwest Political Science Association meeting and the 2011 meeting of the Chicago Area Behavior Workshop, June 14, 2011, http://web.mit.edu/berinsky/www/files/rumor.pdf.

36. Russell Baker, "Gipper, Scrooge and Santa," *New York Times*, September 12, 1981.

37. "Ketchup Is Ketchup Is Ketchup," Associated Press, September 25, 1981.

38. Mary Thornton and Martin Schram, "Hold the Pickles, Hold the Relish, Hold the New School Lunch Regs," *Washington Post*, September 26, 1981.

39. IRS, "Economic Growth and Tax Relief Reconciliation Act of 2001 (EGTRRA),"

June 7, 2001, available at http://www.irs.gov/pub/irs-utl/egtrra_law.pdf; IRS, "Jobs and Growth Tax Relief Reconciliation Act of 2003 (JGTRRA)," May 23, 2003, available at http://www.gpo.gov/fdsys/pkg/PLAW-108publ27/content-detail.html.

40. Thomas L. Friedman, "We Need a Plan to Cut, Save and Invest at the Same Time," *New York Times*, December 7, 2010, available at http://www.chron.com/disp/story .mpl/editorial/outlook/7329089.html.

41. Thanh Tan, "House Gives Early OK to Bills Balancing '11 Budget," *Texas Tribune*, March 31, 2011, available at http://www.texastribune.org/texas-legislature/82nd -legislative-session/house-gives-early-ok-to-bills-balancing-11-budget/; Brandi Grissom, Reeve Hamilton, Ross Ramsey, Emily Ramshaw, Morgan Smith, and Thanh Tan, "House Budget Shrinks Spending, Slashes Services," *Texas Tribune*, April 2, 2011, available at http://www.texastribune.org/texas-taxes/budget/house-budget -shrinks-spending-slashes-services/.

42. Tax Foundation, "State Spending per Capita, Fiscal Year 2007," February 5, 2009, available at http://www.taxfoundation.org/research/show/287.html; Tax Foundation, "State Revenues per Capita, Fiscal Year 2008," accessed April 17, 2011, available at http://www.taxfoundation.org/files/state_revenue_2008pc-20100325.pdf.

43. Center for Public Policy Priorities, "Medicaid and the State Budget: Mortal Injury?," March 9, 2011, available at http://www.cppp.org/files/3/2011_03_09_Medicaid _%20and_state%20budget%20corr%203%2021%202011.pdf; Center for Public Policy Priorities, Eva DeLuna Castro, "Analysis and Charts on the House Appropria- tions Committee's Budget Proposal for 2012–13," March 25, 2011, available at http:// www.cppp.org/research.php?aid=1062&cid=6.

44. George H. Rodriguez, "Let's Have a Budget to Fit Our Times," San Antonio Tea Party, April 3, 2011, available at http://www.sanantonioteaparty.us/103745/ let%e2%80%99s-have-a-budget-to-fit-our-times/.

45. Jeffrey M. Jones, "Perry Zooms to Front of Pack for 2012 GOP Nomination: Leads Romney by 29% to 17%," Gallup, August 24, 2011, available at http://www.gallup .com/poll/149180/Perry-Zooms-Front-Pack-2012-GOP-Nomination.aspx.

46. Gary Strauss, "For the Wealthy, a Return to Luxury Spending," *USA Today*, February 21, 2011, http://www.usatoday.com/money/economy/2011–02–21–1Aluxury21_CV_N .htm.

47. CBS News, "National Exit Polls 2010," 2010, available at http://www.cbsnews.com/ election2010/exit.shtml?state=US&jurisdiction=0&race=H&tag=contentBody ;electionCenterHome.

48. Centers for Medicare and Medicaid Services, Office of Research, Development, and Information, "The Medicaid Analytic Extract Chartbook," 2008, available at http:// www.cms.gov/MedicaidDataSourcesGenInfo/downloads/2008MAXChartbookwith 2004Data.pdf.

49. CBS News, "National Exit Polls 2010," 2010, available at http://www.cbsnews.com/ election2010/exit.shtml?state=US&jurisdiction=0&race=H&tag=contentBody ;electionCenterHome.

50. Francis Fukuyama, "Left Out," *American Interest* (January–February 2011), available at http://www.the-american-interest.com/article-bd.cfm?piece=906.

51. Theodore Roosevelt, "Expansion and Peace," *Independent* (December 21, 1899), available at http://www.bartleby.com/58/2.html.

52. Federal Reserve Bank of New York, "Timelines of Policy Responses to the Global Financial Crisis," accessed April 17, 2011, available at http://www.newyorkfed.org/

research/global_economy/policyresponses.html; Federal Reserve Bank of New York, "Financial Turmoil Timeline," accessed April 17, 2011, available at http://www.newyorkfed.org/research/global_economy/Crisis_Timeline.pdf.

53. Andrew Bacevich, *The Limits of Power: The End of American Exceptionalism* (New York: Henry Holt, 2008), pp. 15–66, available at http://www.americanempireproject.com/bookexcerpt.asp?ISBN=0805090169.

CHAPTER SEVEN: THE BIG ONE

1. Osama bin Laden, interview by John Miller, *Frontline*, PBS, May 1998, available at http://www.pbs.org/wgbh/pages/frontline/shows/binladen/who/interview.html#video.
2. Ibid.
3. Ibid.
4. The Daily *Ummat* of Karachi, "Who Was Behind 9/11?—an Interview with Osama bin Laden," September 28, 2011, available at http://forum.mpacuk.org/showpost.php?p=38960&postcount=41; CNN/Public Action, "Bin Laden Interview: 28th September 2001," Pakistani News Service, accessed June 19, 2011, available at http://iraqwar.mirror-world.ru/tiki-read_article.php?articleId=152029.
5. Amy Belasco, "The Cost of Iraq, Afghanistan, and Other Global War on Terror Operations Since 9/11," Congressional Research Service, September 2, 2010, available at http://www.fas.org/sgp/crs/natsec/RL33110.pdf.
6. Joseph Stiglitz and Linda Bilmes, *The Three Trillion Dollar War* (New York: Norton, 2008).
7. Associated Press, "Pentagon Estimates Libya Costs at $608 Million," *U.S. News & World Report*, April 11, 2011, available at http://www.usnews.com/news/articles/2011/04/11/pentagon-estimates-libya-costs-at-608-million.
8. Miles Mogulescu, "Bin Laden Used a Similar Strategy to Decimate American Capitalism as Reagan Used to Hasten End of Soviet Communism," Huffington Post, October 6, 2008, available at http://www.huffingtonpost.com/miles-mogulescu/bin-laden-used-a-similar_b_132230.html.
9. David Leonhardt, "America's Sea of Red Ink Was Years in the Making," *New York Times*, June 9, 2009, available at http://www.nytimes.com/2009/06/10/business/economy/10leonhardt.html.
10. Office of Management and Budget, "Historical Tables, Table 1.1—Summary of Receipts, Outlays, and Surpluses or Deficits (-): 1789–2016," accessed May 18, 2011, available at http://www.whitehouse.gov/sites/default/files/omb/budget/fy2012/assets/hist01z1.xls.
11. Fact Check, "The Budget and Deficit Under Clinton," February 3, 2008, available at http://www.factcheck.org/askfactcheck/during_the_clinton_administration_was_the_federal.html. "The difference between the federal deficit and the federal debt: A deficit occurs when the government takes in less money than it spends in a given year. The debt is the total amount the government owes at any given time. So the debt goes up in any given year by the amount of the deficit, or it decreases by the amount of any surplus."
12. Office of Management and Budget, "Historical Tables, Table 7.1—Federal Debt at the End of Year: 1940–2016," accessed May 18, 2011, available at http://www.whitehouse.gov/sites/default/files/omb/budget/fy2012/assets/hist07z1.xls.
13. Money Café, "Federal Funds Target Rate from 1955 to 2011" (historical chart),

accessed May 18, 2011, available at http://www.moneycafe.com/library/fedfundsrate
.htm#chart.

14. CNBC, "Boom, Bust and Blame—the Inside Story of America's Economic Crisis,"
accessed June 19, 2011, available at http://www.cnbc.com/id/31187744/.
   "On September 17, 2001, less than a week after 9/11, the Fed began a series of
interest rate cuts that made it easier and cheaper to borrow money. The cuts continued for nearly two years, through June 2003, and created incredible new demand for
mortgages, home equity loans, automobile financing, and other kinds of credit."

15. Zoltan Pozsar, Tobias Adrian, Adam Ashcraft, and Hayley Boesk, "Shadow Banking,"
Federal Reserve Bank of New York (staff report), July 2010, available at http://www
.newyorkfed.org/research/staff_reports/sr458.pdf: "Shadow banks are financial
intermediaries that conduct maturity, credit, and liquidity transformation without access to central bank liquidity or public sector credit guarantees. Examples
of shadow banks include finance companies, asset-backed commercial paper
(ABCP) conduits, limited-purpose finance companies, structured investment
vehicles, credit hedge funds, money market mutual funds, securities lenders, and
government-sponsored enterprises. Shadow banks are interconnected along a verti-
cally integrated, long intermediation chain, which intermediates credit through
a wide range of securitization and secured funding techniques such as ABCP,
asset-backed securities, collateralized debt obligations, and repo. This intermediation chain binds shadow banks into a network, which is the shadow banking system.
The shadow banking system rivals the traditional banking system in the intermediation of credit to households and businesses. Over the past decade, the shadow
banking system provided sources of inexpensive funding for credit by converting
opaque, risky, long-term assets into money-like and seemingly riskless short-term
liabilities. Maturity and credit transformation in the shadow banking system thus
contributed significantly to asset bubbles in residential and commercial real estate
markets prior to the financial crisis. We document that the shadow banking system
became severely strained during the financial crisis because, like traditional banks,
shadow banks conduct credit, maturity, and liquidity transformation, but unlike
traditional financial intermediaries, they lack access to public sources of liquidity,
such as the Federal Reserve's discount window, or public sources of insurance, such
as federal deposit insurance."

16. http://en.wikipedia.org/wiki/Subprime_mortgage_crisis#cite_note-42.

17. A. Michael Spence, "Lessons from the Crisis," PIMCO, November 2008, available at
http://www.pimco.com/EN/Insights/Pages/Viewpoints%20Lessons%20from
%20the%20Crisis%20Spence%20November%202008.aspx.

18. Office of Management and Budget, "Historical Tables, Table 1.1—Summary of
Receipts, Outlays, and Surpluses or Deficits: 1789–2016," accessed May 18, 2011, available at http://www.whitehouse.gov/sites/default/files/omb/budget/fy2012/assets/
hist01z1.xls.

19. Kathy Ruffing and James R. Horney, "Critics Still Wrong on What's Driving Deficits
in Coming Years: Economic Downturn, Financial Rescues, and Bush-Era Policies
Drive the Numbers," Center on Budget and Policy Priorities, June 28, 2010, available
at http://www.cbpp.org/cms/index.cfm?fa=view&id=3036.

20. Office of Management and Budget, Historical Tables, Table 7.1—"Federal Debt at
the End of the Year: 1940–2016," accessed June 19, 2011, available at http://www
.whitehouse.gov/sites/default/files/omb/budget/fy2012/assets/hist07z1.xls.

21. Kate Zernike and Megan Thee-Brenan, "Poll Finds Tea Party Backers Wealthier and

More Educated," *New York Times*, April 14, 2010, available at http://www
.nytimes.com/interactive/2010/04/14/us/politics/20100414-tea-party-poll-graphic
.html?ref=politics#tab=2.

22. Ibid.

23. Ibid.

24. Ibid.

25. Public Religion Research Institute, "Survey: Plurality of Americans Believe
Capitalism at Odds with Christian Values," April 20, 2011, available at http://www
.publicreligion.org/research/?id=554.

26. Ibid.

27. Ibid.

28. C. Eugene Steuerle and Stephanie Rennane, "Social Security and Medicare Taxes
Benefits over a Lifetime," Urban Institute, January 2011, available at http://www
.urban.org/UploadedPDF/social-security-medicare-benefits-over-lifetime.pdf.

29. Kaiser Family Foundation, "Facts at a Glance: Medicare Enrollees," accessed May 18,
2011, available at http://www.statehealthfacts.org/comparecat.jsp?cat=6.

30. Lori Montgomery, "Social Security Splinters Democrats in Debate over Reining
in Budget Deficits," *Washington Post*, March 24, 2011: "Social Security is the single
largest federal program, dispensing about $700 billion last year to nearly 60 million
people, the vast majority of them retirees. Since the program's creation in 1935, the
cost of Social Security benefits has been entirely covered by payroll taxes paid by
current workers. This year, however, payroll tax revenues are projected to fall $45 bil-
lion short of covering benefits, and the problem is projected to grow as the number
of retirees balloons compared with the number of working adults."

31. Social Security Administration, "How Is Social Security Financed?," accessed May 18,
2011, available at http://www.ssa.gov/pressoffice/factsheets/HowAreSocialSecurity.htm.
"In 2010, $649 billion (82%) of total OASI and DI income came from payroll taxes.
The remainder was provided by interest earnings ($118 billion or 15%) and revenue
from taxation of OASDI benefits ($24 billion or 3%)"; U.S. Census Bureau, "Resi-
dent Population by Race, Hispanic Origin, and Age: 2000 and 2009," Washington,
D.C.: U.S. Department of Commerce, accessed May 18, 2011, available at http://www
.census.gov/compendia/statab/2011/tables/11s0009.xls.

32. Barack Obama, "Remarks by the President at a DNC Event, Chicago, Illinois,
N9NE Restaurant," April 14, 2011, available at http://www.whitehouse.gov/the-press
-office/2011/04/14/remarks-president-dnc-event.

33. James Hibberd, "FOX News Has Oldest Cable Audience," *Hollywood Reporter*,
November 30, 2010, available at http://www.hollywoodreporter.com/blogs/live-feed/
fox-news-oldest-cable-audience-54230.

34. Michael Barone, "The Transformative Power of Rick Santelli's Rant," *National
Review* (June 10, 2010), available at http://www.nationalreview.com/articles/229927/
transformative-power-rick-santellis-rant/michael-barone.

35. John Boehner, "Speech to the National Religious Broadcasters," February 27, 2011,
accessed May 18, 2011, available at http://www.speaker.gov/News/DocumentSingle
.aspx?DocumentID=226442.

36. Mitch Daniels, "Debt Is the New 'Red Menace' " (speech at the Conservative Political
Action Conference Ronald Reagan Centennial Dinner), February 11, 2011, available
at http://www.realclearpolitics.com/articles/2011/02/12/debt_is_the_new_red
_menace_108875.html.

37. "Mitch Daniels, Indiana's 49th Governor," *Indianapolis Star*, January 11, 2005, avail-

able at http://www2.indystar.com/library/factfiles/people/d/daniels_mitch/daniels
.html.

38. Martin Wolk, "Cost of Iraq War Could Surpass $1Trillion: Estimates Vary, but All
Agree Price Is Far Higher than Initially Expected," msnbc.com, March 17, 2006,
available at http://www.msnbc.msn.com/id/11880954/.

39. Amy Belasco, "The Cost of Iraq, Afghanistan, and Other Global War on Terror
Operations Since 9/11," Congressional Research Service, September 2, 2010, available
at http://www.fas.org/sgp/crs/natsec/RL33110.pdf; Joseph Stiglitz and Linda Bilmes,
*The Three Trillion Dollar War* (New York: Norton, 2008).

40. Urban Institute and Brookings Institution Tax Policy Center, "Historical Top Tax
Rate," January 30, 2011, available at http://www.taxpolicycenter.org/taxfacts/
displayafact.cfm?Docid=213.

41. Carl Levin, "Where Were the Watchdogs? The Financial Crisis and the Breakdown
of Financial Governance" (speech before the Homeland Security and Governmental
Affairs Committee), January 21, 2009, available at http://hsgac.senate.gov/public/
_files/012109Levin.pdf.

42. Thomas B. Edsall, "Man Versus Machine," Huffington Post, November 2, 2008, available at http://www.huffingtonpost.com/2008/11/02/man-versus-machine_n_140115
.html.

43. Bryan Walsh, "George W. Bush's Last Environmental Stand," *Time* (November 5,
2008), available at http://www.time.com/time/health/article/0,8599,1856829,00.html.

44. Paul Krugman, "Patients Are Not Consumers," *New York Times*, April 21, 2011,
available at http://www.nytimes.com/2011/04/22/opinion/22krugman
.html?scp=2&sq=krugman&st=cse.

45. Clifford Marks, "In Media Coverage, Deficit Eclipses Unemployment," *National
Journal*, May 16, 2011, available at http://www.nationaljournal.com/economy/
in-media-coverage-deficit-eclipses-unemployment-20110516.

46. House of Representatives, House Budget Committee, "The Path to Prosperity;
Restoring America's Promise: Fiscal Year 2012 Budget Resolution," April 5, 2011, available at http://budget.house.gov/UploadedFiles/PathToProsperityFY2012.pdf.

47. Daniel Henninger, "A Ronald Reagan Budget: Paul Ryan's Budget Offers Much
More than Deficit-Reduction Brimstone," *Wall Street Journal*, April 7, 2011, available
at http://online.wsj.com/article/SB10001424052748704101604576246900648182340
.html?mod=WSJ_Opinion_LEADTop.

48. Karl Rove, "Obama's Government Shutdown Gambit: the President Sees Political
Profit in Demagoguing GOP Spending Proposals," *Wall Street Journal*, April 7, 2011,
available at http://online.wsj.com/article/SB10001424052748704013604576246740 9075
65666.html?mod=WSJ_Opinion_LEFTTopOpinion.

49. Sojourners, "About Us," accessed June 19, 2011, available at http://www.sojo.net/
index.cfm?action=about_us.mission.
     Sojourners: "Our mission is to articulate the biblical call to social justice, inspir-
ing hope and building a movement to transform individuals, communities, the
church, and the world. . . . We believe that unity in diversity is not only desirable,
but essential to fulfilling God's ultimate desire for God's people, as expressed in
scripture (Acts 2, Revelation 7:9), and thus an essential element of seeking God's will
on earth as it is in heaven. . . ."

50. Roger Pilon, "Is It Immoral to Cut the Budget? The Good Samaritan Parable
Instructs Us to Attend to the Afflicted Voluntarily, Not Through Coercive Government Programs," *Wall Street Journal*, April 7, 2011, available at http://online.wsj.com/

article/SB10001424052748704101604576246441115301636.html?mod=WSJ_Opinion _LEFTTopOpinion.

51. Kaiser Health News, "Census Bureau: Recession Fuels Record Number of Uninsured Americans," September 17, 2010, available at http://www.kaiserhealthnews.org/ Daily-Reports/2010/September/16/uninsured-census-statistics.aspx.

52. Robert Greenstein, "CBO Report: Ryan Plan Specifies Spending Path that Would Nearly End Most of Government Other than Social Security, Health Care, and Defense by 2050. Plan Also Contains Deeper Cuts to Medicare and Medicaid than Ryan Revealed," Center on Budget and Policy Priorities, accessed May 18, 2011, available at http://www.cbpp.org/cms/index.cfm?fa=view&id=3453.

53. Ibid.

54. Ibid.

55. Robert Greenstein, "Chairman Ryan Gets Roughly Two-Thirds of His Huge Budget Cuts from Programs for Lower-Income Americans," Center on Budget and Policy Priorities, April 5, 2011, available at http://www.cbpp.org/cms/index .cfm?fa=view&id=3451.

56. Grover Norquist, interview, *Morning Edition*, National Public Radio, May 25, 2001, available at Lexis-Nexis.

57. Urban Institute and Brookings Institution Tax Policy Center, "Major Tax Provisions of the Roadmap for America's Future Act of 2010, Baseline: Current Law; Taxpayers All Choose the Alternative Tax system, Distribution of Federal Tax Change by Cash Income Level, 2014, Summary Table," Urban Institute and Brookings Institution Tax Policy Center Microsimulation Model (version 0509–5), available at http://www .taxpolicycenter.org/numbers/displayatab.cfm?Docid=2681&DocTypeID=1:
Number of AMT Taxpayers (millions). Baseline: 23.2 Proposal: 0.0
(1) Calendar year. Baseline is current law. Proposal is effective Jan. 1, 2011, and would (a) eliminate the AMT; (b) repeal the income and payroll tax exclusion for employer-sponsored health insurance; (c) provide a refundable tax credit equal to $2,300 ($5,700 for families) for the purchase of health insurance; (d) repeal the corporate income tax; (e) impose an 8.5% business consumption tax (BCT); and (f) allow taxpayers to choose between the current tax system and an alternative simplified tax system. The alternative tax system eliminates all adjustments to income, itemized deductions, tax credits, and the estate tax and has a standard deduction of $12,500 ($25,000 for joint returns), personal exemptions of $3,500, and rates of 10% up to $50,000 ($100,000 for joint returns) and 25% above that level. Interest, dividends, capital gains, and non-wage business income would be excluded from tax under the alternative system. Dollar values for the alternative tax system are indexed for inflation; the refundable credit amount is indexed by the average growth rate of CPI and medical care expenses. Taxpayers are assumed to all opt into the alternative system.
(2) Tax units with negative cash income are excluded from the lowest income class but are included in the totals. For a description of cash income, see http://www .taxpolicycenter.org/TaxModel/income.cfm.
(3) Includes both filing and non-filing units but excludes those that are dependents of other tax units.
(4) After-tax income is cash income less: individual income tax net of refundable credits; corporate income tax; payroll taxes (Social Security and Medicare); and estate tax.

(5) Average federal tax (includes individual and corporate income tax, payroll taxes for Social Security and Medicare, and the estate tax) as a percentage of average cash income.

58. Bruce Bartlett, "Imbalanced Budget: Ryan Gives Wealthy a Free Pass," Fiscal Times, April 7, 2011, available at http://www.thefiscaltimes.com/Columns/2011/04/07/Wealthy-Get-Free-Pass-in-Ryan-Budget.aspx.

59. Barry Eichengreen, "Is America Catching the 'British Disease'?," Project Syndicate, November 9, 2010, available at http://www.project-syndicate.org/commentary/eichengreen24/English.

60. Kevin D. Williamson, "Socialism Is Back," *National Review* (January 19, 2011), available at http://www.nationalreview.com/articles/257302/socialism-back-kevin-d-williamson?page=3; Haidt quote of Mikhail Gorbachev.

61. Gideon Rachman, *Zero-Sum Future: American Power in an Age of Anxiety* (New York: Simon & Schuster, 2011), accessed May 18, 2011, available at http://books.simonandschuster.com/Zero-Sum-Future/Gideon-Rachman/9781439176610/excerpt.

62. Dana Blanton, "Fox News Poll: 62% Think U.S. Is on the Decline," FoxNews.com, July 30, 2010, available at http://www.foxnews.com/us/2010/07/30/fox-news-poll-%-think-decline/.

63. Jon Cohen, "Few Americans Say U.S. Is Well-positioned to Compete in Global Economy," *Washington Post*, January 21, 2011, available at http://www.washingtonpost.com/wpdyn/content/article/2011/01/21/AR2011012102958.html?hpid opnews.

64. Kerri Shannon, "China Could Overtake the U.S. Economy by 2025 or Sooner," NuWire Investor, August 3, 2010, available at http://www.nuwireinvestor.com/articles/china-could-overtake-the-us-economy-by-2025-or-sooner-55776.aspx.

65. John Hawksworth and Gordon Cookson, "The World in 2050," PriceWaterhouse Coopers, accessed May 18, 2011, available at http://www.pwc.com/gx/en/world-2050/pdf/world_2050_brics.pdf.

66. Phil Izzo, "Nearly 1 in 3 Unemployed Out of Work More Than a Year," *Wall Street Journal*, June 3, 2011, available at http://blogs.wsj.com/economics/2011/06/03/nearly-1-in-3-unemployed-out-of-work-more-than-a-year/.

67. Pew Charitable Trusts, "A Year or More: the High Cost of Long-Term Unemployment," January 27, 2011, available at http://www.pewtrusts.org/uploadedFiles/wwwpewtrustsorg/Reports/Economic_Mobility/long_term_unemployment_update_january_2011.pdf.

68. Michael Powell, "Profits Are Booming. Why Aren't Jobs?," *New York Times*, January 8, 2011, available at http://www.nytimes.com/2011/01/09/weekinreview/09powell.html.

69. David Wessell, "Foreign Firms Aren't Hiring in the U.S.," *Wall Street Journal*, April 20, 2011, available at http://blogs.wsj.com/economics/2011/04/20/foreign-firms-arent-hiring-in-u-s/?KEYWORDS=wessel.

70. Catherine Rampell, "Corporate Profits Were the Highest on Record Last Quarter," *New York Times*, November 23, 2010, available at http://www.nytimes.com/2010/11/24/business/economy/24econ.html.

71. Jon Cohen and Peyton M. Craighill, "Poll: Americans Increasingly View Global Economy as a Negative for U.S.," *Washington Post*, January 28, 2011, available at http://www.washingtonpost.com/wp-dyn/content/article/2011/01/28/AR2011012801651.html?hpid=moreheadlines.

72. "Percent Job Losses in Post WWII Recessions, Aligned at Maximum Job Losses, Summary for Week Ending April 1st," Calculated Risk, April 2, 2011, available at

http://www.calculatedriskblog.com/2011/04/summary-for-week-ending-april-1st
.html.

73. Catherine Rampell, "Average Length of Unemployment Rises Again," *New York Times*, April 1, 2011, available at http://economix.blogs.nytimes.com/2011/04/01/ average-length-of-unemployment-rises-again/.

74. Ibid.

75. Mark J. Parry, "The Good News: Worker Productivity and Profits per Workers Are at Record Highs. The Bad News: That Probably Means a Record Jobless Recovery," Carpe Diem, April 9, 2011, available at http://mjperry.blogspot.com/2011/04/ good-news-worker-productivity-and.html?utm_source=feedburner&utm _medium=email&utm_campaign=Feed%3A+blogspot%2FmmMP+%28CARPE +DIEM%29.

76. Ibid.

77. Paul Kennedy, *The Rise and Fall of the Great Powers* (New York: Random House, 1987), pp. xvi, 51.

78. Joseph Stiglitz and Linda Bilmes, *The Three Trillion Dollar War* (New York: Norton, 2008).

79. Paul K. Kerr, "Nuclear, Biological, and Chemical Weapons and Missiles: Status and Trends," Congressional Research Service, Report RL30699, February 20, 2008, available at http://www.fas.org/sgp/crs/nuke/RL30699.pdf.

80. Niall Ferguson, "Complexity and Collapse: Empires on the Edge of Chaos," *Foreign Affairs* (March–April 2010), available at http://www.informationclearinghouse.info/ article24874.htm.

81. Graham Bowley, "Uncle Sam Wants His AAA Rating," *New York Times*, January 13, 2011, available at http://www.nytimes.com/2011/01/14/business/economy/14place .html?hp.

82. Chris Giles and James Politi, "U.S. Lacks Credibility on Debt, Says IMF," *Financial Times*, April 12, 2011, available at http://www.ft.com/cms/s/0/dc1aadea-652e-11e0 -b150-00144feab49a.html?ftcamp=rss&ftcamp=crm/email/2011412/nbe/InTodaysFT/ product#axzz1JRFfOdzT.

83. Standard & Poor's, "Fiscal Challenges Weighing on the 'AAA' Sovereign Credit Rating on the Government of the United States," April 18, 2011, available at http://www .standardandpoors.com/ratings/articles/en/us/?assetID=1245302919686.

84. Congressional Budget Office, "The Budget and Economic Outlook: Fiscal Years 2011 to 2021," January 2011, available at http://www.cbo.gov/ftpdocs/120xx/doc12039/ SummaryforWeb.pdf.

85. Urban Institute, Alan J. Auerbach and William G. Gale, "Tempting Fate: The Federal Budget Outlook," February 8, 2011, available at http://www.urban.org/ uploadedpdf/1001497-Auerbach-Gale-Tempting-Fate.pdf.

86. Walter Mondale, "Mondale's Acceptance Speech," 1984, accessed May 18, 2011, available at http://www.cnn.com/ALLPOLITICS/1996/conventions/chicago/facts/famous .speeches/mondale.84.shtml.

87. Barack Obama, "Remarks by the President on Fiscal Policy, George Washington University, Washington, D.C.," April 13, 2011, available at http://www.whitehouse .gov/the-press-office/2011/04/13/remarks-president-fiscal-policy.

88. Ibid.

89. "Republican Members of the House of Representatives Hold a News Conference," transcript, press conference, April 13, 2011, available on Nexis.

90. Emi Kolawole and Rachel Weiner, "Gingrich: Ryan Budget Plan 'Right-Wing Social

Engineering,' " *Washington Post*, May 15, 2011, available at http://www.washingtonpost.com/blogs/44/post/gingrich-ryan-budget-plan-right-wing-social-engineering-sunday-talk-shows/2011/05/15/AF4OtE4G_blog.html.

91. Lydia Saad, "Americans Divided over Ryan vs. Obama Deficit Plans: Favor Congressional Republicans over Democrats on Federal Budget, Generally," Gallup, April 27, 2011, available at http://www.gallup.com/poll/147287/americans-divided-ryan-obama-deficit-plans.aspx.

92. James Galbraith, e-mail message to author, May 1, 2011.

93. Council on Foreign Relations, Michael Spence and Sandile Hlatshwayo, "The Evolving Structure of the American Economy and the Employment Challenge," March 2011, available at http://www.cfr.org/industrial-policy/evolving-structure-american-economy-employment-challenge/p24366.

94. Ibid.

95. Ibid.

96. Ibid.

97. Ibid.

98. Ibid.

99. Ibid.

100. Bill Gross, "America's Debt Is Not Its Biggest Problem," *Washington Post,* August 10, 2011, available at http://www.washingtonpost.com/opinions/americas-debt-is-not-its-biggest-problem/2011/08/10/gIQAgYvE7I_story.html.

101. U.S. Census Bureau, "Statistical Abstract of the United States, 2011, Income, Expenditures, Poverty, & Wealth: Gross Domestic Product (GDP)," Washington, D.C.: U.S. Department of Commerce, accessed May 18, 2011, available at http://www.census.gov/compendia/statab/cats/income_expenditures_poverty_wealth/gross_domestic_product_gdp.html.

102. Ibid.

103. Ibid

104. U.S. Census Bureau, "Table P-1, CPS Population and per Capita Money Income, All Races: 1967 to 2009," Washington, D.C.: U.S. Department of Commerce, accessed May 18, 2011, available at http://www.census.gov/hhes/www/income/data/historical/people/P01AR_2009.xls.

105. U.S. Census Bureau, "Table H-17, Households by Total Money Income, Race, and Hispanic Origin of Householder: 1967 to 2009," Washington, D.C.: U.S. Department of Commerce, accessed May 18, 2011, available at http://www.census.gov/hhes/www/income/data/historical/household/H17_2009.xls.

106. Rick Newman, "4 Reasons to Cheer When China Overtakes America," *U.S. News & World Report*, April 28, 2011, available at http://money.usnews.com/money/blogs/flowchart/2011/04/28/4-reasons-to-cheer-when-china-overtakes-america.

107. Michael Hirsh, "Feldstein, Krugman Agree: Another War Would Help: Economists from Both Sides of the Political Spectrum Envision Grim Employment Scenarios for Years to Come," National Journal Online, October 5, 2010, available at http://nationaljournal.com/njonline/ec_20101005_5357.php.

CODA

1. Richard A. Clarke, "Bin Laden's Dead, Al Qaeda's Not," *New York Times*, May 2, 2011, available at http://www.nytimes.com/2011/05/03/opinion/03clarke.html?ref=opinion.

2. Peter S. Goodman, "Osama's Legacy: American Drift," Huffington Post, May 2, 2011,

available at http://www.huffingtonpost.com/2011/05/02/osamas-legacy-american
-drift_n_856365.html.

3.   Barry Ritholtz, "Bin Laden's (Long Overdue) Day of Reckoning," Big Picture, May 2,
     2011, available at http://www.ritholtz.com/blog/2011/05/bin-ladens-long-overdue
     -day-of-reckoning/.

4.   Giles Foden, "Review: The Black Swan: The Impact of the Highly Improbable by
     Nassim Nicholas Taleb," *Guardian*, May 12, 2007, available at http://www.guardian
     .co.uk/books/2007/may/12/society. "Until the 19th century and the discovery of
     mutant black swans in Australia, it was assumed all swans were white. 'Black swan' is
     a catch-all phrase for 'outliers' or wildly unexpected events and processes: something
     such as 9/11, for instance, or the rise of Google. The underlying probability of these
     black swans has been 'mispriced' as if they were undervalued stocks or other con-
     tainers of latent value. The other quality of black swans is that the events themselves
     have wide-ranging, society-changing effects that go far beyond their initial apparent
     import."

5.   U.S. Energy Information Administration, "International Energy Outlook, 2010,"
     2010, available at http://www.eia.doe.gov/oiaf/ieo/world.html.

6.   World Resources Institute, "How Much of the World's Resource Consumption
     Occurs in Rich Countries?," August 31, 2007, available at http://earthtrends.wri.org/
     updates/node/236.

7.   Paul Collier, *The Bottom Billion: Why the Poorest Countries Are Failing and What Can
     Be Done About It* (New York: Oxford University Press, 2007).

8.   Juana Summers, "Ovide LaMontagne Kicks Off New Hampshire GOP Primary,"
     Politico, April 29, 2011, available at http://www.politico.com/news/stories/0411/
     53969.html#ixzz1L35rNSgd.

# Selected Bibliography

Abramowitz, Alan I. *The Disappearing Center: Engaged Citizens, Polarization, and American Democracy.* New Haven: Yale University Press, 2010.

Abramowitz, Alan. "Diverging Coalitions: The Transformation of the American Electorate," University of Virginia Center for Politics, April 9, 2009, http://www .centerforpolitics.org/crystalball/articles/aia2009040901/.

Alterman, Eric. *Kabuki Democracy: The System vs. Barack Obama.* New York: Nation Books, 2011.

Altman, Roger C. "American Profligacy and American Power: The Consequences of Fiscal Irresponsibility," *Foreign Affairs,* November/December 2010, http://www.foreignaffairs .com/articles/66778/roger-c-altman-and-richard-n-haass/american-profligacy-and -american-power.

———. "Globalization in Retreat: Further Geopolitical Consequences of the Financial Crisis," *Foreign Affairs,* July/August 2009, http://www.foreignaffairs.com/ articles/65153/roger-c-altman/globalization-in-retreat.

Ansolabehere, Stephen, and James M. Snyder. *The End of Inequality: One Person, One Vote and the Transformation of American Politics.* New York: W. W. Norton, 2008.

Ansolabehere, Stephen, and Shanto Iyengar. *Going Negative: How Political Advertisements Shrink and Polarize the Electorate.* New York: Simon and Schuster, 1997.

Auerbach, Alan J., and William G. Gale. "Tempting Fate: The Federal Budget Outlook," Urban Institute, February 8, 2011, http://www.urban.org/uploadedpdf/1001497 -Auerbach-Gale-Tempting-Fate.pdf.

Bacevich, Andrew. *The Limits of Power: The End of American Exceptionalism.* New York: Henry Holt, 2008, http://www.americanempireproject.com/bookexcerpt .asp?ISBN=0805090169.

Bafumi, Joseph, and Robert Y. Shapiro. "A New Partisan Voter," *The Journal of Politics* 79:1 (2009), http://www.temple.edu/ipa/events/documents/Shapiropaper-S00223816080900 14.pdf.

Balz, Dan, and Ronald Brownstein. *Storming the Gates: Protest Politics and the Republican Revival.* New York: Little, Brown, 1996.

Bartels, Larry M. "Base Appeal: The Political Attitudes and Priorities of Core Partisans," http://www.princeton.edu/~bartels/core.pdf.

————. *Unequal Democracy: The Political Economy of the New Gilded Age.* Princeton University Press, 2010.

Belasco, Amy. "The Cost of Iraq, Afghanistan, and Other Global War on Terror Operations Since 9/11," Congressional Research Service, September 2, 2010, http://www.fas.org/sgp/crs/natsec/RL33110.pdf.

Berinsky, Adam J. "Rumors, Truths, and Reality: A Study of Political Misinformation," Working Paper, June 14, 2011, http://web.mit.edu/berinsky/www/files/rumor.pdf.

Bernstein, Peter L. *Against the Gods: The Remarkable Story of Risk.* Hoboken: Wiley, 1998.

Besharov, Douglas J. "Social Welfare's Twin Dilemmas: Universalism Versus Targeting and Support Versus Dependency," American Enterprise Institute, January 25, 1998, http://www.aei.org/paper/22208.

Betts, Richard K. *Conflict After Cold War: Arguments on Causes of War and Peace,* 3rd Edition. London: Longman, 2008.

Blumenthal, Sidney. *The Rise of the Counter-Establishment: The Conservative Ascent to Political Power.* New York: Union Square Press, 2008.

Brady, David W., and Craig Volden. *Revolving Gridlock: Politics and Policy from Carter to Clinton.* Boulder: Westview, 1997.

Brecher, Charles, and Raymond D. Horton. *Power Failure: New York City Politics and Policy Since 1960.* New York: Oxford University Press, 1993.

Brinkley, Alan. *American History: A Survey Since 1865.* New York: McGraw Hill, 1999.

Brockman, John. *The Third Culture: Beyond the Scientific Revolution.* New York: Touchstone, 1996.

Brownstein, Ronald. *The Second Civil War.* New York: Penguin, 2007.

Burghart, Devin, and Leonard Zeskind. "Tea Party Nationalism: A Critical Examination of the Tea Party Movement and the Size, Scope, and Focus of Its National Factions," Institute for Research & Education on Human Rights, Fall 2010, http://www.teapartynationalism.com/pdf.

Burtless, Gary, and Joseph F. Quinn, "Retirement Trends and Policies to Encourage Work Among Older Americans," presented at the Annual Conference of the National Academy of Social Insurance, Washington, D.C., January 26–27, 2000, http://fmwww.bc.edu/ec-p/wp436.pdf.

Carney, Dana R., John T. Jost, Samuel D. Gosling, and Jeff Potter. "The Secret Lives of Liberals and Conservatives: Personality Profiles, Interaction Styles, and the Things They Leave Behind," *Political Psychology* 29 (2008): 807–40, http://www.psych.nyu.edu/jost/Carney,%20Jost,%20&%20Gosling%20(2008)%20The%20secret%20lives%20of%20liberals%20.pdf.

Citrin, Jack, and Benjamin Highton. *How Race, Ethnicity, and Immigration Shape the California Electorate.* San Francisco: Public Policy Institute of California, 2002.

Collier, Paul. *The Bottom Billion: Why the Poorest Countries Are Failing and What Can Be Done About It.* New York: Oxford University Press, 2007.

Collins, Gail. *When Everything Changed: The Amazing Journey of American Women from 1960 to the Present.* New York: Harper Perennial, 2007.

Cowen, Tyler. *The Great Stagnation: How America Ate All the Low-Hanging Fruit of Modern History, Got Sick, and Will (Eventually) Feel Better.* New York: Dutton, 2011.

DeLuna Castro, Eva. "Analysis and Charts on the House Appropriations Committee's Budget Proposal for 2012–13," Center for Public Policy Priorities, March 25, 2011, http://www.cppp.org/research.php?aid=1062&cid=6.

Dobson, James C. *Dare to Discipline*. Wheaton, Ill.: Tyndale House, 1977.

Dooling, Richard. *Rapture for the Geeks: When AI Outsmarts IQ*. New York: Harmony Books, 2008.

Edsall, Thomas B., and Edsall, Mary D. *Chain Reaction: The Impact of Race, Rights, and Taxes on American Politics*. New York: W. W. Norton, 1992.

Edsall, Thomas B. *Building Red America: The New Conservative Coalition and the Drive for Permanent Power*. New York: Basic Books, 2006.

Federal Reserve Archival System for Economic Research. "The 1970s: Inflation, High Interest Rates, and New Competition," accessed June 12, 2010, fraser.stlouisfed.org/publications/erp/page/6688/ . . . /6688_ERP.pdf.

Feld, Lowell, Nate Wilcox, and Markos Moulitsas Zúniga. *Netroots Rising: How a Citizen Army of Bloggers and Online Activists Is Changing American Politics*. Westport: Greenwood, 2008.

Ferguson, Niall. *The Ascent of Money: A Financial History of the World*. New York: Penguin, 2008.

Ferrante, Joan. *Sociology: A Global Perspective*. Belmont, Calif.: Wadsworth, 2010, http://books.google.com/books?isbn=0840032048.

Fiorina, Morris P., Jeremy C. Pope, and Samuel J. Abrams. *Culture War? The Myth of a Polarized America*. London: Longman, 2004.

Foer, Franklin. *How Soccer Explains the World: An Unlikely Theory of Globalization*. New York: Harper Perennial, 2005.

Frank, Robert H., and Philip J. Cook. *The Winner-Take-All Society: How More and More Americans Compete for Ever Fewer and Bigger Prizes, Encouraging Economic Waste, Income Inequality, and an Impoverished Cultural Life*. New York: Free Press, 1995.

Frank, Robert H. *Luxury Fever: Why Money Fails to Satisfy in an Era of Excess*. New York: Free Press, 1999.

———. *The Darwin Economy: Liberty, Competition, and the Common Good*. Princeton University Press, 2011.

Freedman, Samuel G. *The Inheritance: How Three Families and the American Political Majority Moved from Left to Right*. New York: Simon and Schuster, 1998.

Freeman, Richard. "The Global Expansion of Higher Education," National Bureau of Economic Research, May 2009, http://www.nber.org/digest/oct09/w14962.html.

French, K. R., Martin N. Baily, John Y. Campbell, and John H. Cochrane. *The Squam Lake Report: Fixing the Financial System*. Princeton University Press, 2010.

Friedman, Thomas L. *Hot, Flat, and Crowded: Why We Need a Green Revolution—And How It Can Renew America*. New York: Farrar Straus Giroux, 2008.

Gelman, Andrew. *Red State, Blue State, Rich State, Poor State: Why Americans Vote the Way They Do*. Princeton University Press, 2009.

Gitlin, Todd. *The Bulldozer and the Big Tent: Blind Republicans, Lame Democrats, and the Recovery of American Ideals*. Hoboken: Wiley, 2007.

———. *The Twilight of Common Dreams: Why America Is Wracked by Culture Wars*. New York: Henry Holt, 1995.

Graham, Jesse, Jonathan Haidt, and Brian A. Nosek. "Liberals and Conservatives Rely on Different Sets of Moral Foundations," *Journal of Personality and Social Psychology* 96 (2009): 1029–46, http://www4.gsb.columbia.edu/rt/null?&exclusive=filemgr .download&file_id=7214828&rtcontentdisposition=filename%3DGraham_Jesse _paper.pdf.

Greenstein, Robert. "CBO Report: Ryan Plan Specifies Spending Path that Would Nearly

End Most of Government Other Than Social Security, Health Care, and Defense by 2050: Plan Also Contains Deeper Cuts to Medicare and Medicaid than Ryan Revealed," Center on Budget and Policy Priorities, accessed May 18, 2011, http://www.cbpp.org/cms/index.cfm?fa=view&id=3453.

Hacker, Jacob, and Paul Pierson. *Off Center: The Republican Revolution and the Erosion of American Democracy*. New Haven: Yale University Press, 2005.

Hacker, Jacob, with Paul Pierson. *Winner-Take-All Politics: How Washington Made the Rich Richer—and Turned Its Back on the Middle Class*. New York: Simon and Schuster, 2010.

Hacker, Jacob. *The Divided Welfare State: The Battle over Public and Private Social Benefits in the United States*. Cambridge: Cambridge University Press, 2002.

Haidt, Jonathan, and Jesse Graham. "When Morality Opposes Justice: Conservatives Have Moral Intuitions that Liberals May Not Recognize," *Social Justice Research* (2007), http://papers.ssrn.com/sol3/papers.cfm?abstract_id=872251.

Haidt, Jonathan. *The Righteous Mind: Why Good People Are Divided by Politics and Religion*. New York: Pantheon Books, forthcoming February 2012.

Hall, Matthew, Audrey Singer, Gordon F. De Jong, and Deborah Roempke Graefe. "The Geography of Immigrant Skills: Educational Profiles of Metropolitan Areas: Immigration, Jobs and the Economy, Demographics, Ethnicity," Brookings Institution, June 9, 2011, available at http://www.brookings.edu/papers/2011/06_immigrants_singer.aspx.

Halperin, Mark, and John F. Harris. *The Way to Win: Taking the White House in 2008*. New York: Random House, 2006.

Harris, Frederick C., Valeria Sinclair-Chapman, and Brian McKenzie. *Countervailing Forces in African-American Civic Activism, 1973–1994*. Cambridge: Cambridge University Press, 2006.

Harvey, David. *A Brief History of Neoliberalism*. New York: Oxford University Press, 2007.

Hawksworth, John, and Gordon Cookson. "The World in 2050," PriceWaterhouse Coopers, accessed May 18, 2011, http://www.pwc.com/gx/en/world-2050/pdf/world_2050_brics.pdf.

Heilemann, John, and Mark Halperin. *Game Change: Obama and the Clintons, McCain and Palin, and the Race of a Lifetime*. New York: HarperCollins, 2010, http://www.ontheissues.org/Archive/Game_Change_Immigration.htm.

Huntington, Samuel P. *Who Are We? The Challenges to America's National Identity*. New York: Simon and Schuster, 2004.

Inglehart, Ronald, and Pippa Norris. "The True Clash of Civilizations," *Foreign Policy*, (March/April 2003): pp. 63–70, http://ksghome.harvard.edu/~pnorris/Acrobat/Inglehart%20Foreign%20Policy.pdf.

———. *Rising Tide: Gender Equality and Cultural Change Around the World*. Cambridge: Cambridge University Press, 2003.

Isaacs, Julia B., Isabel V. Sawhill, and Ron Haskins. *Getting Ahead or Losing Ground: Economic Mobility in America*. The Brookings Institution, http://www.brookings.edu/~/media/Files/rc/reports/2008/02_economic_mobility_sawhill/02_economic_mobility_sawhill.pdf.

Jacobs, Lawrence R., and Robert Y. Shapiro. "The American Public's Pragmatic Liberalism Meets Philosophical Conservatism," *Journal of Health Politics, Policy and Law*, 1999, 24(5).

Jacobson, Gary C. *The Politics of Congressional Elections*. Boston: Addison Wesley Publishing Company, 1996.

Jones, Robert P., and Daniel Cox. "Old Alignments, Emerging Fault Lines: Religion in the 2010 Election and Beyond: Findings from the 2010 Post-election American Values Survey," Public Religion Research Institute, November 2010, http://www.publicreligion.org/objects/uploads/fck/file/AVS%202010%20Post-election%20report%20FINAL.pdf.

————. "Religion and the Tea Party in the 2010 election," Public Religion Research Institute, October 2010, http://www.publicreligion.org/objects/uploads/fck/file/AVS%202010%20Report%20FINAL.pdf.

Judis, John B., and Ruy Teixeira. *The Emerging Democratic Majority.* New York: Scribner, 2002.

Judis, John B. *The Folly of Empire: What George W. Bush Could Learn from Theodore Roosevelt and Woodrow Wilson.* New York: Oxford University Press, 2006.

Katsillis, John, and J. Michael Armer. "Education and Mobility," in *Encyclopedia of Sociology*, Edgar F. Borgatta and Rhonda J. V. Montgomery, eds. New York: Macmillan, 2000, http://edu.learnsoc.org/Chapters/20%20education/4%20education%20and%20mobility.htm.

Katznelson, Ira. *When Affirmative Action Was White: An Untold History of Racial Inequality in Twentieth-Century America.* New York: W. W. Norton, 2005.

Kemmelmeier, Markus. "Social Dominance Theory," in Ritzer, George, ed., Blackwell Encyclopedia of Sociology. Blackwell Publishing, 2007. Blackwell Reference Online. 05 September 2011. http://www.sociologyencyclopedia.com/public/tocnode?id=g9781405124331_yr2010_chunk_g978140512433125_ss1–321.

Kennedy, Paul. *The Rise and Fall of the Great Powers.* New York: Random House, 1987.

Kochhar, Rakesh, Richard Fry, and Paul Taylor. "Wealth Gaps Rise to Record Highs Between Whites, Blacks, Hispanics Twenty-to-One," Pew Research Center, July 26, 2011, http://pewsocialtrends.org/2011/07/26/wealth-gaps-rise-to-record-highs-between-whites-blacks-hispanics/.

Kurzweil, Ray. *The Age of Spiritual Machines: When Computers Exceed Human Intelligence.* New York: Viking, 1999.

Lakoff, George. *Moral Politics.* Chicago: University of Chicago Press, 2002.

Langberg, Jason, and Cary Brege. "The Racial Achievement Gap in the Wake County Public School System," Legal Aid of North Carolina, March 2010, http://www.legalaidnc.org/public/Learn/Statewide_Projects/ACS/ACS_Publications/IssueBrief_Mar-10_WCPSSAchievementGap.pdf.

Lanier, Jaron. *You Are Not a Gadget: Being Human in a Technological Age.* New York: Knopf, 2010.

Leege, David, Kenneth D. Wald, Brian S. Krueger, and Paul D. Mueller. *The Politics of Cultural Differences: Social Change and Voter Mobilization Strategies in the Post-New Deal Period.* Princeton, NJ: Princeton University Press, 2002.

Leiserson, Greg, and Jeffrey Rohaly. "The Distribution of the 2001–2006 Tax Cuts: Updated Projections," November 2006, Tax Policy Center, Brookings-Urban Institute, http://www.taxpolicycenter.org/UploadedPDF/411378_tax_cuts.pdf.

Lemann, Nicholas. *The Promised Land: The Great Black Migration and How It Changed America.* New York: Vintage, 1992.

Lewis, Michael. *The Big Short: Inside the Doomsday Machine.* New York: W. W. Norton, 2010.

Mamun, Arif, Paul O'Leary, David C. Wittenburg, and Jesse Gregory. "Employment among Social Security Disability Program Beneficiaries, 1996–2007," *Social Security*

*Bulletin* 71: 3 (2011), Social Security Administration, Office of Retirement and Disability Policy, http://www.ssa.gov/policy/docs/ssb/v71n3/v71n3p11.html.

Mann, Thomas E., and Norman J. Ornstein. *The Broken Branch: How Congress Is Failing America and How to Get It Back on Track.* New York: Oxford, 2006.

Marable, Manning. *The Great Wells of Democracy: The Meaning of Race in American Life.* New York: Basic Books, 2003.

Massey, Douglas S., and Robert J. Sampson. "Moynihan Redux: Legacies and Lessons," *The Annals of the American Academy of Political and Social Science* 621 (2009): 6–27.

Mayhew, David R. *Divided We Govern: Party Control, Lawmaking, and Investigations, 1946–1990.* New Haven: Yale University Press, 1993.

McCarty, Nolan, Keith T. Poole, and Howard Rosenthal. *Polarized America: The Dance of Ideology and Unequal Riches.* Cambridge, Mass.: MIT Press, 2006.

Morgenson, Gretchen, and Joshua Rosner. *Reckless Endangerment: How Outsized Ambition, Greed, and Corruption Led to Economic Armageddon.* New York: Times Books, 2011.

Nacos, Brigitte L., Yaeli Bloch-Elkon, and Robert Y. Shapiro. *Selling Fear: Counterterrorism, the Media, and Public Opinion.* University of Chicago Press, 2011.

Nye, Joseph S., Brent Scowcroft, Martine Feldstein, and David Leonhardt. *The Global Economic Crisis and Potential Implications for Foreign Policy and National Security.* Washington, D.C.: Aspen Institute, 2009.

Nye, Joseph S. "The Future of American Power: Dominance and Decline in Perspective," *Foreign Affairs* (November/December 2010), http://www.foreignaffairs.com/articles/66796/joseph-s-nye-jr/the-future-of-american-power.

Piketty, Thomas, and Emmanuel Saez. "Income Inequality in the United States, 1913–1998," *The Quarterly Journal of Economics* 118:1, February 2003.

Pinker, Stephen. *The Blank Slate: The Modern Denial of Nature.* New York: Viking, 2002.

Pratto, Felicia, James Sidanius, and Shana Levin. "Social Dominance Theory and the Dynamics of Intergroup Relations: Taking Stock and Looking Forward," *European Review of Social Psychology* 17 (2006).

Pratto, Felicia, James Sidanius, Lisa M. Stallworth, and Bertram F. Malle. "Social Dominance Orientation: A Personality Variable Predicting Social and Political Attitudes," *Journal of Personality and Social Psychology* 67 (1994): 741–63, http://dash.harvard.edu/bitstream/handle/1/3207711/Sidanius_SocialDominanceOrientation.pdf?sequence=1.

Rabinowitz, Joshua L., David O. Sears, James Sidanius, and Jon A. Krosnick. "Why Do White Americans Oppose Race-Targeted Policies? Clarifying the Impact of Symbolic Racism," *Political Psychology* 30 (2009): 805, http://communication.stanford.edu/faculty/krosnick/Why%20do%20white%20Americans%20oppose%20racial%20policies.pdf.

Rachman, Gideon. *Zero-Sum Future: American Power in an Age of Anxiety.* New York: Simon and Schuster, 2011, http://books.simonandschuster.com/Zero-Sum-Future/Gideon-Rachman/9781439176610/excerpt.

Rajan, Raghuram G. *Fault Lines: How Hidden Fractures Still Threaten the World Economy.* Princeton University Press, 2010.

Reinhart, Carmen, and Kenneth Rogoff. *This Time Is Different: Eight Centuries of Financial Folly.* Princeton University Press, 2011.

Rodrick, Dani. "Has Globalization Gone Too Far?," Institute for International Economics, Washington, D.C., 1997.

Rosin, Hanna. *God's Harvard: A Christian College on a Mission to Save America.* New York: Houghton Mifflin Harcourt, 2007.

Roubini, Nouriel, and Stephen Mihm. *Crisis Economics: A Crash Course in the Future of Finance.* New York: Penguin, 2010.

Sachs, Jeffrey D. *Economics for a Crowded Planet: Common Wealth.* New York: Penguin Press, 2008.

Schaller, Thomas F. *Whistling Past Dixie: How Democrats Can Win Without the South.* New York: Simon and Schuster, 2006.

Shapiro, Robert Y., and Lawrence Jacobs. *Politicians Don't Pander: Political Manipulation and the Loss of Democratic Responsiveness.* University of Chicago Press, 2000.

Sidanius, Jim, and Felicia Pratto. *Social Dominance: An Intergroup Theory of Social Hierarchy and Oppression.* Cambridge: Cambridge University Press, 2001, passim.

Skerry, Peter. "Islam in America," *The American Interest* 2:5, http://www.theamerican -interest.com/article.cfm?piece=283.

Skitka, Linda J., and Philip E. Tetlock. "Providing Public Assistance: Cognitive and Motivational Processes Underlying Liberal and Conservative Policy Preferences," *Journal of Personality and Social Psychology* 65 (1993): 1205–23, http://faculty.haas.berkeley.edu/ tetlock/Vita/Philip%20Tetlock/Phil%20Tetlock/1992–1993/1993%20Providing %20Public%20Assistance. . . . pdf.

Sniderman, Paul M. *Race and Inequality: A Study in American Values.* London: Chatham House, 1985.

Snyder, Timothy. *Bloodlands: Europe Between Hitler and Stalin.* New York: Basic Books, 2010.

Solow, Robert M. *Work and Welfare.* Princeton University Press, 1998.

Sorkin, Andrew Ross. *Too Big to Fail: The Inside Story of How Wall Street and Washington Fought to Save the Financial System—and Themselves.* New York: Penguin, 2011.

Spence, Michael, and Sandile Hlatshwayo. "The Evolving Structure of the American Economy and the Employment Challenge," Council on Foreign Relations, March 2011, http://www.cfr.org/industrial-policy/evolving-structure-american-economy -employment-challenge/p24366.

Stephanson, Anders. *Manifest Destiny: American Expansion and the Empire of Right.* New York: Hill and Wang, 1996.

Steuerle, C. Eugene, and Stephanie Rennane. "Social Security and Medicare Taxes Benefits over a Lifetime," Urban Institute, January 2011, http://www.urban.org/UploadedPDF/ social-security-medicare-benefits-over-lifetime.pdf.

Stewart, James B. *Den of Thieves.* New York: Touchstone, 1992.

Stiglitz, Joseph E., and Linda J. Bilmes. *The Three Trillion Dollar War: The True Cost of the Iraq Conflict.* New York: W. W. Norton, 2008.

Stimson, James A., and Carmines, Edward G. *Issue Evolution: Race and the Evolution of American Politics.* Princeton University Press, 1989.

Swendiman, Kathleen S., and Thomas J. Nicola. "Social Security Reform: Legal Analysis of Social Security Benefit Entitlement Issues," Congressional Research Service, August 11, 2010, http://aging.senate.gov/crs/ss2.pdf.

Taleb, Nassim Nicholas. *The Black Swan: The Impact of the Highly Improbable.* New York: Random House, 2007.

Tanenhaus, Sam. *The Death of Conservatism: A Movement and Its Consequences.* New York: Random House, 2010.

Tesler, Michael, and David Sears. "President Obama and the Growing Polarization of

Partisan Attachments by Racial Attitudes and Race," American Political Science Association, September 2010, http://mst.michaeltesler.com/uploads/sample_2.pdf.

Tetlock, Philip E. "Cognitive Style and Political Ideology," *Journal of Personality and Social Psychology* 45 (1983): 118–26, http://faculty.haas.berkeley.edu/tetlock/Vita/Philip %20Tetlock/Phil%20Tetlock/1977–1983/1983%20Cognitive%20Style%20and %20Political%20Ideology.pdf.

Tetlock, Philip E., and P. G. Mitchell. "Liberal and Conservative Approaches to Justice: Conflicting Psychological Portraits," *Psychological Perspectives on Justice*, B. Mellers and J. Baron, eds. Cambridge: Cambridge University Press, 1993, http://faculty.haas .berkeley.edu/tetlock/Vita/Philip%20Tetlock/Phil%20Tetlock/1992–1993/1993 %20Liberal%20and%20Conservative%20Approaches%20to%20Justice.pdf.

Thurow, Lester. *The Zero Sum Society: Distribution and the Possibilities for Economic Change.* New York: Basic Books, 1980.

Wattenburg, Martin, George C. Edwards, and Robert L. Lineberry. *Government in America: People, Politics, and Policy.* Boston: Allyn & Bacon, 2004.

Westen, Drew. *The Political Brain: The Role of Emotion in Deciding the Fate of the Nation.* New York: PublicAffairs, 2007.

Winter, Nicholas. "Masculine Republicans and Feminine Democrats: Gender and Americans' Explicit and Implicit Images of the Political Parties," American Political Science Association (2009), http://papers.ssrn.com/sol3/papers.cfm?abstract_id=1451343.

Zuniga, Markos Moulitsas. *Taking on the System: Rules for Radical Change in a Digital Era.* New York: Penguin, 2008.

# Grateful Acknowledgments

Grateful acknowledgment is made to the following for their permission to reprint previously published material:

Cambridge University Press: Excerpt from "Liberal and Conservative Approaches to Justice: Conflicting Psychological Portraits" by Philip E. Tetlock and Gregory Mitchell, from *Psychological Perspectives on Justice: Theory and Applications,* edited by Barbara A. Mellers and Jonathan Baron, copyright © 1993 by Cambridge University Press. Reprinted by permission of Cambridge University Press.

Barry Eichengreen and Project Syndicate: Excerpt from "Is America Catching the 'British Disease'?" by Barry Eichengreen and Project Syndicate, from the Project Syndicate blog (http://www.project-syndicate.org/commentary/eichengreen24/English), copyright © 2010 by Project Syndicate. Reprinted by permission of Barry Eichengreen and Project Syndicate.

Roger Pilon: Excerpt from "Is It Immoral to Cut the Budget?" by Roger Pilon, originally appearing as an editorial in the *Wall Street Journal* on October 7, 2011, copyright © 2011 by Roger Pilon. Reprinted by permission of Roger Pilon.

Barry Ritholtz: Excerpt from "Bin Laden's (Long Overdue) Day of Reckoning" by Barry Ritholtz, from the Big Picture blog (http://www.ritholtz.com/blog/2011/05/bin-ladens-long-overdue-day-of-reckoning/), copyright © 2011 by Barry Ritholtz. Reprinted by permission of Barry Ritholtz.

# Illustration Credits

*Fig. 4.3:* Courtesy of the Economic and Business Research Center at the Eller College of Management, University of Arizona. Available at: http://ebr.eller.arizona.edu/DataEntry/CurrentIndicators.aspx?CurrID=3. Accessed March 21, 2011.

*Fig. 4.4:* Courtesy of the Economic and Business Research Center at the Eller College of Management, University of Arizona. Available at: http://ebr.eller.arizona.edu/DataEntry/CurrentIndicators.aspx?CurrID=8. Accessed March 21, 2011.

*Fig. 4.5:* Courtesy of the Economic and Business Research Center at the Eller College of Management, University of Arizona. Available at: http://ebr.eller.arizona.edu/DataEntry/CurrentIndicators.aspx?CurrID=9. Accessed March 21, 2011.

*Fig. 4.6:* From "National Population Projections," Population Profile of the United States, published by the United States Census Bureau, Population Division. Available at: http://www.census.gov/population/www/pop-profile/natproj.html.

*Fig. 4.7:* From "Beyond 2010: Demographic Change and the Future of the Republican Party" by Alan J. Abramowitz. Courtesy of University of Virginia Center for Politics and Alan J. Abramowitz. Reprinted with permission. Available at: http://www.centerforpolitics.org/crystalball/articles/aia2010031101/.

*Fig. 5.2:* Copyright © 2010 Fruzsina Eordogh.

*Fig. 5.3:* Copyright © 2010 Fruzsina Eordogh.

*Fig. 5.4:* From *State of the Dream 2011: Austerity for Whom?* Copyright © 2011 United for a Fair Economy. Reprinted with permission. Available at: http://www.FairEconomy.org/Dream.

*Fig. 5.5:* From *State of the Dream 2011: Austerity for Whom?* Copyright © 2011 United for a Fair Economy. Reprinted with permission. Available at: http://www.FairEconomy.org/Dream.

*Fig. 5.6:* Copyright © 2011 Public Agenda. Reprinted with permission. Available at: http://www.publicagenda.org/charts/race-tanf-recipients.

*Fig. 5.7:* From *State of the Dream 2011: Austerity for Whom?* Copyright © 2011 United for a Fair Economy. Reprinted with permission. Available at: http://www.FairEconomy.org/Dream.

*Fig. 5.8:* From *USA, Inc: A Basic Summary of America's Financial Statements*, February 2011, created and compiled by Mary Meeker for Kleiner Perkins Caulfield & Byers. Reprinted with permission. Available at: http://www.kpcb.com/usainc/.

*Fig. 5.9:* © 2011 Jezevec.

*Fig. 5.10:* From *Understanding the Economy: Long-Term Unemployment in the African American Community*, published by the United States House of Representatives Joint Economic Committee (Carolyn B. Mahoney, D-NY, Chair). Available at: http://jec.senate.gov/public/index.cfm?a=Files.Serve&File_id=e9a910b5-8bb3-484f-a176-6257a24e27bb.

*Fig. 6.1:* From "Why Half of Americans Pay Nearly No Income Tax" by Roberton Williams. Copyright © 2010 Tax Analysts/Urban-Brookings Tax Policy Center. Reprinted with permission. Available at: http://www.taxpolicycenter.org/UploadedPDF/412106_federal_income_tax.pdf.

*Fig. 6.2:* From "Is 'Tax Day' Too Burdensome for the Rich?" Copyright © 2011 Citizens for Tax Justice. Reprinted with permission. Available at: http://www.ctj.org/pdf/taxday2009.pdf.

*Fig. 6.3:* From "9/11 and Birther Misperceptions Compared" by Brendan Nyhan. Reprinted with permission. Available at: http://www.brendan-nyhan.com/blog/2009/08/911-and-birther-misperceptions-compared.html.

*Fig. 6.4:* From "Poll Shows False Obama Beliefs a Function of Partisanship" by Adam J. Berinsky. Courtesy of Pollster.com and Adam J. Berinsky. Reprinted with permission. Available at: http://www.pollster.com/blogs/poll_shows_false_obama_beliefs .php?nr=1. See also: Adam J. Berinsky, "Rumors, Truths, and Reality: A Study of Political Misinformation," June 14, 2011. Available at: http://web.mit.edu/berinsky/ www/files/rumor.pdf.

*Fig. 7.1:* "Critics Still Wrong on What's Driving Deficits in Coming Years" by Kathy A. Ruffing and James R. Horney. Courtesy Center on Budget and Policy Priorities. Reprinted with permission. Available at: http://www.cbpp.org/files/12-16-09bud.pdf.

*Fig. 7.2:* From "Survey: Americans Believe Capitalism at Odds with Christian Values." Copyright © 2011 Public Religion Research Institute. Reprinted with permission.

*Fig. 7.3:* From "In Media Coverage, Deficit Eclipses Unemployment" by Clifford Marks, copyright © 2011 National Journal Group, Inc. Available at: http://www .nationaljournal.com/economy/in-media-coverage-deficit-eclipses-unemployment -20110516.

*Fig. 7.4:* From "Chairman Ryan Gets Nearly Two-Thirds of His Huge Budget Cuts from Programs for Lower-Income Americans" by Robert Greenstein. Courtesy Center on Budget and Policy Priorities. Reprinted with permission. Available at: http://www .cbpp.org/files/4-5-11bud2.pdf.

*Fig. 7.6:* From http://www.calculatedriskblog.com/ by Bill McBride. Copyright © 2011 Bill McBride. Reprinted with permission. Available at: http://www.calculatedriskblog .com/2011/04/summary-for-week-ending-april-1st.html.

*Fig. 7.8:* From "The Good News: Worker Productivity and Profits per Workers Are at Record Highs. The Bad News: That Probably Means a Record Jobless Recovery." Copyright © 2011 Mark J. Perry. Reprinted with permission.

*Fig. 7.9:* From *The Evolving Structure of the American Economy and the Employment Challenge* by A. Michael Spence. Copyright © 2011 Council on Foreign Relations Press. Reprinted with permission.

*Fig. C.1:* From *International Energy Outlook 2010: World Energy Demand and Economic Outlook* (Report #: DOE/EIA-0484), published by the United States Energy Information Administration. Available at: http://www.eia.gov/oiaf/ieo/world.html.

*Fig. C.2:* From "Ask EarthTrends: How Much of the World's Resource Consumption Occurs in Rich Countries?" by Amy Cassara. Available at: http://earthtrends.wri.org/ updates/node/236.

# Index

Page numbers in *italics* refer to illustrations.

### BEYOND OUTRAGE
*What Has Gone Wrong With Our
Economy and Our Democracy, and How to Fix It*
by Robert B. Reich

The American political system is in crisis—paralyzed by gridlock, beset with cynicism, and sabotaged by competing interests that have perversely made even common-sense policy virtually impossible. In this urgent book, Robert Reich argues nothing important can happen in Washington unless citizens are energized and organized to make sure politicians honor their promises. But in order to be effectively mobilized, we need to see the big picture. *Beyond Outrage* connects the dots for us, showing why the increasing share of income and wealth going to the top has hobbled jobs and growth for everyone else, undermining our democracy; caused Americans to become increasingly cynical about public life; and turned many Americans against one another. Here's a blueprint for action for everyone who cares about the future of America.

Business

### THE WORKING POOR
*Invisible in America*
by David K. Shipler

Shipler journeys deeply into the lives of individual store clerks and factory workers, farm laborers and sweatshop seamstresses, illegal immigrants in menial jobs and Americans saddled with immense student loans and paltry wages. They are known as the working poor. They perform labor essential to America's comfort. They are white and black, Latino and Asian—men and women in small towns and city slums trapped near the poverty line, where the margins are so tight that even minor setbacks can cause devastating chain reactions. Shipler shows how liberals and conservatives are both partly right—that practically every life story contains failure caused by both society and the individual. Braced by hard fact and personal testimony, he unravels the forces that confine people in the quagmire of low wages. competition from abroad.

Social Science